#EdJourney

#EdJourney

A ROADMAP TO THE FUTURE OF EDUCATION

Grant Lichtman

JB JOSSEY-BASS
A Wiley Brand

Published by Jossey-Bass
A Wiley Brand
One Montgomery Street, Suite 1200, San Francisco, CA 94104-4594
www.josseybass.com

Jossey-Bass books and products are available through most bookstores. To contact Jossey-Bass directly call our Customer Care Department within the U.S. at 800-956-7739, outside the U.S. at 317-572-3986, or fax 317-572-4002.

Wiley publishes in a variety of print and electronic formats and by print-on-demand. Some material included with standard print versions of this book may not be included in e-books or in print-on-demand. If this book refers to media such as a CD or DVD that is not included in the version you purchased, you may download this material at http://booksupport.wiley.com. For more information about Wiley products, visit www.wiley.com.

Library of Congress Cataloging-in-Publication Data

Lichtman, Grant, 1956-
EdJourney : a roadmap to the future of education/Grant Lichtman.
    pages cm
Includes bibliographical references and index.
ISBN 978-1-118-89858-1 (cloth)
ISBN 978-1-118-89887-1 (ebk.)
ISBN 978-1-118-89888-8 (ebk.)
1. School improvement programs. I. Title.
LB2822.8.L54 2014
371.2'07—dc23

                                    2014013590

Printed in the United States of America

FIRST EDITION

HB Printing   10 9 8 7 6 5 4 3 2

CONTENTS

■ ■ ■

PART ONE: ROADBLOCKS: HOW CAN WE OVERCOME THE BIGGEST OBSTACLES TO SCHOOL REFORM?

ABOUT THE AUTHOR

Grant Lichtman has thought, taught, and written about transformational education for more than 20 years. His first book, *The Falconer: What We Wish We Had Learned in School*, is based on his seminar in problem solving, strategy, and creational thinking in which he and his students explore a novel interpretation of *The Art of War*. Grant spent fifteen years as a senior administrator, trustee, and teacher at Francis Parker School in San Diego, one of the largest independent schools in the United States. He consults with, keynotes, and facilitates workshops with both private and public schools and school groups. He is currently senior fellow of the Martin Institute for Teaching Excellence, a Memphis-based public-private partnership for educational professional growth, and a collaborating consultant with the National Business Officers Association.

Before working in education, Grant directed business ventures in the oil and gas industry in the former Soviet Union, South America, and the US Gulf Coast. Grant graduated from Stanford University with a BS and MS in geology and studied the deep ocean basins of the Atlantic and Pacific Oceans and the Bering Sea. Grant and his wife, Julie, live in Poway, twenty miles north of downtown San Diego. Their son, Josh, is a PhD candidate in systems biology at Stanford. Their daughter, Cassidy, graduated with her BA in political science and MA in history from Stanford, and is currently a member of the USA National Volleyball Team.

Grant's Prius is in fine shape, with just over 115,000 miles on the odometer as of this writing.

For Julie, Josh, and Cassidy,
without whom my journeys don't exist

ACKNOWLEDGMENTS

I AM GRATEFUL TO THE FACULTY, STUDENTS, AND ADMINISTRATORS, MANY OF WHOM I HAD not met in advance, who took time out of their busy days to facilitate my visits to their schools on this trip, or who have talked to me via phone and video chat; and for the even larger number who have attended subsequent workshops and events where we have exchanged and refined ideas. This book is a representation of their work, every day, in the service of our students.

My trip was sponsored by generous donations from the Martin Institute for Teaching Excellence, WhippleHill, Lake/Flato Architects, and Bickmore Risk Management Services. I am thankful to those who took me into their homes or provided a night's lodging at a local hotel. A number of the schools I visited were kind enough to donate small stipends to help cover trip expenses.

Having met with and interviewed more than six hundred people on this trip, it is impossible to thank all of those who have contributed to my thinking. Many are cited in the narratives that fill these chapters, but many more contributed, and I am equally indebted to all who took the time to meet and talk with me.

Both along the way and in many other ways before and after this journey, I have been supported by a remarkable network of educators who freely share their ideas in pursuit of a transformed learning experience for our children. Two friends and colleagues in particular supported my work over a number of years, well before anyone else thought that some of these ideas had value. Bo Adams urged me to take this journey and spent hours each week conducting and uploading video interviews with me to chart my progress. Jill Gough has been one of my most passionate supporters for years, especially as an advocate and practitioner of the art of questioning. Bo, Jill, and Alyssa Gallagher read a preview of the manuscript and contributed very helpful comments.

Other educational thought leaders who are not cited in the book but who have greatly contributed to and directed my thinking include Jamie Baker, Greg Bamford, Pat Bassett, Jennifer Bjornstad, Suzie Boss, Don Buckley, Holly Chesser, Earl Cleope, Laura Deisley, Bill Dunkel, Michael Ebeling, Keith Evans, Peter Gow, Lee-Anne Grey, Scott Griggs, Chris Harrington, Josie Holford, Megan Howard, Ken Kay, Brad Lichtman, Jonathan Martin, Bob Ogle, Dave Ostroff, Billy Peebles, Jay Rainey, Meenoo Rami, Gretchen Reed, Will Richardson, Diane Ryan, Jeff Shields, Thomas Steele-Maley, Chris Thinnes, John Thorsen, Bernie Trilling, Sonya Wrisley and the Design 39 Campus team, Laura Vetter, and Yong Zhao. In addition to those named are the hundreds of educators who have participated in many workshops where we have generated ideas for the future success of schools, many of whom have contributed to the synthesized suggestions I am now putting forward.

I am particularly thankful to Shoshana Zuboff for taking the time to meet with me, share and refine my ideas on emerging trends in educational consumerism, and provide me access to both her published works and her work in process. I am also grateful to Adrian Bejan for his communications and clarifications of the constructal law and how it might apply to emerging structures of a more connected system of information age education.

I am extraordinarily grateful to Kate Bradford at Jossey-Bass for taking on my project as editor, for her thoughtful comments and guidance, and to the entire Jossey-Bass/Wiley publishing team for giving me the opportunity to publish under their legendary name.

Most of all I am grateful to my wife, Julie, who did not try to dissuade me from taking an open-ended and unusual trip, supported me in jumping off into a new career, and put up with by far the longest time we have been apart in the past thirty years.

INTRODUCTION

THE VETERAN ADMINISTRATOR AT THE END OF A CROWDED CONFERENCE TABLE HELD HER head in her hands.

"It shouldn't be this hard."

I left Charleston late that afternoon on the four-hour drive to Greenville. Over the past eight weeks I had visited more than fifty public and private schools on my solo drive around the country, and at many of these schools I had the same discussion about how organizational change is hard, particularly in schools with strong traditions of success or those subject to the fierce winds that blow from every point of the political compass. It is black-letter law on the subject of organizational innovation: *Change is hard.* Change brings displacement and even grief; it takes a long time; and all of that is OK. Every school I visited is undergoing some form of organizational and cultural change, and at almost every one, the forces opposing change seem to be at least holding their own against the brush-fires of innovation. So we talked about the obstacles and disruptions of change, surfacing those points of difficulty, taking them from the shadows and admitting their power.

As I chased the setting sun westward through the rolling late-fall piney woods of South Carolina, I had a moment of epiphany, the fulcrum of my trip, two-thirds in the rearview mirror and still four thousand miles to go. It must have been the last two books I had read: *Armageddon*, the story of the

Berlin airlift, by Leon Uris, and *War*, the story of a year at forward operating base Restrepo in the Kharangal Valley of Afghanistan, by Sebastian Junger.

Kicking the Nazis out of Europe was hard. That was what my father's generation did. That was really hard stuff.

The Berlin airlift was hard. Homesteading the Kansas prairie was hard. The list kept growing in my head, each idea so vivid I knew I did not need to pull the car over to a rest stop to write them down.

Going to the moon.
Giving birth after twenty-four hours of labor.
Raising kids in poverty as a single mom.
Standing your post at a firebase in the grit of the Kharangal Valley for a year.
Saying goodbye to your child as he deploys to spend that year.

Those are hard.

Change at most schools is not hard; it is *uncomfortable*. Sometimes it might be *very* uncomfortable for some people. It can be messy, complicated, and tiresome. *Uncomfortable* means making some tough decisions. But using the excuse that we can't change schools because "it is hard"?— well, we need to get some perspective on the difference between *hard* and *uncomfortable*. *Hard* is fighting against every odd with no certainty of success or even of survival. The job ahead for Eric Juli, principal of the Design Lab school in the heart of the most depressed, gang-ridden section of Cleveland, is *hard*. This is a school with one floor in a crumbling old building, where Eric spends most of his day finding a snack for a pregnant girl who did not get breakfast or pants for a boy whose one pair is just too dirty for decency, a school where the teachers don't come to school and the students don't care—and yet Eric is going to change that learning experience against every force imaginable and won't rest until every graduate gets an acceptance to college. That's *hard*.

My Journey

For eighty-nine days I drove my 1997 Prius around the country visiting sixty-four public and private schools. I interviewed more than six hundred teachers, administrators, students, and parents, asking them the same basic questions:

- What does innovation mean to you?
- How has your school changed to meet the challenges of a rapidly changing world?
- Is your school organized more for the benefit of the children or the adults?
- What do we really need to teach and learn in schools, and how are you doing that?
- What does that look like?
- What has worked?
- What has not?

The night before I set out on this trip, I packed the back of my car, got ready to leave my wife for the longest separation we have had in thirty years, and wrote in my journal:

Tomorrow morning before dawn I will drive off for three months on the road. I will miss my wife, Julie, who is putting up with the unknowns of this journey as much as I am. The last time I did something like this, I was single, twenty-four, filled a backpack with a few clothes and many rolls of film, and bought a one-way ticket to Kathmandu. My goal then was to have no goal, to see, learn, absorb, and understand a world far removed from that in which I had grown up. That journey took me through much of southern Asia, steered me into a teaching and research opportunity in the Philippines, and set my rudder in many ways for the rest of my life. Now, much older, back, joints, and patience less well attuned to sleeping on train platforms, my new step-off journey will be more physically comfortable. Sixty-dollar hotels may not be luxurious, but they are warm, dry, and safe. And of course I have already received hospitable and welcoming invitations to visit with many thoughtful and innovative educators . . . welcome mats mitigate discomfort in so many ways!

Though separated by thirty-two years and 180 degrees of longitude, in one way these two journeys are similar. My goal is still to see, learn, absorb, and understand. My questions may be more focused after three decades of thinking, writing, teaching, and talking about how and why we learn, but I will try to be just as open to what the journey has to teach me as I was when my belongings filled a backpack, not the back of a Prius.

What This Book Is About

Our world is changing at a dramatic rate, and nowhere more rapidly than in relationship to the creation and management of knowledge. Public or private, across a range of structures, grade levels, traditions, demographics, and resource bases, K–12 schools share a number of common obstacles in "pro-acting" and reacting to these changes, and are overcoming those obstacles in ways that can be translated and leveraged by most or all schools. The future of education is being created right now, today. I know because I saw it and talked to the adults and students who are creating it. It is not an easy process, and the obstacles to change are big and real. But schools across the country are painting the strokes of a fundamentally different and better type of student learning. Taken together, these different strokes make up the picture of what that learning looks like and how we get there.

A number of authors have written compelling books that show us what good education looks like at a few schools. I take a different approach in looking at a large number of schools, connecting the common threads of great education at many of them, and charting a roadmap not only of what transformed learning for the future looks like, but also of how school leaders and organizations can get there. I didn't send out a survey or do phone interviews with a few dozen schools and educators who are leading educational change. I did not even select most of the schools I visited based on their track record of innovation. I visited schools along my route and asked them about *their* definition of innovation, about *their* paths, obstacles, and successes. I watched and listened to hundreds of teachers, administrators, students, and parents, some who had planned to meet with me weeks in advance and others who I stopped in the hall or observed informally from the back of their classroom. These are *their* stories, voices, and pathways to the future. To use a metaphor that will crop up throughout the book, my goal is to link the many wonderful, exciting, stimulating, energizing, passion-driven brushfires of innovation I found at almost every school I visited and help fan them into a conflagration.

Thirty years ago I sat down and asked myself a simple question: *What defines great learning?* I had no formal background in education other than my own experience as a student and a bit of teaching. I am only a little embarrassed to admit that I had never read Dewey or Piaget or Bloom. I decided that great teaching and learning required much more focus on student engagement and direction; students asking questions instead of regurgitating answers; students and teachers co-creating knowledge instead of consuming it; teaching systems thinking; problem finding instead of just problem solving. Some very prominent educators told us at the time, "You can't teach that to students; they won't get it." Unfortunately we let those supposedly bright people sway us from what we knew was right.

As we entered a new century, bright educators and forward-looking people from many walks of life made the argument that the world was changing at a dramatic rate, the economic and social worlds have flattened, and technology has irrevocably disrupted traditional knowledge-based industries, including education. They said we needed to prepare students with a different set of skills, those needed for the twenty-first century. While I did not agree that these skills are any more relevant to this century than to any other time in human history, the conversation had suddenly changed.

The Goal of Education Has Changed

Today, most thoughtful educators agree that the industrial age model of content-driven education no longer serves our students. Here is the remarkably simple argument in a nutshell. The rate of change in the world is accelerating, and nowhere more than with respect to information. The sum of all human knowledge will soon be *doubling* every year, a frightening concept even if you are not good at math. Schools in the past have been tasked with teaching human knowledge to the next generation, knowledge young people can use to conduct themselves later in life in civil society. It is no longer possible to convey the amount of information they will need or to be certain that the information we do convey will be relevant for very long. Technology has made knowledge nearly universally accessible, disrupting the foundation of education that has existed since people first gathered around fires thousands of years ago. The goal of education has changed from the transfer of knowledge to the inculcation of wisdom, born of experience, which will help students to succeed in an increasingly ambiguous future. Schools must either radically change what they do or very quickly become utterly irrelevant. If schools do not change, they will simply be bypassed, an outmoded mechanism that has served its purpose and passed into history. Simply, in order to not only survive but thrive, schools must develop comfort with, and capacity for, ongoing change.

If you are an educator, or if you care about the future of education and have a stake in education because you are a parent or an employer and know that our current system of education is rapidly losing relevancy, this book is for you.

How the Book Is Organized

The book has three sections. The first section identifies major obstacles to educational innovation that were most commonly reported in my visits, giving examples of schools that have successfully overcome those very same obstacles. Here are a few of the highlights:

- Time in schools is allocated according to an outdated assembly-line model based on subject, classroom space, and student age, not on optimum conditions for improved learning of each student.
- Schools are not fundamentally structured to accommodate or promote connectivity, risk taking, and nimbleness, skills the students will need in their futures and characteristics that will lead to schools to effectively innovate.
- Teachers are not given the time and resources to develop professionally, to connect with colleagues outside of narrow ranges of interest, or to become active learners.

- Leadership is frequently stuck in rigid, outmoded "Management 1.0" practices that are antithetical to innovation in knowledge-based organizations.
- Outcomes in both public and private schools are currently driven by inertia, college admissions offices, fearful parents, and political forces, not by the best practices of education and learning.

The good news is that for every combination of intransigent obstacles there is an example of a school that has successfully solved the problem. I will connect these dots of success. At nearly every school I visited, I identified processes, structures, and practices that have helped schools overcome the obstacles to innovation. Many of these schools are operating in a radically different fashion than they were just five years ago. These schools are finding creative ways to align five key resources (time, people, space, knowledge, and money) in ways that support desired teaching and learning outcomes. Class schedules are changed, sometimes radically, in order to allow and promote a pedagogy that is deep, contextual, and focused on the student, not the teacher. Leaders courageously promote risk taking and set up intentional, sustainable structures, processes, and lines of authority that promote the best practices of innovation. Leaders hire employees more for their ability and willingness to grow and learn over time than for content expertise and find the time and money to help those adults continuously upgrade their expertise as educators. These schools recognize that the options for education are radically expanding, so they focus on delivering value to their student and family customers.

The second section paints a mosaic of a dramatically changing learning experience taking place in schools that are successfully innovating. I found that we can group these brushfires of innovation into five categories that, together, define the learning experience of the postindustrial age:

- *Dynamism:* Teachers and students use time and space in dramatically new ways. They take advantage of new knowledge about how the brain works and how individuals learn, leveraging technology to differentiate the learning experience for each individual child. Teachers and students are co-learners, with students taking increasing ownership of their learning experience.

- *Adaptability:* Teachers develop a growth mindset, not just tolerating but actively embracing a level of constant change that reflects the world outside of class. Courses change and merge, and the boundaries of departments and subjects disappear. Teachers figure out how to improve standards-based outcomes with project, group, and student-centered activities.

- *Permeability:* School programs, and in fact physical schools themselves, are highly permeable, with students and teachers spending significant time off campus, in their communities and, through technology, connected with other knowledge participants around the world. In fact, the concept of "school" as differentiated from the "real world" disappears.

- *Creativity:* Learning increasingly emphasizes the creation of knowledge along with a balanced consumption of foundational elements of a liberal arts education. Students lead their own learning through design of problems, activities, and even course materials. Students and teachers become creators as well as consumers of knowledge.

- *Self-correction:* The institution becomes self-evolving, not slave to conflicting outside forces that are de-linked from educational best practices. Students and teachers take time for frequent and authentic reflection. They embrace the concept of empathy as a guiding beacon in what they teach and learn. They gain comfort with constant change and learn to break or avoid the chains of inertia.

Each chapter is fleshed out with concrete examples of schools and teachers who have already implemented and reimagined the learning experience.

The third section begins with a description of the global challenges that face education and a roadmap for how schools must retool their foundational assumptions to meet those challenges. The changes that futurists see in the evolution of education are dramatically larger than those being contemplated by most educators. We are perched on the cusp of two fundamentally different learning systems: the industrial age assembly-line model that has been in place for 150 years, and the evolving ecosystem model that more accurately reflects our best understanding of effective education for the future. The reason so many educators and parents are frustrated with our current educational system is that the characteristics of these two systems are incompatible; we can't get where we want to go by just tweaking the controls on the assembly line. The driving characteristics of dynamism, adaptability, permeability, creativity, and self-correction are more closely aligned with the driving mechanisms of successful natural ecosystems, of rain forests, coral reefs, and prairie grasslands, not engineered assembly lines. Those who continue to try to cram the square peg of the industrial model and mindset into the round hole of learning for the future will become increasingly marginalized.

The penultimate chapter outlines the case for a forward-looking strategy for school communities based on a foundation of new design thinking. Since I finished my journey around the country I have been privileged to facilitate workshops with hundreds of educators who, given the opportunity, find many ways to challenge and reimagine the concept of what we call "school." The new foundation of what I call zero-based strategic thinking helps school communities to continuously, systematically, and sustainably increase the value of what they do well, instead of working from outdated models of strategic planning that largely revise goals based on legacy assumptions about what has and has not worked well in the past. Strategy becomes a continuous process of thinking, an organizational habit and capability that promotes ongoing innovation practices among all of the valued and valuable members of the school community.

The final chapter summarizes what I think are the big takeaways from my work and this book.

A Few Clarifications

I want to be clear on several points at the outset:

- The discussion of what good education *should* look like for the twenty-first century has run its course, and I am not going to reargue it. For more than a decade, educators and pundits have been discussing what good education looks like in the twenty-first century. I have sat with hundreds of thoughtful educators, students, and parents and asked them what they think students need to be successful in their future. Many more thousands of such discussions have taken place in schools across the country. Nearly all of them end up with about 80 percent agreement on a list of skills that looks something like this: persistence, confidence, resilience, patience, openness, creativity, adaptability, courage, perspective, empathy, and self-control. (By the way, high school seniors at three schools in Dallas generated that short list. It took them a total of nine minutes.) We need to agree that this is a good approximation of the skills our young people need to survive in the future. We need to stop talking about what "it" is, and start *doing* "it."

- Innovation is not about technology. In setting up the complicated calendar for my trip I asked school leaders to give me a few hours to learn about their most exciting new ideas and programs. Many asked me, "What do you want to see?" I left it to them with the caveat that I was not interested in talking about 1:1 laptop programs and iPad rollouts. Plenty of others have researched and written extensively about the role of technology in a new learning paradigm. In many visits I asked principals, heads of school, and other leaders this question: "If I walked down the halls today and asked all of your teachers, 'What does innovation mean to you?' how many would immediately default to something about technology?" Many nodded their heads, knowing this to be the case. We still think of technology too much as the goal of innovation and not a tool. Technology provides some of the arrows in the quiver of innovation. Real innovation in learning means reframing the mindset of the archers—the students and teachers—and that is the subject of this book.

- Change leadership busts, rather than reinforces, the silos of classroom and the administration office. On my visits and as I wrote the book I was frequently asked, "Who is this book for? Administrators? Leaders? Classroom teachers? Parents? Will you share concrete ideas for what I can do in the classroom?" The answer to all is a resounding "Yes!" We have to get past the mindset that leadership is the job of those at the top of the pay scale. Both leadership and innovation are vastly more effective and rapid in distributed, not hierarchical, organizations. Change is *not* outside the reach of everyone in the system. Leading change should be part of the "job description" of every student, teacher, administrator, and parent. We are *all* leaders of educational change, so this book is for *all* of us.

- I visited public, private, and charter schools; my own work background was with independent schools, so I started my trip with more of them on my roadmap. Different schools face different political, demographic, monetary, and inertial challenges. This book is about what connects schools in their pursuit of innovation more than what separates them. Almost by definition, change is easier in private and charter schools than in many public school settings. By citing examples from private schools I am not showing disrespect or disregard for the challenges faced in public education. For more than a century, some schools have acted as laboratories for the larger field of education, and the lessons learned in these risk-taking lab schools are valuable for all of us. Public or private, we can all learn from each other, taking what is transferable and scalable for our own needs.

- My connections with schools did not stop when I finished this trip; in fact they accelerated, like the rate of change in the world of education. I am aware of new brushfires of innovation burning at schools I did not visit, and I have seen innovative schools connect and leverage each other's working pilot programs at an ever-increasing rate. Some examples I managed to work into this book before it went to press, and others I will find and report on via my blog, *The Learning Pond*, as quickly as I can. The schools I visited were the tip of the burning spear; there are hundreds of other schools where the same changes are smoldering, sparking, and in various stages of incipient combustion. If your school does not appear, I did not leave you out intentionally!

To get us kicked off in the right direction, here is my best stab at a rationale for the innovations that we need to encourage, embrace, and embolden in our system of education:

- Students and teachers need the skills to be successful in a fluid, rapidly changing, and ambiguous future.

- For students and teachers to be prepared for that future, they need to become self-evolving learners with a growing individual and collective comfort and capacity for change.
- Our schools must rapidly realign our systems and resources in support of that overarching goal. Failure to do so will lead to institutional irrelevancy.
- Innovation is the process of that realignment through creation and implementation of new ideas that bring value to your school community.

The obstacles are significant, but for every obstacle there is already at least the start of a solution. We just need to reach out, and add those solutions to the ever-evolving mosaic that is great education.

Hitting the Road

When I left my driveway before dawn on September 9, 2012, I did not have many solid expectations for the trip and certainly no pre-ordained ideas to validate. I was overwhelmed by the number of people who agreed to meet with me and who were eager to share their ideas, successes, and failures. A few I knew as colleagues from my fifteen years working in education; the vast majority were strangers, passionate about their life mission to prepare young people for their own futures. For many of them, I was just a guy in a Prius with questions to ask. This book is really their story, sifted through the filter of the guy who got to ask the questions, listen, record, and then get back in the car for a long drive to the next town or city. Many of those I met on the road said they were jealous of my time to explore, question, synthesize, and reflect. They have every right to be jealous; this trip was an extraordinary privilege. But what does it say about our education system when the best educators, knowing full well that learning thrives only with those nutrients—deep thinking, exploration, synthesis, and reflection—can't find the time for them?

Highway motels are not bad places. They all look the same and run together with the trappings of the road, plastic key cards to room numbers I almost forgot, cereal and yogurt in the morning if the buffet is free, a granola bar in my room if it is not. Fast food is just calories you consume when you have somewhere better to be. Gas is gas. Nothing can replace an early Sunday morning drive down from the cool pines and green, late summer pastures of Richland, Utah to red, yawning sandstone canyon lands, Van Morrison on the sound system; or a stack of thick pancakes drowning in maple syrup on the first day of the Massachusetts winter; or a rolling patch of North Carolina Appalachia in all of its fall splendor, leaves blowing across the two-lane in a final bow before the trees are bare.

Ten thousand miles, eighty-nine days, one major car repair, and long drives in the slow lane are a small price to pay for the chance to spend hundreds of hours learning with people who know and care about what learning really means.

#EdJourney

Roadblocks

How Can We Overcome the Biggest Obstacles to School Reform?

BEFORE I LEFT ON MY TRIP, PAT BASSETT, THEN PRESIDENT OF THE NATIONAL Association of Independent Schools, urged me to keep track of the obstacles to innovation that schools are facing—the things that don't work as much as the things that do work. It was great advice, and as I interviewed teachers, students, administrators, and parents representing schools of all kinds and grade levels, I kept a log of these obstacles. As you might imagine, I started to hear similarities in the issues as the trip progressed. By the end of the tour I had captured nearly three hundred specific comments about why innovation and change are challenging and often uncomfortable at schools—why, despite years of discussion and agreement that we have to change education in order to prepare our students for a very different world, change is sluggish, stalled, or set aside. I waited until I got home, sat down with my log, and sorted the list into manageable buckets of similar comments.

I found four obstacles repeated most frequently that appear to present a truly existential challenge to a school's ability to change what it does:

- Use of time
- Developing people and their ability to change
- Leadership
- Organizational structures

The next set of obstacles, cited or reflected at many schools but not with the same level of prominence or not as firmly blocking the critical path to innovation, are these:

- Changing learning modalities
- Inertia

- Inward focus
- Failure to clarify the school's differentiated value
- Reluctance to systematically work the problem

Before we get into specific stories and examples, I want to offer some context for the subject of change in knowledge-based organizations. I did not start my road trip completely devoid of preconceptions. For the previous two years I had studied, purchased a small library, and loaded my blog reader with ideas and insights from authors, business leaders, and change agents whose expertise draws from both inside and outside the world of education. It is a world of lessons gleaned from the past five hundred years of human history, tracing the success and failure of knowledge-based industries and organizations since at least the Renaissance.

I have already talked about what is perhaps the most commonly cited obstacle to innovation: *change is hard*. Assuming I got my point across in the introduction, let's replace *hard* with *uncomfortable*. Although this is an important distinction, the reasons for this discomfort are real. If we don't have to do something uncomfortable, we generally will not. Change is uncomfortable because it is about the future, and most predictions about the future turn out to be wrong.

> *Change is uncomfortable because it is about the future, and most predictions about the future turn out to be wrong.*

Organizations that have to commit large amounts of resources—make big bets—on what will happen a long way into the future take big risks that their visions of the future are just plain wrong. Think about NASA and plans for going to Mars. What happens to all of that human and financial capital if someone comes along and figures out a better rocket engine? What happens if electric car designers are wrong and hydrogen proves the more efficient renewable energy source? What if we build a magnetic-levitation bullet train and halfway into the project someone invents the 2.0 version that is cheaper, faster, and safer? These are enormous risks.

Schools are fortunate in this regard. The main job of schools is to prepare students for the future, and the amount of capital risk is relatively low. We just have to continually upgrade what we are supposed to be good at: managing the flow of knowledge. So why do we think that innovation and change are hard? Here are a few large-scale reasons gleaned from the long history of organizational change that pertain particularly to schools:

• Successful organizations tend to be inwardly focused on what they *have done*, instead of what they *might do*, and that can lead to doubling down on past success. If schools are not imagining a different future, they will amplify their efforts to do what they have always done, only better.

• Through either omission or commission, leaders may fail to clearly articulate that innovation is an organizational imperative that is critical to the future. If the organization does not see its collective interests aligned with the need to promote innovation, there will be no real change. Schools are very busy places, and when things are generally going well or according to plan, innovation takes a back seat.

• Innovation is not just the creation and implementation of new ideas. Successful innovation demands that these new ideas create new value. The failure to link innovation strategies to value will result in the creation of lots of interesting new ideas that may or may not benefit the organization. Educators are creative people, but not all creativity results in value to the organization. Educators are also collegial and often averse to telling their colleagues that a good idea is not necessarily an idea that will make the school better at serving an evolving mission.

• Organizations fail to innovate if they lack either internal or external networks. If an organization fails to seek *external* insights, it will become convinced that its way is the best or only way. If the organization fails to develop collaborative *internal and external* networks, it will lose the advantages of idea leverage and cultivation that have proven over time to be *the* critical factor in successful innovation. Schools have been much slower to recognize the key role that networks play in innovation than other successful knowledge-based organizations.

• Innovation requires matching change vectors, which combine speed and a direction, to the rate of change in the external environment. Technology is the prime reason that organizations are now forced to innovate much more rapidly than even a decade ago. Knowledge-based organizations like schools have to keep pace with those changes, while also dealing with a nearly vertical curve in the rate of change of the sum of human knowledge.

• Educators tend to be conservative when it comes to change. Educators tend to enjoy working in a highly democratic environment of decision making where consensus is a common goal. Teachers don't like to ruffle each other's feathers; they prefer to work together as a collective. This tendency has powerful positive effects when it comes to developing collaborative working groups, but it generates overwhelming frictional resistance to change if there is cultural reluctance to ask hard questions of one's colleagues and oneself.

• Schools have always been a special case with respect to failure. In schools, risks are taken in small, slow increments, and failure is not generally celebrated. There are few, if any, institutional benefits or rewards for those who want to take risks, and there is plenty of downside for both students and employees who try and fail.

These are just a few of the challenges to innovation that translate from other knowledge-based organizations to education. There are many more challenges, but we will now focus on those obstacles most common to schools and see how educators all over the country are overcoming them.

CHAPTER ONE

Time
The Most Common Obstacle
to Change in Schools

At the end of a long day of school visits in Denver, I spoke with Alan Smiley, head at St. Anne's Episcopal School. He talked about the need to balance rapid innovation with maintaining a center of focus for students and adults that does not change. I knew that he had touched on a very important theme, but I also knew I was tired from eight hours of interviews at two schools that day and would not grasp his real meaning without time to reflect. This idea was there, teasing me, just past the range of my understanding, as I wrapped up at St. Anne's, drove out of Denver in a rainstorm, and settled in for the long drive to Kansas City.

As it turned out, I did not get to Kansas City that night. My car died just across the Colorado-Kansas border; I will save that tale for later in the book. So it was not until the weekend, having left Kansas on my way to St. Louis, that I finally had the chance to think about time and the pace and rate of change. With a full day to make the drive, I turned off of I-70 East, the major six-lane swath of asphalt that boldly pounds across the American heartland, onto Highway 50, a small two-lane byway which winds through the green, rolling hardwoods and rich bottomlands of the Missouri countryside. Speeds are slower, small crossroad towns flicker by, John Deere dealers and red-roofed, back-road burger stands more common than Arby's and McDonald's. Sometime in the midafternoon I slowed down, pulled over to a deserted picnic stop, and turned off the ignition. As I looked across the cloudy countryside, I finally got Alan's point.

The same rapid changes in the world that drive innovation also drive an ever-more-hectic pace of learning. We pile on increasingly competitive college admissions; parents, students, and educators press the pedal to the floor even harder. Yet we all know that we think best, find connections, experience important and sometimes life-changing "aha" moments—not in the rush of the day or when information is swirling at us as we try to grab it, write notes, or complete an assignment—but instead when we take a walk or a long drive, or meditate, or just sit with a cup of tea in the afternoon or at the end of the day. Few schools have time set aside for drinking tea.

Our Most Precious Resource

Ask any randomly selected group of American adults, "What do you wish you had more of?" Some will say "money," but almost all will say "time"— the time to do many of the things they would like: visiting with family, pursuing an interest outside of their normal work, helping a charity. The traditional industrial age model of education, as much as any manufacturing assembly line, is slave to the concept of time. Students' lives are segmented into twelve or thirteen yearlong blocks of time according to their age and birthdate. Years are broken down into school time and nonschool time, semesters, trimesters, quarters, summer school, and vacations. Days are strictly bound by the time that schools must start and end within a remarkably narrow set of options. During those days, students and teachers march to the unnatural rhythm of bells and class changes, many still in blocks of 50 or 55 or 49 minutes that suggest that learning is best accomplished in exactly these quanta parsed out according to subject. Some schools have modified the daily routine to allocate two-hour blocks for one subject and not for another, or fewer, longer blocks for all subjects.

Schools that truly challenge their use of time find that it holds the key to liberating innovation. In my research with schools, *by far* the most frequently cited obstacle to meaningful change is time. The two areas for which teachers, administrators, and students consistently

Schools that truly challenge their use of time find that it holds the key to liberating innovation.

told me they wish they had more time, or more flexibility in time, were the organization of class time in the daily schedule and time for adults to meet, collaborate, and learn. Both public and private schools are finding solutions to the problem of time. Some create new time, not by extending the school day or year, but by shifting where people have to be during the day. Some reprioritize how time is spent and find that the school survives, and thrives, following what were formerly thought of as impossibly difficult changes to the school's schedule. And we will hear of a ninth-grade student who came up with an elegant solution to one of the most intransigent problems in every school: finding time for teachers to meet and work together on their own learning pathways.

Why Is Time Chopped Up?

During my visit to a highly respected school in the Midwest, I sat in on a third-grade class. Recognizing the benefits of working across subject matter areas, this school had created a two-hour block of time to teach humanities. Sitting in the back of the class, perched on the tippy edge of a chair made for third graders, I noticed that the well-organized teacher had listed the day's agenda on the whiteboard. She had parsed the day into about a dozen blocks of time. This is absolutely routine at most elementary schools. Student time is chopped up into so many minutes for math, so many minutes for art, so many for reading, and so on.

Not a single educator has ever told me that students learn best in twenty-minute or hour-long blocks of time segmented by subject, yet almost every school structures time that way. Why is school organized this way? I asked this question of many educators I met on my trip, and the answers varied little. The responses fell into two groups: (1) "I need that time in order to teach my students what they need to know," and (2) "It's done that way because that is the way we have always done it." In an overgeneralized way, these two themes characterize the vast majority of responses about why daily schedules are the way they are.

As I discussed in the introduction, there is an enormous disconnect between what educators say are the key learning outcomes they want for their students and the allocation of our precious resources: time, people, money, space, and knowledge. Educators overwhelmingly agree that the essential qualities of their graduates are things like creativity, love of learning, good citizenship, empathy, effective communication, deep understanding of the challenges that face us in the world, and curiosity. Yet the organizing element of both student and teacher lives, day in and day out, week after week, year after year, is that the allocation of time has nothing to do with those essential outcomes.

Daily life at school is organized this way because that is how we always have done it, and changing the allocation of time can be extremely uncomfortable. Teachers have been hired, trained, labeled, organized, and evaluated by how well they control their time, their classroom, and their subject. A change to the daily schedule is a threat to who and what they are as teachers. Can we blame teachers for not welcoming a major change in their daily routine with open arms when this has been the source of their individual and community identity for as long as any of us can remember?

Daily life at school is organized this way because that is how we always have done it, and changing the allocation of time can be extremely uncomfortable.

Most educators agree in principle that long periods of time that allow for deep inquiry, accumulation of experience, and iterative practice of critical skills will yield the best long-term results. Ask the same question to teachers and administrators about changing the *specific* schedule of *their* school, and it scares the heck out of them. Even asking the question often generates fear, skepticism, and push-back: "You are trying to steal my time."

What if we were starting a school from scratch, with no preconditions other than creating the best possible learning environment for students? Would we break the day up into 55- or 75-minute chunks according to the same six or seven age-old subject areas? Would we all move in lockstep at the beginning and end of these increments of time and tell everyone to switch their brain patterns when a bell rings? Would it be set in stone that every student study math or a foreign language for the same number of minutes each day? Nearly every educator I met on the trip told me that learning at schools has evolved in response to time schedules as a precondition, and not the other way around.

Reimagining the School Calendar

The annual agrarian-driven school calendar has been a fixture of most schools for 150 years. We start school in the fall and take breaks for the major winter holidays, a week in spring, and then summer. Many public and private schools have found opportunities within these "vacation" gaps to offer enrichment programs, which often turn out to be the fun- and passion-filled activities that do not fit into the traditional scaffold of subject-driven curriculum. Some schools have asked why those "other" programs are relegated to summer school or spring break and have reimagined the entire school year schedule.

The Hawken School is a private K–12 school on the eastern outskirts of Cleveland. Educators at the school started talking seriously about time and transformational learning about five years ago, and what they have done to align the use of time with their vision of innovative education has become something of a legend among independent schools in the United States. Head of School Scott Looney asked the faculty to look at their use of time and advise him on how well that usage aligned with their school-wide essential learning outcomes. He got a lot of feedback. At the end of a year he came back to the faculty and pointed out that their own stated goals were for graduates to become "lifelong learners," "creative and independent thinkers," "good citizens," and "people who serve others." Yet students spent their days in school locked into a rigid routine focusing almost exclusively on science, history, math, and the rest of the traditional subject-driven curriculum.

Scott asked the faculty to create a schedule for the high school division that would align the use of time with the desired learning outcomes. The faculty had three years to get it done; there were no other options. "We held up who we wanted to be as educators, and our daily schedule, and pretty much said, 'We can't get there from here,'" Scott told me. "We could not achieve our educational goals when time was ruled by the traditional daily schedule. I did not tell the faculty what the new schedule should look like; I left it completely up to them. What I did say was this: 'You have three years to

"We held up who we wanted to be as educators, and our daily schedule, and pretty much said, 'We can't get there from here.'"

develop a schedule that aligns with our vision. We are not going to start the school year in 2010 with a schedule that fails to meet that test.'"

Hawken now has a remarkable Upper School schedule that includes large blocks of time for "normal" or so-called "rotation" classes, as well as two three-week "intensive blocks," when the students take just one class in the three weeks. This schedule allows Hawken teachers to create new classes and students to spend much more time off campus, learning in the downtown community. And the new schedule created an explosion of creative thinking and practical innovation. Doug Smith, associate director of the Upper School and history teacher, said that "having students for longer periods of time, up to an entire day, requires teachers to put a lot more thought into how they are constructing any particular class than they had to before." Doug said that the schedule change really challenged the faculty to reflect on their craft and role as teachers. "You could always go in and wing it for a fifty-five-minute period if you had to, but if you have them for six hours, you can't do that. When you have students for these more intensive periods of time, you have a richer connection with each other."

Teacher Dorothy Walthrup told me that the redeployment of time in the daily schedule allows students to access a completely different learning experience. "Now our students have the opportu-

"If you have the courage to push through the initial resistance to change, the other side is lovely, and more often than not you look back and say, 'What were we so worried about?'"

nity to go learn in ways that are very different than traditional education. Before, teachers were not encouraged to do things outside of the classroom because you were taking time away from other classes. There was a big mind shift on the part of teachers from taking a field trip to a really experiential learning opportunity. I see it as a manifestation of more real-world learning. The students learn more about how to collaborate during the intensive courses, and they bring those skills back and use them in the more traditional classes, rather than just working by themselves."

Scott says, "If you have the courage to push through the initial resistance to change, the other side is lovely, and more often than not you look back and say, 'What were we so worried about?' Schools are so resistant to change that changes that feel radical, aren't. We only changed one-sixth of the actual schedule, yet people look at it as a revolutionary change in how we use time. In hindsight what we did was evolutionary, not revolutionary. The next big change we go through will be easier because people know we can do it."

Making Time an Elective

Thousands of American educators know the story of Science Leadership Academy (SLA) in Philadelphia. SLA is a public magnet school in partnership with the Franklin Institute, a major museum and science center in Philadelphia. The school has a rigorous college prep program, though it offers no Advanced Placement (AP) courses. All classes are taught in a project-based environment, and the school community embraces the core values of inquiry, research, collaboration, presentation, and reflection.

SLA students are a cross section of urban America. The students come from every zip code in Philadelphia. About half qualify for free or reduced lunch, which means their families are not financially well off. There are about thirty students in each class, which is the same number as in any other Philadelphia public school. Teacher salaries are the same as those of other schools in the district. SLA gets the same funding from the public coffers as does any other school of the same size. The difference is that 90 percent of the school's graduates go on to four-year colleges.

The schedule at SLA allows students to work with the downtown Franklin Institute. Students and teachers are frequently at school late at night or working together online from home. Jeremy Spry, SLA's assistant principal, succinctly summarized their view of time: "We make 'time' the elective. The schedule allows students to pursue their own passions in blocks of time. What they do with it is up to them, both on campus or with off-campus partners."

Schools are starting to think about and adopt the concept of what has come to be known as "Google time," applying it to new learning opportunities for students as well as teachers. At Google, one of the most innovative companies on the planet, employees are expected (not allowed—expected) to spend 20 percent of their time doing something that has nothing to do with their real job. They can think, learn, explore, ponder, interact, and hopefully create something that will help the company to succeed in a new and different way. Don Wettrick teaches media at Franklin Community, a public high school outside Indianapolis. In 2012, he had a brainstorm. "If we think the 'Google 20 percent time' model makes sense, and want to provide students an opportunity to stretch in that modality, why not create time and space for them each day, one period out of their daily class schedule? What would that do for enhancing creativity, student ownership of the learning space, and that all-critical key to learning, passion?"

"The schedule allows students to pursue their own passions in blocks of time. What they do with it is up to them, both on campus or with off-campus partners."

Don pitched the idea to his principal and in 2012 kicked off the "Innovations" class. Students in this elective come up with their own ideas of projects to pursue and then use social media to connect to resources outside of the school—in the community, the region, or anywhere in the world—to help meet their project goals. When I first interviewed Don, one student was pursuing ideas related to autistic learning and iPads. Another was working on a blended fuel project. A third was helping to negotiate contracts for installation of a renewable solar energy system at the school. A few students were struggling to merge projects and passions, which of course one would expect in an authentic program. Not all students immediately take to the freedom of time to think on their own. They have been constrained by class schedules for their entire developmental lives. Classes like Don's allow them a first glimpse of what the real world, beyond fifty-five-minute slices, looks like and expects.

Molding Time to Purpose

In most schools, use of time is a nearly sacred driver of life and decisions. Time is viewed as a fixed term in the learning equation, rather than as perhaps the most flexible variable. Some schools have never been captive to this relationship or are starting to break away from it. They deliberately identify the best learning environment for their students and then warp time to fit the learning model.

Poughkeepsie Day School (PDS), a humble independent school nestled in the Hudson River Valley, has been a standard bearer of classic Progressive Era education for decades. PDS has a creative schedule that includes long interdisciplinary blocks of time. To PDS, innovation means keeping aware of the world the students are living in and providing learning and support within that world. Educators at the school feel it is critical for the students to become fully connected to their community, and they use the larger blocks of time in their daily routine to allow these connections to evolve way beyond the occasional field trip. The school has chosen to trade short blocks of time driven by subject content for larger blocks of time driven by broad, deep themes. In every eight-day cycle there is one full day for intensive courses, which can occur on or off campus. The kindergarten class partners with a local farm to learn about the economics, science, and work of growing food. Students go out to the farm, work in the soil, and bring food back with them to school. First-grade students survey and interview shop owners and residents along Market Street in Poughkeepsie to learn about how a city uses resources, what makes a community, and the connection between the economy and jobs. The entire school takes a weekly break called "choice time" when students of mixed ages work on projects or subjects of their choosing and help lead the courses.

Shifting the use of time does not always require changes to the daily schedule. Teachers are reviewing curriculum, units, and the flow of work within a class and finding they can create time even within a traditional hour-long class period. Norfolk Academy is one of the oldest and most respected college prep schools on the Atlantic seaboard. Math teacher Katy Woods told me how educators at the school sat down with the traditional curriculum and rethought what was actually critical for the students to learn. "What we found is that you can actually teach geometry in about six weeks if you have to. Having that flexibility to decide when to do a lecture and when to let the students explore problems allows us to use time in a much more creative way. The students are engaging in projects that actually use math in ways that interest them. They have designed a locker room. They designed new athletic shoes all the way from how to make them to getting celebrity sponsors, to marketing the final product, and all that uses math. We found that by streamlining the content portion of the curriculum we could create all this time for the students to 'play' with math, which is what the real world is all about."

Time for Adult Collaboration

A few teachers want to be left alone to teach in ways they are comfortable, to do what they have always done. Most teachers desperately want more time to work with their colleagues and to learn about new teaching practices, to try out new ideas, to constantly develop themselves into better teachers. It is one of the marvelous common threads of the profession: Most teachers got into teaching because they really care about kids and want to do whatever they can to be the best teachers they can be. Teachers tend to be eager to learn, just as they are eager to promote a love of learning in their students. But few schools allocate significant chunks of time for professional development. When teachers are not in class they are preparing for class, grading papers, talking with students, or attending meetings. Most teachers take work home at night and on weekends. Many teachers teach during the summer months or work on units for the following year. The problem of finding time for authentic, productive, collaborative professional development has stumped nearly every school I visited.

The daily class schedule dictates more than just the learning experience for students. The schedule also controls the amount and type of time that adults have for their own learning and professional development. Few adults, particularly teachers, have time to adjust to our rapidly changing world, to learn about new technologies or brain research that impacts how and what we teach, to collaborate with their colleagues at school or across school boundaries, to learn about and adopt successes that others have found. At most schools, teachers meet with colleagues in their respective departments every few weeks, with teachers from their own divisions perhaps once a month, with other teachers in their own schools once or twice a year, and rarely or ever with teachers from other schools. Many attend workshops or a conference once every year or every two years. This poverty of collegial connection is antithetical to everything we know about the importance of networking to organizational innovation. In the business world, companies increasingly live and die based on rapid innovation that is fostered and nurtured by the time and opportunity for employees to constantly grow. Why should schools be different?

Fortunately, some school leaders are finding all kinds of ways to create time for team-based professional collaboration. The mechanism for creating time in an apparently overloaded schedule is the same: Leaders refuse to let traditional time allocations deprive them of the chance to meet and learn from each other. As with student learning, they treat time as a manageable variable, not a fixed driver.

Lyn Hilt was principal of Brecknock Elementary School, a public pre-K–6 school, when I visited the school, in the rolling hills of rural Lancaster County, Pennsylvania. I spent the morning with Lyn and her teachers, talking about the difficulty of integrating critical learning skills into a curriculum that is largely focused on teaching to standards-based tests. Third-grade teacher Stephanie Ciabatinni told me it came down to Lyn making collegial connections a top priority for her faculty: "She found time for us during the day. We have time every week to get together with the other grade-level teachers, and we decided to use this time to review upcoming units through the lens of the state standard curriculum and figure out how to integrate all of the twenty-first-century skills that we know are critical for our students. By working together we can achieve this in a way we just would not be able to if we were each working just in our own classroom." Lyn is also one of a growing number of school leaders who not only use Twitter as a way to connect professionally with educators around the country and the world, but also strongly urge teachers to do the same. "I want my teachers connected with people with other ideas as often as possible. Some people see Twitter as a distraction. Used correctly, it is an ideal tool for faculty professional growth. It does not take up a lot of time, yet it connects people who would never have met each other."

School leaders like Lyn and highly paid scheduling consultants have struggled for years with how to create frequent blocks of time for teachers to work with each other. Following my trip, I was working with the students and faculty of St. Andrews' Episcopal School in Fort Worth for a day, and a ninth-grade student offered a solution that I think can, and should, utterly transform how we solve this problem. I asked the students to take a few minutes to think about how learning takes place on their campus. After a short observational walk around campus, the students itemized their thoughts and then pitched ideas to each other about how learning might be more closely tied to their own lives and personal objectives.

One of the students commented that adults needed time by themselves to learn, just as students do. He recognized that many of the classrooms at all grade levels were becoming project-based, and good projects are designed to include time for student collaboration, research, making, designing, building, and creating. His group asked, "What if we just aligned the days and times when many classes were doing this kind of independent work? What if, say, every other Thursday for a half-day, all or many classes at the school had 'project time'? We need time to work on these projects together and don't really need teachers hovering around at those times. A few adults could supervise a large number of students during these collaborative work times, releasing the rest for large, frequent blocks of professional growth time." Remember, four ninth graders came up with this idea after just twenty minutes studying the problem!

I have subsequently put this idea in front of a large number of teachers and administrators from both public and private schools. As of this writing, no one has offered any significant reason why this idea would not work.

Bringing the Outside In

For their own learning, educators have traditionally gone to conferences, read books, taken a course in their credentialing program and . . . that was pretty much it. Each adult viewed himself or herself as a stand-alone learning project. Now we see how powerfully the entire organization can leverage an ever-widening knowledge base by creating time and pathways for adults to share their learning with each other. We see school as a learning environment for adults as well as children. As I say when I facilitate an active learning workshop with educators, the most important mechanism we have for professional growth is to "leverage the brainpower in the room." Innovative schools are finding

Innovative schools are finding time in their annual schedule for teachers and administrators to do what they do best: share and teach each other.

time in their annual schedule for teachers and administrators to do what they do best: share and teach each other.

Pam Moran is the superintendent of the Albemarle County Schools, a 13,000-student district that serves a diverse community ranging from high-tech suburbanites to remote, low-income farms an hour west of Richmond, Virginia. Among the many innovative practices Pam and her team of forward-looking educators have incorporated is a professional sharing program, an in-house annual conference where teachers and administrators from the entire county put on poster sessions about what they are doing in the classroom. Pam and her team showed me the lineup of presentations for the 2012 conference. They had more than 160 separate sessions presented in a single day, a massive outpouring of shared knowledge, each offered by a teacher who is passionate about what she or he is doing in the classroom. These educators don't rely on outside consultants to tell them about the next great thing. They give their own teachers a platform and a little bit of time to share.

I found this poster session mechanism repeated at several other schools I visited, including St. Andrew's Episcopal in Potomac, Maryland, and Parish Episcopal in Dallas. Once or twice a year, the teachers take a half-day or full-day break for professional development, and active sharing is a centerpiece. Teachers who have been to a conference or who piloted a new idea in their classroom share the results. Teachers who have developed a new resource or published a new workbook put them out on display. The school celebrates their creativity. Most schools have built-in professional growth days when the students are absent, so these in-house conferences do not add time to the yearly schedule or a penny of expense to the budget. In fact, for schools that bring in outside consultants to lead a professional growth day, this leveraging of internal brainpower is a significant cost savings.

The Denver Green School (DGS) is another public school we will revisit several times in this book. The school was founded by a unique partnership of veteran local educators that I will discuss more in the chapters on leadership and organizational structures. DGS operates under the oversight of the Board of Denver Public Schools, but also under an innovation initiative that gives the school a great deal of autonomy. The school serves students from a lower–middle class demographic, with 60 percent qualifying for free and reduced lunch. The school is dedicated to teaching concepts and practices of sustainability in relationship to the classroom, the community, and students themselves, through a host of project-based learning activities.

Developing faculty's comfort with a fluid, dynamic academic program is key to the DGS mission. The school tweaked the daily schedule to allow extra time every day for faculty to meet with each other, and every Friday the students come for only a half-day, with the remainder of that day allotted for faculty professional growth. In addition, teacher contracts include a week in June and two weeks before school starts in the fall that are totally dedicated to collaboration and school coordination issues. The site leaders found money in a tight budget to pay teachers to spend that extra week or two at school, devoted solely to developing themselves into better teachers.

At the College School, a small, early childhood–sixth-grade private school serving middle class families in St. Louis, faculty collaboration and professional development is a top priority of the school. The school's tuition is not substantially more than what local public schools receive in support from the tax base, so time and money are both precious resources. Teachers get released for one period a day and an additional three mornings a week for program and professional development. Teachers are expected to keep a keen eye on best practices and innovative programs at other schools, constantly try out new ideas, and tweak their own programs. Each fall the faculty

Leaders were able to create time for authentic, sustained, high-frequency professional collaboration without increasing teaching loads, the number of employees, or, for the most part, the number of hours or days that teachers work.

gets together and creates a school-wide template for professional development to guide common discussions. In 2012, the main headings under which the teachers thought about their growth were "inspiration," "student care," and "customer experience." Teachers help create the template and are expected to show, over the course of the year, how they have expanded their understanding and implementation of the annual themes and goals.

In each of these cases, leaders were able to create time for authentic, sustained, high-frequency professional collaboration without increasing teaching loads, the number of employees, or, for the most part, the number of hours or days that teachers work. These educators made choices and came up with creative solutions to reimagine their use of discretionary time during the day and year.

REFLECTION

Educators at nearly every school I visited mentioned the need to reevaluate the school's daily schedule to align time with their vision of what our students need to be successful in their futures. Most schools will end up with some form of modified block schedule that gives each teacher a longer period for subject-based learning on a less frequent meeting rotation. Educators at these schools will think that this is the best they can do, the closest they can come without making any of their stakeholders too uncomfortable. It will be a lukewarm solution. A few schools will do what truly forward-leaning schools have started to do. They will set aside the traditional chain that binds us to subject matter and class schedule, line up their learning and teaching priorities, and not rest until the highest priorities get the most time in the day, the week, and the school year.

How can a school team turn time from a limitation into a powerful tool? The process starts with reimagining what our schools would look like if we had no traditions of short, subject-based time slots. As we will see in the penultimate chapter of this book, we need to construct our schools without the preconditions placed upon us by the industrial age model. What if you asked your teachers, students, and parents to design a school with no constraints on time? What might they offer? Schools that have undertaken this exercise never default back to a series of fifty-minute classes. If schools are also able to transcend the rigid boundaries of traditional subjects, they may envision long blocks of time, unconstrained by bells, when students and teachers are free to focus on passion-centered learning, not a fixed quantum of content. Would this kind of school require us to retool how students and teachers engage? Absolutely. But we will not deconstruct the assembly line unless we change the use of time in schools. We can't create more minutes in a day or days in a year, but we can absolutely twist time to better meet our learning goals.

CHAPTER TWO

People
The Changing Job of an Educator

On the road, weekends are a time to catch up on work and sleep, to find a park, a hiking trail, a driving range, or a back-road nine-hole course where tee times are not required, even on Sunday. Weekends are a time to restock the snack box in the car, repack a suitcase, and eat free breakfast twice, once in the early light of day and once with the other weekend travelers, late risers with dogs in their rooms and kids who swim in the noisy little indoor hotel pool.

Cheap hotels are cheaper on weekends, and cheaper yet in Naugatuck, Connecticut, an old New England town nestled along both sides of the river that shares its name, a few miles south of Waterbury. Naugatuck used to have more mills and factories and people than it does today. I got in late on Friday afternoon, hungry from a rainy three-hour drive from Boston with nothing to eat but peanuts, raisins, and water. I drove around town looking for dinner. If you like pizza, you would love Naugatuck. I found six pizza parlors and a McDonald's.

On Saturday I got a haircut, my first trip to the barber in more than thirty years. Back in the day I had hair, though never much, and my wife started cutting my hair before we were married. Now I just run the clippers over my balding pate every few weeks. It was nice to visit a barber, chat about the town and the Patriots' season, even if he took twenty minutes for a two-minute job. Renting his chair and conversation was worth the fifteen dollars. That evening I went out again, looking for something to eat other than pizza and found a family diner with salads, burgers, and red-checkered vinyl tabletops. I drove around town and passed a sunset wedding unfolding on the green of a small church with a tall Protestant steeple, guests sitting on white chairs while the bride in her off-shoulder gown and the groom in his traditional tuxedo exchanged vows under a bandstand cupola and the wind knocked the chill factor into the thirties. New Englanders are tough, even brides. Factories and mills close, once-urgent towns become sleepy byways, but people stay. I think schools, like towns, are largely defined by their people.

Risk, Fear, and a Growth Mindset

Schools are people places. Change makes people uncomfortable, and schools generally don't like to make people uncomfortable. But facing and overcoming those points of resistance opens up an entirely new future of learning opportunities for both students and adults. Over and over, school leaders told me that the single most impactful driver of effective change was creating a "growth mindset" among employees: the recognition and willingness that next year can, and probably should be, different from this year.

By a *growth mindset*, I mean a willingness to change what you are doing, which means shifting the equation of risk, fear, failure, and reward. Alan Deutschman, in *Change or Die* (2007), lays out three keys to becoming comfortable with this kind of growth. First, you form relationships "with a person or community that inspires and sustains hope" to the point that you believe you have the ability to change. Second, you learn and practice the skills you will need to direct and embrace change. Third, you "learn new ways of thinking about your situation and your life." You focus on the upside of what is possible instead of the fear that it will fail. Ultimately, Deutschman concludes, "change is learning." As educators we know and embrace the elegance of this simple reduction; as innovators we know that people with this mindset are the drivers who keep pace with a changing world.

Taking risks in a traditional school has both real and perceived downsides and very little upside. Fear of change manifests in many ways at the schools I visited. When schools begin the discussion of incorporating distance-learning programs, teachers worry: "We are the experts in what we teach. Why are you trying to outsource our jobs?" When new technologies appear on the horizon that can make learning more tailored to the individual student, teachers worry: "You are trying to replace me with a computer." When school leaders try to tackle the problem of the daily schedule, the immediate response from many is this: "You don't value what I do. If you did, you would not be trying to take time away from me." Risky behavior has not been traditionally rewarded in schools; schools treat failure by assigning a unique letter grade that is absent from almost any other system in the real world. Adults who comply with the repetitive status quo get good evaluations and are promoted. People who take a risk that goes wrong do not. In a traditional school model, a discussion of "risk" raises concerns about student safety, rather than the opportunity for both students and teachers to develop skills to deal with adversity or failure.

Educators default to their own histories of what good education looks like. We all had great teachers in our own youth, teachers who inspired us and changed the way we look at the world. We remember those personal heroes and seek to emulate them, to create in our own classrooms what those heroes created for us. The problem is that the outcomes we seek have changed and that mental model is now an obstacle, not a template. John Dewey (1916) spoke of the importance of the educational growth mindset more than a century ago when he told us, "If we teach today as we taught yesterday, we rob our children of tomorrow."

Today, as in the past, most teachers are hired because they know their subject, can convey it to students, and can control a classroom, not because they adapt or lead change well. Teachers are evaluated on how well they meet an assessment rubric that has little, if any, focus on how well they promote or lead change from year to year. Administrators are evaluated on how smoothly the school runs. Most adults at schools have the mindset that things usually do not change and, when they do, they change slowly. This mindset has fit past conditions well. The rate of change in the world was such that we expected the next decade to look more or less like today. That expectation no longer matches reality. As one principal told me, "If you are not willing to change, you should not be a teacher. It is now part of the job. Period."

I find that most teachers *beg* for more opportunities to grow and excel as a teacher. Many recognize that some of the basic skills that have served teachers well in the past are no longer adequate. They ask to attend conferences and workshop trainings to learn and practice new techniques to elevate student engagement but have access to vanishingly little time, free rein, or resources to pursue those passions. Other teachers are justifiably wary of top-down mandated change. "Just wait a few years and it [whatever is being discussed] will come around again." Fads in education come and go with the changing political winds, publishers with statewide contracts, research data, and the flux of societal pressures. Teachers are buffeted by all of these fads, and they nod warily to the most recent "flavor of the month." On my trip, many great teachers asked one simple question: "How do we know that this time the change is for real?"

Constant Growth

Jeremy Spry, assistant principal at Science Leadership Academy (SLA) in Philadelphia, told me that both teachers and students at the school share a common language based on a set of core values and a common progression through grade and subject level. Beyond that, he said, members of the school community are always looking at the next change they can make to enhance an authentic learning experience. In the hallway we waylaid teacher Alexa Dunn, who told me, "We make program decisions all the time; we never really take a time-out of thinking about how we can be better. The faculty get together every week to present to each other, and that creates a mindset that we are learners. We learn from our students, which makes the classroom truly transactional. We pursue new knowledge together, which ties directly into the model of project-based learning."

> *"The faculty get together every week to present to each other, and that creates a mindset that we are learners. We learn from our students, which makes the classroom truly transactional."*

SLA's founder and principal, Chris Lehmann, crystallized *why* and *how* SLA is making so much headway relative to other schools that seem stuck in the traditional model: "The systems and structures we have put in place make people better teachers. I am a better principal here." He believes that "the history of other progressive schools shows that they become places where adults are free to do their own thing, but there is not a through-going pathway for the students." Teachers at SLA spend an enormous amount of time connected with their jobs. Some told me that they are still e-mailing their students at midnight. Some come in on the weekends because the students ask them to. Teachers take over each other's classes when needed, which is pretty much all the time because there is always something that is pulling a teacher and group of students in a new and exciting direction. Teachers can't use last year's syllabus for this year's class since courses take new directions as the students pursue unpredictable passions and teachers deal with that frequent ambiguity. Every one of the teachers I met walking the halls of my morning visit said they would not trade their school for any other learning environment. They talk like soldiers, charging up a hill, committed to do anything needed to take the summit—committed to each other to not let the obstacles beat them back.

Teacher as Lead Learner

Many educators have recognized that the role of teacher is no longer a "sage on the stage," lecturing to a quiet and often sleepy or distracted class. I increasingly hear teachers and their students talking about the adults becoming "lead learners" and "co-learners" alongside their students. I found this emerging relationship displayed in many ways at the schools I visited. Teachers rebuild their curriculum each year, rather than repeating what they taught last year. They increasingly connect with colleagues to develop learning strategies that incorporate new research into how the brain works and how students learn. Teachers are willing to try new technologies that provide students with direct access to content or improve the efficiency of differentiated learning, even if these teachers are not completely comfortable with the technology when it first becomes available. Perhaps most important, teachers develop a view of themselves as participating in a constantly evolving journey of exploration *with* their students, as opposed to teachers' traditional role of providing knowledge *to* their students.

When I met Geoff Wagg he was the Upper School principal at Episcopal Academy outside Philadelphia, one of the oldest schools in the United States. Geoff has been a leading voice for innovation in schools ever since he left graduate school the year after the World Wide Web was invented. He talked about how taking risks with new ideas, with teachers pushing beyond what they have done in the past, grabs hold in schools and ends up utterly changing the learning culture. "I think the two greatest technological innovations we have had in schools in a long time are the graphing calculator and the word processor. If you talk to math teachers who taught before the era of the graphing calculator and ask them, 'Did you think it was going to make a real difference, become a critical technology in the classroom?' most will say 'absolutely not.' If you ask them would they ever go back and teach the way they did before we had graphing calculators, almost all will say 'absolutely not.' What we can teach now as a result of that technology is so much higher up the thinking taxonomy that we will never give it up. And of course we would say the same for the word processor. Neither one of those are profound technologies. They were just continuations of technologies that were in development. The transformation in learning took place when teachers who were open-minded to those technologies understood how they could be used, and were willing to go ahead and try without any real game plan or training. That made them so revolutionary. And now they have infiltrated our learning completely."

"For schools, innovation is about taking different things that already exist and piecing them together and making them work in a profoundly different way that makes teaching and learning better."

For learning to keep pace with changes in the world, Geoff says, schools have to adopt a culture that is widespread throughout the business world, a culture that recognizes the value of risk and the process of learning from failure. "Innovation is not invention. This is not my example, but I will use it: 3M did not invent glue or cellophane, but they did invent Scotch tape. For schools, innovation is about taking different things that already exist and piecing them together and making them work in a profoundly different way that makes teaching and learning better. And that requires people being free to make these connections in their classrooms or their offices and take advantage of them. We need to embed that same mindset in schools where people feel comfortable that they are going to try something new. If it works, great, but if it fails, that is OK, too, because what you are doing is trying to get better."

Desire to Learn

Not all schools, even those that view themselves as innovative and adaptive, exude the sense that they want, as an organization, to change for the better. Virtually every school I visited was running a pilot project that they felt was "innovative" or aligned with a "twenty-first-century" mindset. But in some of those schools, the pilots were isolated; there was no intentional or pervasive expectation or urgency regarding change from the traditional school format. There was no collective understanding that we need to move ourselves along with changing times. Where present, however, this collective desire to learn and grow among the adults is a tangible lever that keeps the entire organization from becoming stuck in outmoded ruts.

Innovation Charter Academy is a public charter school about forty minutes northwest of Boston. It was started in the 1990s as a middle school and later added a high school. The school is now housed on what was the building and grounds of a monastery, which became a small Wang outpost and then a satellite of Boston University before Innovation Charter bought the site. The library occupies the old chapel, and the school just put in a turf athletic field. It is starting to look like an East Coast prep school, except it is tuition-free. In 2012, the school had 660 students, on the way to about 800 students over the next two years.

Their students come from the surrounding ten towns. The school doesn't admit the brightest kids; it gets a random selection of those who apply. Demand to attend is double the available spots. In the school's two graduating classes so far, 100 percent of the seniors have received acceptances at four-year colleges. The stipend the school receives from the local districts varies, but averages about $10,000 per student per year, which is low relative to many public schools around the country and a fraction of what many private schools charge. That pays for everything, including expenses that the public schools do not have to pay. When snow piles up, the school pays a vendor out of the annual allotment; the public works crews plow driveways for the regular public schools. When the sewer lines need to be replaced, Innovation has to find money in the budget. The school has to take care of all of its own administrative expenses. Teachers generally make less than their counterparts in the regular public schools.

I spent about three hours with Middle School Director Melissa Kapeckas and High School Director Greg Orpen. I asked Melissa what she thinks lies at the heart of the school's ability to generate improved student outcomes with less money than other public schools and vastly less than most private schools. Her answer sounded almost exactly like what I heard from Chris Lehman at SLA in Philadelphia: "We have an incredible staff who want to be at the school and enjoy learning from each other. We insist on teachers having the mindset that they will always grow and always change. We are never satisfied and always refining our teaching practices and programs, not once a year or every few years, but all the time. As a group we set continuous goals at the same time we are thinking about what is next. We have these core values and that really creates a sense of community."

"We insist on teachers having the mindset that they will always grow and always change. We are never satisfied and always refining our teaching practices and programs, not once a year or every few years, but all the time."

As the school has grown, administrators have had to adapt to retain faculty, many of whom were young and single when the school started. Now those same teachers have families of their own and can't continue putting in the long nights and weekends. Administrators have shifted resources to support teachers as the school ethos requires those teachers to continually realign themselves. The school has reduced the number of different courses each teacher must prepare and increased time for collaboration in teams to spread the curriculum development load. The school modified the schedule to release students early three out of every four Wednesdays, at 12:45 pm, so teachers get a good chunk of time to work together. Melissa told me that simply reducing the administrative drag in the school makes teachers feel better about their ability to change what they do: "We intentionally play down any sign of red tape; if teachers want to do something, it gets done. Teachers feel a lot of ownership of their work."

Finding and Hiring Innovators

Savvy school leaders know that they can dramatically accelerate the rate of change in their school if they hire people with "innovation DNA" who are also good teachers, rather than hiring knowledge experts who are locked into a traditional teaching role. Ten or even five years ago, nearly all schools looked exclusively at the teaching pedigree of an applicant: years of experience, mastery of subject, and the ability to manage students in a classroom. Now, schools with a vision of innovation realize that those characteristics are important but not the *most* important qualities. Administrators at these schools look for evidence of creativity in applicants' past. Does the applicant work well on a team? Have they taken risks in their professional career or do they want to teach a course the same way they have always taught it? Will they need extensive training in how a growth mindset applies to the school setting? One school I visited brings a group of job applicants in together, and the first-stage interview involves giving the group a design task to complete, while the hiring team watches the dynamics of the struggling pool of applicants.

The fastest way to ensure long-term comfort with change is to hire people who are immediately comfortable with constant change. In his best seller *Good to Great*, Jim Collins (2001) made popular the phrase and concept of "getting the right people in the right seats on the bus." Organizations can twist themselves into knots trying to change, but if the right people are not on "the bus," the likelihood of success is drastically reduced.

In *The Myths of Innovation*, Scott Berkun (2010) tracks the history of innovation and provides a rich description of why innovation does and does not occur. "Developing new ideas requires questions and approaches that most people won't understand initially, which leaves many true innovators at risk of becoming lonely or misunderstood." He says that innovation is nonlinear: "Mistakes and complexity are everywhere. There is no playbook that removes risk." Key challenges that innovators confront include finding an idea, sponsorship or funding, timing, and reproducing a positive result. "Ideas are generally not rejected on their merits; they are rejected because of how they make people feel." Innovators are bombarded by negative feedback from people who don't believe their ideas will work, don't understand them, don't see the problem, are threatened by the solution, or just don't care enough to put in the effort to give it a good chance to succeed. It is therefore a unique set of skills that sets the successful innovator apart, and those are skills for which schools can, and should, hire.

Shirley Hord and Edward Tobia, in *Reclaiming Our Teaching Profession* (2012), say that the starting point in developing our people resources at school is "development of a mindset that is centered on continuous improvement." These authors see teachers as "independent heroes" who need to begin acting as "contributing members of a community of professional learners." Hord and Tobia offer a clear list of attributes that we can use to help distinguish teachers who have a growth mindset from those who do not:

> *"Teachers must be honest about student progress, open enough to receive ideas and feedback from colleagues, competent enough to share strategies with team members, and talented enough to access best practices in their field."*

> Teachers must be honest about student progress, open enough to receive ideas and feedback from colleagues, competent enough to share strategies with team members, and talented enough to access best practices in their field. . . regularly scan the literature . . . take on mentoring roles, engaging in curriculum development projects, and designing professional learning experiences. (pp. 14–15)

The literature is full of templates for what kind of person makes the best innovator. Carol Dweck's body of work, and particularly her book *Mindset* (2007), have made the connection of innovation with a growth mindset highly accessible and relevant to the educational community. To add to this awakening among educators, I think a school can dramatically increase the organizational innovation DNA in a short period of time by finding, hiring, training, and retaining people who exhibit some of these characteristics of a growth/innovation mindset:

• *Innovators tend to be dissatisfied with the status quo and willing to risk something in order to effect a change.* Innovative educators are willing to upset decades of education history in order to align their practice with their desired outcomes. A common thread among innovators is that they focus on the future, not on the past or present. They see what needs to happen at some point that may be years ahead and have the ability to work backward from that vision to initiate action today.

- *Good innovators can look at large amounts of data or information from disparate sources and recognize patterns others will not see.* Sometimes these patterns are obscure or meaningless; not all information that correlates in interesting ways has value. Good innovators are able to predict which of these patterns might have value and judge potential outcomes in light of an entire playing field of possibilities.

- *People who can speak or understand many "languages" or the basics of many different disciplines are more likely to be better at this kind of pattern recognition.* In a school, this means that employees who have experience teaching multiple subjects or multiple grade levels, who worked in the private sector before coming to teaching, or who have a major side focus or "superpower" like technology, music, athletics, art, community service, or travel may be more likely to recognize a new idea of undiscovered value than would those with more narrowly focused backgrounds or interests.

- *Innovators are good at prioritizing options and assessing possible outcomes at various points in the creative process.* Innovators in schools recognize the importance of budget stress, admissions demands, time constraints on the faculty, community politics, and other resource and market constraints that will impact the process of an innovation and still try to innovate within or around these constraints.

- *Innovators tend to be creative, even to the point of being playful.* They have fun with trying new ways of doing what has been done in the past, just for the sake of trying something new. They see their work as a blank canvas on which they love to sketch, draw, and paint, even if that means constantly reworking the picture in real time. They are not afraid to have others comment on their work and in fact enjoy leading others through what innovators see as fun and games, rather than a grinding process.

- *Innovators love to exchange ideas.* Innovators enjoy acting as the conduit for an exchange of ideas among groups that find this difficult—connecting people and vision, making contacts where none previously existed. Innovators love to ask questions. Innovators are those most eager to break down internal boundaries and connect across disciplines or campuses.

• *Innovators are naturally empathetic, particularly with their students.* Schools are the core of a community of interlocking stakeholders. Schools need to ensure that they have institutional empathy with the changing needs and wants of their customers, which requires direct communication between the customer (students and parents) and producers (teachers).

• *Innovators are often the most stubborn employees in the organization.* While some employees stubbornly resist new ideas, innovators stubbornly refuse to give up on a good new idea. They are evangelical in their pursuit and support of what they believe is the next great thing. They acquire community resources, both tangible and intangible, and are driven to see their new idea become adopted.

Building an Innovative Teaching Team

Maplewood Richmond Heights (MRHMS) is a public middle school that serves a blue-collar community in the St. Louis urban core. When I visited then principal Bob Dillon and his team at MRHMS, he reported getting about 150 applications for every teaching opening he posted. He focuses on building teams that, over time, embody the kind of cultural DNA that promotes innovation: "I want someone who adds to the team, who brings some set of ideas and skills that we lack or want. The best hires are those that can embrace the current system as well as help the program and culture to grow. In addition, I want people who are intellectually robust with a huge belly fire for changing the lives of kids in a positive way. Couple those elements with a strong desire to learn, a deep sense of creativity and positive risk-taking, and you have created the very high likelihood that your newest team member will enhance your place of learning."

Across town, the College School is a small private early childhood–sixth-grade school serving a modest middle- and lower-middle-class section of St. Louis. Now retired head of school Sheila Gurley told me that it all starts in the hiring process. Sheila hires and retains people with a strong record of creativity, not just strong subject teachers: "Not everyone is cut out to teach in this environment of constant reflection and refinement. We have created a mindset that change is good and can be both comfortable and rewarding. I try to get people to understand that changes are not permanent. People won't agonize over temporary change or pilots or trials if they don't think of them as becoming automatically permanent. We try to hire people who understand this from the outset and find that they automatically fit into our style of constantly refining the learning process."

Porter Gaud School lies just across the salt marsh from Fort Sumter and a cannon shot away from the harbor in Charleston, South Carolina. If any school could hide from innovation behind tradition, it would be here, but it is not. Around a conference table with the entire school leadership team assembled, I asked one of my key questions from the school visits: "What is very different here from what it was just five years ago?" At most schools the answers had to do with pedagogy and classroom practices. The first hand that shot up belonged to Barbara West, director of human resources: "In the hiring process, the number of degrees or years of experience as a teacher is less important. We place more emphasis on the skills that a candidate has, their ability to work with others, and their entrepreneurial spirit. If we hire teachers who are adaptable, they will teach adaptability to their students."

"If we hire teachers who are adaptable, they will teach adaptability to their students."

New Paths of Professional Development

School leaders are not naive; they know they can't just wave a hand and suddenly find that their teachers and junior administrators will embrace risk, change what has worked for years or decades, and break the comfortable molds that define schools. They won't suddenly assume all the traits of innovators. But over time, and with focus, change is possible. As we saw when discussing the use of time at school, leaders understand that time for professional development, for learning these new skills and mindsets, is the highest priority if we are going to truly transform the learning environment. Developing our most critical resource, people, is really about giving them the time and opportunity to accept and embrace change.

The path to developing teacher as leader, teacher as risk taker, or teacher as learner is not the same at every school. The core of what principal Eric Juli needs to do at the urban public Design Lab School in Cleveland is change the way teachers and students view the reason they come to school each day. The night before I visited Design Lab, Eric invited me to dinner at his house. He told me the story of his first few days at the school: "The first day of school, of twenty-five faculty assigned, eight showed up. We had some substitutes, but in a lot of the classrooms there was no adult. The entire first year our faculty absenteeism rate was about 50 percent. I have three teachers who actually know what teaching and learning should look like, or want to learn what it looks like. My goal is to keep those three and get three or four more each year. In four years I will have a faculty of good teachers, and without that we can't break the cycle of poor performance in the classroom."

The venerable Collegiate School in Richmond, Virginia, is a galaxy away from Design Lab in terms of the challenges the school community faces, but educators there also see professional development of their adults as a key to breaking out of a purely traditional learning practice. Two years ago, Head of School Keith Evans asked the University of Richmond Business School to develop and deliver a tailored leadership course for Collegiate middle managers. By the time of my visit, the school had sent about thirty employees through semester-long sessions to learn about and practice the principles of decision making, strategic thinking, and project management. Each employee chose a project that they wanted to tackle and learned critical management skills by developing and presenting an action plan viewed through the lens of the course. The managers I met with told me they "learned specific skills in understanding personal strengths and weaknesses, creating good arguments, team building, overcoming obstacles, and developing buy-in." There were additional benefits to the course that were not part of the curriculum. It went a long way to busting the silos the adults worked in, as they went off campus for three-hour blocks to work and learn together. They learned that they had much more in common than they had realized, and now they have a shared language with which to engage their work at school and their interests beyond. They produced highly relevant work, improved internal communication, and now say they have a much better understanding of the complexity of the school.

Woodward Academy in Atlanta started a leadership training program for selected faculty and administrators. According to Coordinator of Teaching and Learning Shelley Paul, the school put cohorts of about sixteen teachers and administrators through an intensive yearlong program that has "inspired a lot of people to do things they would not have dreamed of. It gives you a feeling of freedom and inspiration to try something new." A group of faculty came out of the program and created Woodward Academy Innovation in the Classroom, or "WA, Inc.," a group of faculty that meets once a month, with each teacher bringing at least one student to the group. According to Shelley, the teachers who have joined have not been just those who might be labeled the most progressive or innovative. It is a broadly ranging group representing divergent viewpoints, and the students are often the most vocal. One of the faculty members told me, "We are all surrendering a little bit of control."

Growth *Is* the Job Description

MC2 School was originally a public alternative school that has since been converted to charter status. The school currently operates a campus in Manchester, New Hampshire, and additional schools in development will also operate under the charter. In 2009, MC2 won a New Hampshire state award for competency-based learning, which is now a standard for all New Hampshire schools. The school offers a highly personalized learning program to students from a very wide range of backgrounds, and it is not through large allocations of dollars; MC2 receives just over $5,400 per student per year to operate the school.

MC2 has developed a system of differentiated, student-owned, performance-based learning that really does put the student into the driver's seat of their learning trajectory. On the school wiki site, the school shares clearly articulated rubrics for a full range of essential performance standards, tools that students and teachers use for cooperative assessment, templates for student portfolios of demonstrated performance, and more. How do they do it? Self-titled "lead learner" Kim Carter says that the key to providing such an individualized program is not money but building the capacity of teachers to be effective in a different way of learning. "We had a second-year teacher who conducted her own study. She tracked every minute of time she spent during the week and compared that to how a traditional teacher spends her time. What she found was that she is *not spending any more time*; she is just *spending her time in very different ways*. Teachers here spend time on weekly reflections, helping students through a cycle of inquiry, and in developing their own learning habits and portfolios of work."

Kim says that the only way to develop the human capacity of teachers to build this system is to engage them in the process of developing a new belief system. "The number one belief we share is that every kid is capable of this kind of learning. Most teachers come with the baggage of a traditional learning style. We structure the day differently; we structure our expectations differently. Teachers learn to give up their roles of creating lesson plans and tracking grades. We don't set a predetermined pace at which every child, and frankly every teacher, will learn. We learn at what we call a 'negotiated pace,' and the student and teacher need to be part of the conversation in negotiating what that pace will be. Over time, as the individual learns the skills of managing and taking ownership of their own learning, we gradually release more of the responsibility to them."

Ravenscroft School is a large pre-K–12 school in Raleigh, North Carolina, which celebrated its 150-year anniversary in 2013. Ten-year Head Doreen Kelly says that school adults need to acquire skills to deal with a more ambiguous future: "The innovation is stepping back, seeing what we have been doing, and adjusting the lens to focus on core values. There is nothing new to invent in our plan; we just have to get out of the students' way. We recognized that there is a set of skills required to do that, that the faculty need to know themselves first. In some ways we have to be less congenial and more collegial, more courageous. A few people that we tolerated in the past have had to move on; for the vast majority this is liberating, allowing people to be up front and open about what frustrates them and doing something about it."

The recognition that developing core skills to deal with change is key led to a unique relationship with the nonprofit Center for Creative Leadership (CCL). The CCL has a long history of working with both for-profit and nonprofit organizations in change and leadership development. Working with Ravenscroft, they created a professional development program to help the faculty become leader-learners, to have the skills to infuse all of their classes with the leadership and citizenship skills that are at the core of the Ravenscroft "values tree." Assistant Head Colleen Ramsden quotes management icon Peter Drucker: " 'Culture eats strategy for breakfast.' Culture can wait out change, and we could not let that happen. We are creating a common language and mindset of what the pedagogy of leadership is, from adult through student, so every teacher feels confident about how to infuse leadership and citizenship training into their classroom and content area. The faculty did not want this focus on leadership and citizenship to be another flavor of the month. In the past, teachers have seen themselves as the purveyors of knowledge. We have to get past that. We have to help them acquire the self-knowledge and skills to become mentors and leaders of others in their own path of learning discovery."

"In the past, teachers have seen themselves as the purveyors of knowledge. We have to get past that. We have to help them acquire the self-knowledge and skills to become mentors and leaders of others in their own path of learning discovery."

Parish Episcopal School in Dallas is taking a similarly aggressive approach to make faculty professional growth transparent, intentional, and highly aligned with the core vision of what education should look like in the future. Like most schools, teachers create individual plans for professional development. At Parish, these plans are public, transparent, and part of the teachers' annual evaluation. All of the faculty are encouraged to review and comment on one another's annual plans. Anyone can go online, look at what their colleagues' priorities are for the year, follow their progress posts, make comments, copy and paste, or whatever. Head of School Dave Monaco says this is key to the process of strategic professional development: "We have eliminated the disparate, fairly weak goal process where teachers simply choose a goal like attending a conference, which offered little connection to the strategic direction of the school. Those were empty exercises that yielded little value; people were just checking a box and everyone was working as an independent entity. Now our professional development is centered on our core 'Practices of Definitive Preparation,' and every teacher's goals are public. The overall process is a top-down template, but after that, what practice a faculty member chooses to focus on, which unit or assessment they apply it to, or whether they work individually or in collaboration with peers, are completely up to the individual."

REFLECTION

"It's all about the kids" is an almost universal mantra at schools and pretty much expresses our collective mission. But in the case of changing education to meet the needs of a rapidly changing world, it's really all about the adults. The kids get it; they are naturally adaptive and flexible thinkers; they use new technology easily; they see learning as fun as long as we allow it to be playful and interest-based and not dreary. Changing what and how learning takes place is an exercise in retooling the adult skill set, and I found that this process really boils down to two steps.

First, we need to paint a picture for educators of what a transformed learning experience looks like, and I hope this book helps. By far the best way for teachers to see this vision, though, is to get out and visit other schools where transforming learning has taken root. I found that, for many teachers, even just a few hours in a school like some of those I visited and describe in this book is all they need to understand that they, too, can adopt a more student-centered, co-learning, growth-minded approach to their practice. One veteran teacher in Atlanta told me that she thought all this talk about innovation was just the next fad until she saw it in a classroom, and "the light went off in my head; I knew I could do that too, and the weight of the world was off my shoulders."

And then we need to give our teachers the resources, chiefly time, to retool. Our adult-leaders have grown up in a system of education that rewards a certain type of behavior, and now we are asking them to change. That takes time—especially time to work together with their colleagues to develop confidence, learn new teaching skills, and overcome a natural fear of change.

I found that schools that do these two things—paint the picture and provide resource support for change—are able to imagine, design, map, and build a dramatically new and improved learning environment in a remarkably short period of time.

CHAPTER THREE

Leadership
Building Vision While
Keeping the Lights On

Eric Juli is passionate about changing the cycle of poverty through education, so he has chosen to make his career in the toughest places. Design Lab School is an identified "new and innovative" high school in the Cleveland public school system. The doors open at 7:30 am. I stand off to the side and Eric gives me a quiet play-by-play: "The day here starts with kids walking through the metal detectors. Nobody wants to start the day that way, but the culture here has adapted to that. The community wants it. It is only negative if we make it negative, but it is certainly not how I want to start my day. A girl came through yesterday wearing her one shirt; it is the only one she has and she was wearing it. I saw several kids wearing the same thing they were wearing yesterday and last Friday."

Free breakfast is served. Two girls walk in yelling at each other, the follow-on to a fight the previous afternoon. Eric and a security guard defuse it for now. A tenth grader nods to Eric; she sits up most of the night with her mother, who is on oxygen at home, feeds her younger siblings, does the laundry, and gets to bed around 4:30 am. About half of the teachers lock their doors in class. The computers in the back of the classrooms are ancient, and most don't work. An eleventh grader walks up to me, a stranger, smiles, sticks out his hand and introduces himself. I ask him why he goes to school here. He says, "I like school." By midmorning, students are lined up outside Eric's office, sent by teachers who don't want them in their class. Eric sends them back; he will not suspend students except in extreme cases. He says the students need more time in school, not less. His teachers are slowly learning. A hungry pregnant girl stops by, and Eric gives her a fruit bar. A boy stops by, not wearing the required khaki pants, and Eric finds a pair. A substitute teacher tries to get a class to take their seats; they ignore him.

Eric walks the halls, talks to every teacher, talks to all the students, and knows who slept where last night and when they had their last meal. Last night was Open House; for 240 students, thirty-five parents came, which is a record for the school. Eric is going to recruit the heck out of incoming ninth graders. He is meeting with pastors and parents. He wants his teachers to call parents on the phone and meet them in their homes or at a church. He wants to change how an entire community thinks about this place called school.

Courage to Change

In 2012, Design Lab School had 240 students, 98 percent African American, almost all on free or reduced lunch. Many are working at two to four grades below level when they arrive as ninth graders. Some students travel an hour and a half each day on the bus to get there. In Cleveland public schools as a whole, 47 percent of African American males graduate high school; in 2012, Design Lab graduated almost 90 percent. I asked Eric how he sorts out the challenges he faces, how he decides at which windmills to tilt. "Our priority challenge here is to create a real learning environment where the students feel cared for. How do we create this culture of care? How do we get students and teachers to understand that there is more than this, that there is a different future they can have? That is our dance, and it is incredibly easy for any principal to be consumed with the daily stuff, but those things don't move the school forward. Our charge here is to get the culture right. So many of our kids come to us hungry and angry and desensitized to violence and have no idea about what school can be. Our mission is to first get to the point where we can talk about math, science and social studies and thinking and writing. We have to have a safe place for those things to occur."

I asked Eric to define success for the 2012–13 year. "Success this year is about getting to the point where we can focus on 'what do we want to learn today' as opposed to 'what are we going to do today.' We need to stop doing and start learning." His teachers don't know what that looks like, so he will need to find professional growth opportunities to show them. His students don't know what that looks like. School has always been a place where you do worksheets and there is a cultural accommodation between teachers and students that sets a low bar and allows everyone to get by. Eric has a few teachers who know how to teach and a few who are eager to learn. He needs to fill his ranks with teachers who are willing to get on board with his vision. That is going to take some time and a lot of stubborn refusal to allow inertia to win.

More than anything else, education leaders need courage. Fortunately for educators, courage does not involve facing an enemy's machine guns, the winter winds of the Kansas plains, or the other life-testing challenges that I cited in the Introduction, which separate what is hard from what is uncomfortable. Fortunately many of the challenges educators face are less daunting than those Eric is facing in Cleveland. But real courage is necessary, and I did not find a single school implementing meaningful change without a courageous leader willing to create and experience discomfort. Very simply, school innovation requires leaders with the courage to overcome aversion to risk, embrace failure, and to build an organizational upside to testing new game-changing ideas.

School innovation requires leaders with the courage to overcome aversion to risk, embrace failure, and to build an organizational upside to testing new game-changing ideas.

Courageous leadership spills over into every aspect of an organization. This chapter will focus on four specific characteristics of leadership that are key to innovation at schools: cultivating and supporting natural leaders, aligning resources with vision, modeling risk, and communicating in a truly effective way. I found that schools that focused on these key leadership strategies are effective at implementing change in a relatively short period of time.

The Nature of Leadership in Schools

Natural leaders are bold, comfortable with risk, creative, and good at coordinating others by setting a vision and then creating strategies and mechanisms to achieve the vision. The great news is that we have people like this in our schools, even though we have not hired many educators on the basis of their natural leadership qualities. Many teachers who were hired because they are knowledgeable in a subject and can manage a class of students are also tremendous natural leaders. The challenge is in translating those leadership skills and providing opportunities for *all* of our adults to lead the process of organizational change.

This book is not a guide to leadership skills, but I have selected what I think are some key skills that are particularly relevant to leading school innovation:

- *Leading innovation is always best done from the front.* Innovation is not a job responsibility that is listed for some and not for others; it is a system of habits and practices that foster a system-wide change in how the organization adapts to its environment. Innovation cannot be delegated to others.
- *Leaders cannot rely on random events* (Stikeleather, 2012). Leaders must intentionally create a focus on innovation as an organizational mission, and communicate that focus to all stakeholders.
- *Leaders are curious about innovation.* Educators increasingly agree that teachers should be the "first learners" in the classroom. School leaders should be the first, and most curious, learners about the process of innovation.
- *Leaders need to identify innovative entrepreneurs* both inside and outside of their organization, and leverage those people's impact on the organization. School leaders have to change their hiring priorities to bring in more natural innovators.
- *Leaders have to manage less and cultivate more.* School leaders need to get away from the head of every conference table, a seat on every committee, and the top of rigidly vertical organization charts. Leaders need to let go of some of their power.
- *Leaders have to realize that the future is less knowable than it has been in the past.* Principals and boards must be willing to step off into untested waters before they have the objective data that would guarantee that they have made the right choice.

Where change is occurring in schools, it is often because school boards have broken with tradition and hired executives who have a history of innovative practices. Nearly all leaders of both public and private schools are hired today due to their length of service and experience as educators: teacher, junior administrator, principal of a school or division. Many school leaders have been great educators. and many school leaders are very good at their current jobs. Some are good innovators. Few school CEOs are hired based on a demonstrated history of true innovation. In fact the opposite is overwhelmingly true. Successful candidates for senior leadership positions at both public and private schools are generally considered to be good corporate managers with a strong background in the educational systems over the past twenty to thirty years, with little track record of ever taking substantial risks. That needs to change. As Lisa Waller, principal of the high school at the Dalton School in New York City, told me, "Sometimes you have to think of something outlandish in order to land with something truly innovative. If we seek to do that which is obviously attainable, we will come up with something more anemic than we want."

> *"Sometimes you have to think of something outlandish in order to land with something truly innovative."*

Aligning Resources with Vision

We know that the skills and knowledge that students will need for the future are different from those the students have needed in the past. Many schools have defined what those skills are; some call them "the essential qualities of a graduate" or "twenty-first-century skills" or "the portrait of a graduate." The lists are not exactly the same for each school or district, but they are similar. These self-developed lists never declare that a student should know the quadratic formula, be able to recite the causes of the Civil War, or dissect a frog. Given a blank slate, very few educators would suggest that we construct our learning experience around doing well on standardized tests. We know that these do not measure what will be important to the students in their futures.

The essential qualities of our students and graduates frame a school vision and mission. Schools have only a handful of resources: time, people, money, knowledge, and physical space. It is up to leadership to allocate these resources to meet the mission of the school. The mission of most schools over the past fifty to one hundred years has been to graduate students who excel on standardized exams. As a result, we have allocated our resources toward the transmission of content knowledge. Public schools have an even greater burden as they have increasingly been required to allocate resources to provide social, physical, and emotional support that students do not receive from home: food, counseling, transportation, and health care, to name a few.

Sustainable change will occur only when resources are visibly and sustainably aligned with a vision of what education looks like in the future, not in the past. If we want students to learn to be global citizens, they have to engage with

Sustainable change will occur only when resources are visibly and sustainably aligned with a vision of what education looks like in the future, not in the past.

experiences and people off campus. If we want teachers to promote student ownership of learning, we have to provide time and money for the teachers to learn those skills and techniques. If we want students and teachers to co-learn and create in flexible design spaces, we have to build those spaces or repurpose old spaces from their traditional classrooms of rows of desks. If we decide that leadership, entrepreneurialism, community service, or success in science, technology, engineering, and mathematics (STEM disciplines) are key outcomes that we want for our students, then we have to realign money, people, time, and space to those foci, which, in an inelastic system, means that we are going to peel some of those same resources away from traditional subject areas.

Mt. Vernon Presbyterian is an early childhood–twelfth-grade school in North Atlanta that is rethinking, reenvisioning, and rebranding the school. The educators' current mission revolves around three pillars—inquiry, innovation, and impact—which have driven a series of aligning vision and academic efforts. Brett Jacobsen, who was hired four years ago to lead this transformation, says: "We live our mission, good, bad, or indifferent. At every discussion we invoke the mission statement or strategic plan, and even if something sounds like a good idea but it does not align with those, we don't pursue it."

Brett has taken the school through some major structural changes in a few short years. I asked him what the key to innovation is, and he did not hesitate for a second: "assembling the right team." The entire senior team is new to the school over the past five years. The school is retaining the highest-performing teachers and attracting teachers and administrators from all over the country. Brett says, "Our vision is to be the best school in the world at delivering a twenty-first-century education, and that means the best at educating this generation, right now. Our strategic plan allows us to evolve. We are constantly reevaluating the plan for efficiency and effectiveness."

The alignment percolates down to all levels of the school. Lower School Principal Shelley Clifford says, "There is a passion among the faculty that lies behind our key messages. We know we may fail sometimes, and if we do we will fix it quickly as well. We want the highest standards of teaching, so we have a really high standard of expectation for professional development. We rebuilt the teacher assessment protocol, and there is no reference to 'minimum standards'; it is about how well a teacher is working compared to the highest standard. Everybody is part of the mission statement; everyone knows what we are doing and can speak to it. It shows; I am blown away by the support of parents for what we are doing." Upper School Principal Tyler Thigpen adds, "We are aligning our teaching strategies directly with the six habits of mind that we have adopted." Middle School Principal Chip Houston notes: "We meet every week and discuss specific goals for the week that align with the mission."

The senior administrative team and board chair point to Brett's arrival as the key to this laser focus on mission, and say that it did not come without some discomfort. They assessed the community's tolerance for rate of change and "push that tolerance as far and as fast as we can." They have leveraged every available professional development day for aligning teaching with the key habits of mind, extended the school year by a week to increase professional growth time, engage in frequent learning walks, and urge their faculty and staff to connect with colleagues outside the school on Twitter. They say it has taken fortitude, courage, and

"Identifying tension between where we are and where we want to be is a good thing. Steady state will be when we are more comfortable in our ability to change."

confidence, all of which are clearly in ready supply in Brett and his team. As Brett puts it, "Identifying tension between where we are and where we want to be is a good thing. Steady state will be when we are more comfortable in our ability to change."

Making Change Sustainable

Good leaders look for opportunities to jumpstart innovation with the clear intention of percolating those changes across the organization. John Collins, superintendent of the 35,000-student Poway Unified School District north of San Diego, did just that. Opening a new school in 2014, John tasked veteran principal Sonya Wrisley and her handpicked founding team to create a school unbounded by tradition and the industrial age model. "We have the opportunity to really do what we want here," says John. "It will be our district's first K–8 school, so we are breaking the grade-level model. It will be a 'choice' school, so if we are going to make it different we have to give parents and families the information they need to make a good choice. But most importantly, we need to start creating a learning environment that addresses the specific needs of each child. We have pieces of the technology to do that; now we have to put it all together and bring it to scale."

> *"We need to start creating a learning environment that addresses the specific needs of each child."*

John, Sonya, and the team are particularly focused on developing systems that will bring their vision into alignment with sustainable long-term change. Team member Tom Downs says they need to ensure that "whatever we do on the day we open school is irreversible. Educators like to try new things, but then revert to their old ways. That is the cycle we have to break." The district is engaged in a long-term project to develop an adaptive learning platform that tracks progress, strengths, weaknesses, interests, and passions of both students and teachers. The platform will, when fully built out, remove repetitive workloads from teachers, freeing them up for more personalized instruction. The platform will form the basis of a school-wide system built around each student rather than grade level, age, subject, classroom space, or predetermined uses of time. Students, faculty, administrators, parents, and even community participants will all have ownership space within the structure.

"The full resources of our district are behind this new learning direction," says John. "It will impact how we hire and train our faculty and how those faculty continue to prepare our students for a more ambiguous future. We will scale what works up to the entire district, which means making sure our teachers and students have the resources they need to learn differently." Even the naming of the school is seen as a resource that can align with the school's mission. When John took the new name of the school to be validated by the school board, they physically squirmed in their seats. "Design 39 Campus? What does that even mean?" one trustee asked. Sonya showed them a three-minute video prepared by the teachers that led off with the question, "If we are going to 'do' school differently, shouldn't we name schools differently?" Sonya argued, "Design is the core of our mission and this is the thirty-ninth school in the district. And in focus groups the kids *love* it!" The board voted to approve the new name.

The community of Parish Episcopal in Dallas knows something about change; the school has increased its student population from 400 to 1,100 in just five years. Head David Monaco is intensely focused on aligning program, resources, and message. As we toured the main campus, he said that educators at the school have settled on just three guiding principles that they want every student exposed to throughout their pre-K–12 career: the Parish Profile of skills and preparation; STEM disciplines; and creating what they call "Students of Impact" through global and leadership opportunities. Every student is exposed to these core immersions at all grade levels. In order to ensure this alignment and integration, they have restructured authority and hired teachers who embrace their mission. Dave says, "We hire people who are able to work with both middle and top performing students, who are able to create and manage tailored learning experiences. Mostly, though, we hire people who are willing to embed their own interests within the broader vision of the school."

The senior leadership team has been crafted to both create and integrate this embedded alignment. Dave says that they are "pruning the bush" of the entire school program to make sure that the program aligns with the mission. In division meetings, on professional development days, in grade-level discussions, and in quarterly letters, Dave is fanatical about fine-tuning, communicating, reinforcing, and promoting just how the school's resources support core learning outcomes. The leadership team even designed, printed, and laminated a placemat for all families that graphically shows how and when students will progress through their STEM exposures from pre-kindergarten through twelfth grade. And it is not just show. Over the 2012 summer, every faculty member developed examples of how these core practices were applied in their classroom, and they held a massive poster session for sharing and collaborative learning at the beginning of school.

Breaking the Aversion to Risk

My good friend, educational thought leader, and chief learning and innovation officer at Mount Vernon Presbyterian School in Atlanta, Bo Adams, once expressed the irony of how schools view failure: "When your child falls off their bike, do you tell them they have failed? When they are learning to walk, does a parent give them a failing grade when they have toppled over the tenth time? Where else in the world do we discourage risk taking with the big downside of a red 'F' like we do in schools?"

> *"Where else in the world do we discourage risk taking with the big downside of a red 'F' like we do in schools?"*

From the superintendent to the principal to the teacher to the student, there is vastly more downside than upside in taking a risk in schools. School communities fear risk as a threat to our children. Is this valid? Of course! Our children are our treasures, and we equate risk with a threat to their safety. We get only one chance; they go through our schools only once, so risking what we have done in the past for something untested takes on special meaning. The current assembly-line system of learning does not allow do-overs. That is the problem.

Adults in schools have had little upside to risk-taking in their own careers. Most teachers did not go into the business of education because they love risk. Teachers and administrators are not promoted faster or paid more based on their willingness to try new things. They are not given time to come up with new ideas or test new curriculum in their classes without going through multiple levels of approval. Superintendents and headmasters are not traditionally hired to take risks; they are hired to manage and ensure a safe learning environment, elevate test scores, and prepare graduates for admission to an acceptable list of colleges.

How do we break this cycle? Simply, organizations will not embrace risk and failure unless the leaders model those behaviors. In the dozens of schools I have visited, I did not see innovation taking place unless leaders had developed a clear mandate and methodology to embrace risk-taking and had visibly engaged in risk taking themselves. In *Leadership Lessons from West Point*, now retired Major Doug Crandall (2007) wrote that "the comfortable illusion of infallibility is the biggest failure of all." If the adults in school feel compelled to portray themselves as all-knowing, they are unlikely to take real risks in their own personal and professional growth. This aversion to risk trickles down from senior leadership to teachers to students. If the leaders don't model this understanding, neither will the rest of the organization.

Organizations will not embrace risk and failure unless the leaders model those behaviors.

The first stop on my countrywide trip was at Colorado Academy (CA), in Denver. CA is a highly respected, mid-sized, K–12 coed day school. By almost any measure, CA should not take a lot of risk. They have a long track record of success. Several years ago, new Head of School Mike Davis led the school through what has become a multiyear, systematic, thoughtful, strategic evaluation of how the school could better serve students for their own futures. In our current shorthand, these educators decided that they needed to become a truly twenty-first-century school. Why? Because Mike and the other educational leaders at CA understood that they have a moral obligation to create the best, most authentic learning environment for their students that they can, even if there is a risk of failure for which they will be blamed. Mike told his community that at a time when "teacher accountability" drives debates over education policy, "there is little room to encourage innovation and experimentation. We all know that our schools must be more innovative, but how can we do that if we don't give teachers room to explode their curriculum and create new things? Likewise, our students are under such pressure to create these 'perfect' resumes that they become risk averse. That is antithetical to what we want them to learn."

The community of CA has begun to overcome natural fears of change and risk aversion in a remarkably short period of time. Mike established a broad vision and convened a series of collaborative opportunities for teachers, trustees, and administrators to decide and validate major program shifts within their strategic planning process. Teacher Paul Kim was part of that team: "It was an incredibly freeing event. I went to my classroom the week after these meetings and knew that I could be fully as creative as I wanted to be and that would align with Mike's vision for the school. I am now willing to experiment because I know that the safety net is there, that the administration is going to support risk taking."

"I am now willing to experiment because I know that the safety net is there, that the administration is going to support risk taking."

Middle School Head Bill Wolf-Tinsman is one of the change leaders at CA. "We have been working with teachers on developing the mindset that we want all of us, teachers, students, parents, to be in, of how to approach and overcome challenges. This is what we want for our students, so we need to model the same behavior. We are using the metaphor of teacher as innovator. We not only expect this of teachers but we have incorporated these same ideas into our assessment metric for the new curriculum we are designing. There is a common mindset of critical thinking that we want all of our students to be exposed to, and it crosses all subjects and grade levels."

Bill says that this is not a one-time event but forms the ongoing expectation for teachers at CA. "We incorporate the same set of skills in our assessment of the teachers themselves. We ask them how they are developing their coursework to enhance the critical skills that we think students need most. We ask them, 'What about what you have developed is pushing kids and teaching kids these skills? Is this something the kids really got their hands dirty with or was it just another classroom project?' As you move towards these mindset objectives, the quality for the classroom work is going to become increasingly authentic, increasingly real world."

As teachers develop these new habits where risk is not only tolerated but also embraced, they develop a new concept of what teaching can look like. Bill says teachers now "walk into a class and put the students in a group and say 'here are your materials, here is the challenge, here is the scoring rubric, good luck.' That gets kids thinking and acting and doing and learning from the mistakes they make. There are a thousand different options and solutions they can come up with. We are not saying there is any specific answer." Not only does CA ask teachers to take risks along with their students; they actively celebrate risk takers, and not just those who succeed. Every month they give an award to the teacher who took a risk and failed most dramatically, and that award is as highly regarded as awards for teachers who try something new and succeed.

At the end of my daylong visit, I met with several parent-leaders and members of the board of trustees. I asked them how they had felt, as flag-wavers for a school with a long history of success, facing leadership who wanted to take the school in a dramatically different direction. One member of the board summarized: "Mike and his team were so effective at communicating why this was the right thing to do, they took so much time, that at the end of the day we just said, 'We trust these folks; they are great educators.' We know there will be controversy, but we trust them."

The same imperative to change drove some difficult, but profoundly impactful conversations at the Catholic Marymount School in Manhattan. Head of School Concepcion Alvar told me that she pushed their faculty and administrators to ask, "How can we make a real transformation? How can we actually improve education for our girls by replacing primarily content-driven curriculum? What do we replace it with?" Concepcion decided that taking risks was absolutely critical to the school's long-term sustainability. "We want to be a showcase of a school that tries new things all the time. With adults, new things can be scary, but that is OK. Innovation here is pointed toward developing a mindset, not a specific outcome."

"With adults, new things can be scary, but that is OK. Innovation here is pointed toward developing a mindset, not a specific outcome."

Concepcion admitted that big conversations like these can polarize a community, but "traditional teaching is killing the joy of learning. We are trying to disassociate kids' self-worth from SAT scores and college acceptances. Academic leadership is steeped in asking questions, some of which may not appeal to parents"—but that did not stop the team from asking those questions.

The faculty and parents asked for a clear vision and Concepcion told them the truth: "I don't have all the pieces in front of me, but we have enough to start." Her administrative team pushed back, "sometimes pushing back hard." Concepcion credits those hard discussions with creating more success. "I grew as a leader because I was seriously questioned by all of these very smart people. I told them 'if it works, great; if not, we will change it.' This is our professional challenge. We're moving. Don't ask me what we will find at the end of the road, but we are moving. We want to educate the girls to question and grow. We need to model this behavior ourselves for the students. If you do the same thing year after year, you should not be teaching."

Communication

Schools, even in the best of times, are busy communities with diverse interest groups and multilayered missions. School communities consist of students who may cover a wide range of ages and adults who almost always represent a wide range of ages and levels of experience, expertise, and interest. Schools have unwieldy governing structures in which the parent-customer is also the ultimate authority, either as the voting public or the majority of the board of trustees. Keeping all of these groups on the same page in a time

> *Effectively innovating school leaders design and implement massive, coordinated communication efforts well in advance of any real change.*

of stasis requires diligence and the skills of a clear communicator. Moving all of these groups along the same path in a time of dynamic change, when discomfort and uncertainty lie around each corner, requires leaders who are both willing and able to take communication to a whole new level.

I found that effectively innovating school leaders design and implement massive, coordinated communication efforts well in advance of any real change. Communication becomes an obsession of school leaders. They write, speak, and e-mail about the ideas being shared by faculty. They hold parent coffees, not just a few times a year, but month after month, laying out the reasons for considering change, listening to feedback, allowing all members of these highly democratic communities to have their say. They *never* let a meeting of any size or constituency take place without giving an update, or framing the discussion within the context of the evolving vision for the school. Ultimately, it is impossible for a parent or teacher or student *not* to understand how the school is changing, and how resource allocation has to change as well. Members of the community have the chance to understand and embrace the coming changes or, if in disagreement with the new directions, choose to find an alternative.

We have seen how the Denver Green School (DGS) offers a nontraditional academic program to families within the Denver public schools framework. Because DGS is a choice school, families can choose to send their students to DGS or to a more traditional school in the area. The leadership team feels the need to make sure that families are making an informed choice, while at the same time looking to attract students to fill seats at the school. The team hosts events during the year to invite families from the area to see what their brand of learning looks like. Then, each summer in the weeks before the new school year starts, teachers go out to visit new students and their families, either at their home or at a neutral site. Often this is just a half-hour meet and greet, but it gives the family the opportunity to meet a child's new teachers one on one and gives the teachers the chance to make sure that parents are on board with the school's vision and expectations. Educators at the school post on their website a comprehensive outline of the school program and expectations for the students and families who choose to attend their school. As we will note in the next chapter, the management structure of DGS distributes authority and responsibility for running the school to many of the teachers, who become effective day-to-day communicators for the vision of the school, since they are the ones responsible for creating and evolving that vision.

Berkeley-Carroll School (BC) is a private K–12 school in the highly competitive New York City market. Brooklyn-based BC has engaged an all-school conversation about aligning all learning to the school mission, which contains just three main words: "ethical, critical, global." Educators at BC are extremely intentional about ensuring that what goes on in the classroom really does reflect these three words. Liz Perry, the director of educational design and innovation, says, "We want to spend less time thinking about what teachers are teaching and more time thinking about what students are learning. When classes are about content and teacher's charisma, the students are relying on the teacher too much. The world is going toward a more blended learning environment where the students need to rely on themselves and each other more."

This alignment conversation led BC to tackle one of the really thorny program issues of our era: the Advanced Placement program. The faculty decided that their mission was not met by the narrow, content-focused AP curricula. They also felt that tracking students ran counter to the democratic statements of the school's vision. As consensus grew, Head Bob Vitalo reset the target to this: "What will our post-AP world look like?" Director of College Counseling Brandon Clarke told me that Bob took on a real burden. "We were no longer going to teach the APs, and in our market that was a real risk. Bob told our teachers to create the best class they could that includes important topics and outcomes you want to see. He took on the burden of communicating those decisions to the school community."

Bob and the administration team got to work on a multiyear communications plan. Rather than trying to hide the fact that they were breaking from tradition, they shouted it out to all who would listen. They boasted about the powerful new courses in their school guide, admissions material, and school community meetings. The college counselors met with every college admissions representative who came on campus to explain what the new courses were about and how they were just as rigorous as the APs they were replacing. Bob said that his focus was to ensure that teachers and parents were on the same page. "As a leader, my task is to bring perception and reality together. If we are going to make change sustainable, we need our community to clearly understand the added value of what those changes represent. The move away from APs is an example of that added value. The fact that we made that change with strong support from our community means that we can be more comfortable in making additional changes to the program in the future."

> *Rather than trying to hide the fact that the school was breaking from tradition, they shouted it out to all who would listen.*

REFLECTION

So much has been written about leadership; writing about leadership is an industry unto itself. As I reflect on the many leaders with whom I have worked, the authors I have read, and on my own experience, one piece of advice always surfaces: "Good leaders lead from the front." The school leaders whom I saw taking their schools or districts from where they had been in the past to a less certain future are all visible, intentional, and clear, and they strongly communicate their ideas. They also model the behaviors they want to see in others. Not all leaders do this, and many mistakenly think that they are being followed. If there is a single point that sticks out from my school visits it is this: Schools will *not* change unless leaders are willing to model, lead, highlight, and reward innovative practices. If school leaders don't know how to do this, they should visit schools and connect with leaders who do. School leaders are increasingly accessible via social media, and I find they are almost always willing to share their knowledge.

I have the honor of an ongoing relationship with faculty at the United States Military Academy at West Point, including teaching two summer seminars with groups of cadets. Everything that West Point does and teaches prepares young people to become leaders under difficult circumstances. In the seminar based on my book *The Falconer*, we talked a lot about the importance of asking questions. As we wound our way through that discussion, I asked the cadets to imagine the questions they would need to ask when they first stepped off a helicopter in some dangerous, ambiguous part of the world. At the end, one of the cadets raised his hand and said, "Now I get why it's so important for a good leader to ask questions, to not assume you have the answers ahead of time. If I don't ask enough questions, someone I am responsible for is going to die."

Fortunately for the rest of us, most of the issues school leaders face do not have the same downside, but that lesson from the cadet will always stick with me. Leaders often feel that they have become leaders because they have answered more questions right in the past than others. That is the nature of our schools and much of the industrial age corporate model. Really good leaders know this is utterly wrong; they are the ones asking more questions in more ways than anyone else. They are the ones who look at what their organizations are doing and what they have done in the past and are always asking, simply, "How can we be better?"

CHAPTER FOUR

Structure
School Organization and Process
in a Time of Change

In the fall of 2012 the great plains of the Midwest were gripped in an almost biblical drought. I drove for days past fields of stubble corn and heard on the radio that the water levels of the Mississippi were so low that barges had to take turns going upriver and down through the narrowing channels. I left St. Louis late one afternoon with the long drive to Chicago ahead of me, waving off directions from my school hosts, trusting in the efficiency of my GPS . . . which sent me on an almost endless slog through stop signs and boarded-up neighborhoods north of downtown. Finally, with the setting sun already in my rearview window and a six-hour drive ahead, I crossed the "Father of Waters" for the first time by car—and the Father had shrunken to a withered old man, quarter-mile sand bars reaching out from both shorelines, trapping the feeble drought-ridden meanders. For any other river, it was still a big river; for the Mississippi, the bridge seemed to cross more dry land than water.

I could not help thinking of this long bridge connecting the west to the east of America as a metaphor of change. On one end of the bridge is a box holding the sum of our own educational experiences. At the other end of the bridge is a box that holds all of the dreams and aspirations we have for teaching our students to become effective lifelong learners. Few of us have seen what an education system looks like that fulfills all those dreams and aspirations. We have hints; we are starting to see the outlines;

we can see the other end of the bridge over there in the mist that rises off the river. But most educators have never been to the other end of the bridge. That is not their fault; they have lived their lives at the nearer end of the bridge.

We have to cross that bridge. We can say, "Let's just drive over the bridge; let's all start thinking like twenty-first-century educators and make it happen." The problem is that our best understanding of how organizations change flies right in the face of this solution. The mechanism for getting over the bridge is the process of organizational innovation, and right there sits the nasty bridge troll for educators. Our people are not going to get over this bridge by reading a book or attending a couple of professional development courses over the summer. Our commitment must be strong, clear, intentional, sustainable, and permanent. Unless the people in your school understand that they have to cross this bridge, that they have to experience things that they have never experienced, and that the process of organizational innovations is sometimes messy and time-consuming, they are not going to cross the bridge. The great news is that history is clear: once you are over this bridge, the next bridge and the next are going to be a lot easier to cross. Few bridges are as long as that first drive across the Mississippi River.

What Is Organizational Innovation?

Innovation is the creation and development of new ideas that contribute significant value to the organization. New ideas are not innovations unless they create value. Rita Gunther McGrath reminds us that many companies talk about their focus on innovation, but empirical data suggest that not many really innovate:

> Thinking of stuff is not innovation. Tinkering with stuff is not innovation. Even inventing stuff is not innovation. Innovation instead, when it's done right, makes us go "wow, of course, why didn't I think of that?" It creates complete experiences that we want to engage in. It eliminates inconveniences and hassles and improves our overall experiences. At its most dramatic, it creates entire categories of offerings, so new that we find it hard to name them at first. (McGrath, 2012)

The schools I have found that are actually changing how and what they teach to meet the future needs of their students are creating organizational structures and processes that stimulate value-generating innovative ideas to nucleate and rapidly grow. Mount Vernon Presbyterian School in Atlanta may be the most innovation-attuned school I visited. Head of School Brett Jacobsen told me that the school is "not interested in red tape, fixed mindsets, low expectations, or blending in. We are interested in solution seekers, ethical decision-makers, communicators, creative thinkers, collaborators, and innovators. I encourage my team to start with questions (not answers), fail up, share well, and have fun. We tell everyone in our community, student and adult, 'we need the work of your hands, the wisdom of your mind, and the discernment of your heart. Look at the familiar as if you have never seen it before. Search for new ideas in new places.'"

"I encourage my team to start with questions (not answers), fail up, share well, and have fun."

Linking Resources to Vision

When I got home from my journey I begged one more favor from my patient wife, Julie, and screwed two large bulletin boards into the wall of our family room. I needed the space to visually map out the hundreds of thoughts, ideas, questions, and obstacles I had uncovered, all translated onto Post-it notes and index cards. In organizing this chapter I pinned, moved, and shifted those cards for days, and finally came up with three questions that I think are being asked and answered by the most effectively innovating schools. I will revisit these three questions in the penultimate chapter, since they form a basis for thinking about ongoing strategy.

- Does your school have a forward-leaning vision that articulates the evolving relationship between students, teachers, and knowledge?
- Are your resources aligned at a systems level with your vision?
- How are you effectively communicating the differentiated value of your school to your customers?

While all three of these questions are essential, the complex work of organizational change centers on the second one. Bo Adams, in his year with the Atlanta-based design thinking firm Unboundary, created a "pedagogical master plan" process to help schools answer these questions, not in order to check the box of a strategic plan or accreditation review, but because lacking such a plan, schools will not develop and implement an integrated roadmap to organizational change. As Bo put it to me, "Schools spend enormous amounts of money creating master plans for campus construction and renovation, but few spend any money at all creating a master plan for how we are actually preparing our students for their futures."

Every school I visited could point to a program, pilot, or classroom that they felt was "innovative," an example of their view of the future, of how they want learning to take place now that they have understood that learning is no longer about transferring content knowledge from one generation to the next. In essence, this group of schools is tinkering with innovation. A much smaller number of schools could identify changes in their organizational functions, structures, processes, or management practices that will intentionally sustain those programs or pilots over time. Most schools are relying on an "organic" percolation of ideas to produce real change. Some recognize that the key to change is to ensure that our resources—time, money, people, space, and knowledge—are clearly, strongly, visibly, and sustainably aligned with a vision of the future as different from the past. If resources remain aligned with a strongly traditional model of learning, change will rarely, and certainly not quickly or sustainably, take hold.

If resources remain aligned with a strongly traditional model of learning, change will rarely, and certainly not quickly or sustainably, take hold.

Empowering Distributed Authority

Strongly vertical, poorly distributed management typical of the industrial nineteenth and twentieth centuries has a nickname: "Management 1.0." Schools have been managed this way for decades or centuries. Many principals, heads of school, and superintendents manage at a very detailed level in a pattern that is vanishing from for-profit, knowledge-based industries. Strong top-down management excises the engine of passion from our teachers and other adults. If decisions are made for us, we find it hard to find relevance; we know this is true for our students, and it is just as true among our employees. Educators may want to teach skills that will allow our students to succeed in the twenty-first century, but many are reluctant to model those skills themselves.

Susanne Ramharter, an innovation agent in corporate marketing, argues that autonomy in most large organizations is largely a fiction:

> Ask managers whether they believe in autonomy for their staff and most will tell you "of course—as far as the work or project allows." Then ask the staff and they will most often tell you that they have very little autonomy, they feel that they are given individual little *tasks* as opposed to *responsibility* for a specific work product. There are many reasons for this, but the increasing desire to industrialize services into efficient factories, where one person on the "production line" can easily be replaced by another is a major factor. (Ramharter & Grams, 2012)

I found the same to be the case at many of the schools I visited. The principal or head of school told me they want their staff to truly "own" their own decision-making. Unfortunately, the staff frequently told me that they did not believe this to be true.

To innovate, organizations need a shared and distributed imagination about what the future holds; a process to create nimble alternatives to address ambiguity in the marketplace; and authority to break silos and push people to collaborate beyond their areas of specific and obvious self-interest. Sam Folk-Williams, of the major software developer Red Hat, writing with Jim Stikeleather and Michele Zanini (2012), argues: "In most organizations, far too much power is linked to positional, rather than personal, or natural authority. While the formal hierarchy can be a matter of public record, natural leaders don't appear on any organization chart." Dave Monaco, head of Episcopal School in Dallas, echoed this idea when he told me, "Innovation is cultural and thus has to be seeded, modeled, and nurtured with intentionality. We have intentionally created and hired for a leadership structure across our organization that empowers key individuals to own, shape, and implement the exciting signature programs that we have germinated. We are fanatical when it comes to asking which leaders and key players have a stake in this conversation and need to be engaged in the shaping and decision-making process."

Traditional organizations reserve authority for making risky decisions to the highest levels. A key tenet of modern "Management 2.0" is that employees throughout the organization must develop the capacity to make good decisions about risk, including considering ways to mitigate the downside of risk and to deal with inevitable failure. Knowledge organizations are becoming better at incorporating experimentation, distributed authority, and effective risk management strategies. In the information age, knowledge workers are frequently mismatched with traditional corporate hierarchies. People who are good at creating and managing ideas are often uncomfortable with strict reporting requirements, working only during daylight hours, and assembly-line production of a product or service. Schools are filled with well-educated, creative, dynamic workforces of teachers who respond better to a flat, open-source, buzzing, collaborative, risk-friendly dynamic than to the controlled, vertical, goal- and assessment-burdened mantras of Management 1.0. Teachers are increasingly called upon to create more tailored information delivery and management strategies alongside their students. It is this letting go of authority that ties together the strengths of good leadership with the strengths of knowledge workers who most positively effect strong organizational innovation.

Schools are filled with well-educated, creative, dynamic workforces of teachers who respond better to a flat, open-source, buzzing, collaborative, risk-friendly dynamic than to the controlled, vertical, goal- and assessment-burdened mantras of Management 1.0.

The Denver Green School (DGS) has the most intentional system of distributed authority of any school I visited. A public, noncharter school in the Denver public school system, DGS was conceived and founded by seven "partners," a group of veteran educators with a combined 150 years of teaching and administrative experience. Since its inception a few years ago, the school has added three more partners and will continue to add partners as teachers rise to the level of interest and commitment of the founders. Three of the partners act, as a group, like the traditional principal, taking care of basic administrative functions. On paper, one is the "lead partner," but in practice they act as a collaborative team, seeking to constantly distribute leadership responsibilities and grow the capabilities of an ever-expanding group of teacher-leaders. One of their expressed goals is that, as teachers join the group of "partners" and gain experience with this management style, they will feel confident enough to spin off and start their own school under the Denver Innovative Schools program.

DGS has addressed one of the critical weaknesses of all knowledge-based organizations: the weak link at the top. Especially in start-ups, the energy demanded to get an organization up and running is ridiculous, and burnout is a real threat. If the vision and leadership are concentrated in just one person, it only takes one point of failure to put the organization at risk. Sometimes this means real failure; sometimes it just slows down what had been great progress. DGS is run by a true partnership of intellectual equals who are committed to ensuring long-term sustainability by designing out the weak link. At an operational level, the management structure has trickled down; DGS is a democratic, teacher-led organization that fosters—in fact, demands—open inquiry and exploration from the adults. Everyone is expected not only to contribute to the overall success of the school, but to lead that success, as well as to be effective in their own classrooms.

Acting Small

When it comes to the ability of an organization to innovate in the face of changing market demands, agility is often inversely proportional to size. Large companies that are known as leaders of innovation in their respective markets find ways to "act small" when it comes to managing innovation. Management 2.0 leaders promote a culture that can evolve without express permission from the top at every step. Characteristics include less centralized control, bottom-up or multilateral planning, open access to planning and information, distributed authority for project-level decisions, and collaboration among employees across more permeable, flexible departmental boundaries.

Schools that are effectively innovating act small by flattening the organizational chart and letting go of authority from the top. They create open spaces in the decision-making process that

Schools that are effectively innovating act small by flattening the organizational chart and letting go of authority from the top.

allow natural leaders to emerge and claim a spot in the decision chain. Flatter organizational charts rely less on imposed positional authority like department chairs and more on mutual and clear commitments between individuals to provide support and collaboration in pursuit of a common goal. In order to truly innovate, schools have to become messier, less rigid in their organizational reporting and responsibilities.

Distributed authority is clearly an opportunity for schools to act small and to be more agile. Traditional schools are tremendously steep pyramids of authority. It is not uncommon for one to two hundred teachers in a public school to report directly to a single principal. In private K–12 schools, those same teachers may report through three division heads to a head of school. Many decisions, including hiring, evaluation, and firing, are made at the top of this pyramid. Management 2.0 practices deflect these decisions away from the top, empowering individuals at the "production level" of the organization to make more decisions on their own. For example, division leaders or department chairs might have the authority to hire and assess teaching faculty; departments set their individual assessment rubrics without having them vetted by the principal, superintendent, or head of school; innovation teams have the authority to commit resources to test a new program in the classroom; a professional learning community (PLC) of teachers decides to try a new teaching approach for a year.

Chris Lehmann of Science Leadership Academy (SLA) says shared decision-making enables his school to act with much greater speed. "We develop that by trying to make sure that people 'check in' frequently so we can leverage the power that comes from being smarter together than we are apart. We also give more weight to those who are doing the actual work; I trust them and they know I trust them, so when we get together to make a shared decision, we honor the people who have done the work; they have a lot of say in the outcome. One thing that is hard is balancing positional authority with situational authority. We constantly are working to reduce that inevitable tension, and I think the key is that those of us with positional authority have to develop relational trust. I have learned a lot about that working here at SLA. As a leader I have to ask others to do more, to take on that authority, but also I have to do less in terms of making decisions on my own."

Large companies often act small by breaking into functional or market-oriented teams that operate like much smaller, more nimble companies. Hathaway Brown School in Cleveland started doing this almost fifteen years ago, and they have developed a remarkable structure that is studied by educators from all over the world. The academic program revolves around their Institute for 21st Century Education, a matrix of ten "Centers" that help students focus their studies on passions and interests. Students choose a Center in which to participate, much as college students choose a major: writing, technology, civic engagement, business and finance, environmental sustainability, STEM disciplines, and more. The faculty and students collaborate to meld the activities of the centers with the core curriculum in ways that amplify the goals of both. For example, they told me, students might write a paper or conduct a self-directed project in the community as part of their Center work, and those efforts would be used in their core classes as well.

In talking with Head of School Bill Christ, who has grown this program from a simple idea over a decade and a half, it is clear that both the administration and faculty have evolved significantly as a result of the fundamental structural change. The structure demands a high level of collaboration based on the interests of the students, not a set of subjects and departments. Centers rise and fall along with student and teacher interests; the academic program is in a process of constant evolution that does not reach stasis. Bill said that educators at the school first conceived of a model akin to a liberal arts college, with purpose, people, and even places dedicated to large thematic issues that would serve to contextualize the "regular" classroom curriculum. He said that a key to their success was that they "started small but had big dreams. We started with just a couple of Centers, and used those to help nurture and build on additional Centers over time. We don't really have a formal process of permission to start a Center; anyone with a good idea can propose a Center and test it out with their colleagues and the students." The Centers allow a large school to act more like a group of collaborating smaller schools, each with its own mission and program, but cooperatively aligned with the mission and program of the entire school.

Networks and Teams

Four or five years ago, if you had walked into a large room of educators anywhere in America and started talking about "silos," most people in the room would have guessed the subject was grain storage. In a very short time, that has radically changed; most educators know that "silos" are the hard boundaries and divisions that keep people in an organization from frequent or meaningful interaction. The solution to siloed structures is found in the power of networks, which many business leaders and authors cite as the single most important key to developing innovative ideas and practices. In *Where Good Ideas Come From*, Steven Johnson explores the terrain and formation of networks: "An idea is not a single thing; it is more like a swarm. . . As long as there is spillover between minds, useful innovations will be more likely to appear and spread through the population at large" (2010, pp. 46, 58). Few really good or new ideas arise from a single individual; truly isolated epiphanies are either rare or mythical.

> "An idea is not a single thing; it is more like a swarm. . . As long as there is spillover between minds, useful innovations will be more likely to appear and spread through the population at large."

Schools have been traditionally organized around rigid concentric silos of classroom, grade level, department, division, and administrative offices that restrict or retard connectivity among people. In most schools, no one person or group is assigned the task to promote or monitor collaboration across those boundaries. In most schools, teachers in one department or division rarely know about what another department or division is doing, even if it is exciting and successful. There are few mechanisms to translate one success story to a different class, subject, or grade level.

Nearly every school I visited that was effecting real change in the learning experience for its students shared a common characteristic: a person or team was specifically charged with encouraging, defining, designing, developing, assessing, or implementing innovative practices, however those were defined for the particular school. This process was not left to chance, and it was not another responsibility of the CEO. The individual or team was given a name, a public charge, a written charter, and clear authority to promote real change. Increasingly, schools and districts are hiring or naming individuals with titles like "chief innovation officer" or "chief imagination officer." These are generally veteran educators with a specific capacity to see and implement new ideas, not just new technologies, across a complex system that is often resistant to their initial attempts. They generally report directly to the CEO, and their job is to promote, nurture, and track nontraditional programs, pilots, and processes to make sure those efforts have the resources to be successful.

Other schools form teams or committees that rotate members on and off to increase percolation of ideas through this group and out to the larger organization. These groups have strong *situational* authority, even if the members have virtually no *positional* authority. Rachel Friis, head of the Winsor School in Boston, told me that her vision when she came to Winsor nine years ago was to "have a school that really thinks about the instructional practices of teaching and learning, not just outcomes." She wanted to take the time and energy to build the case for change with her faculty, expose them to new ideas, encourage them to increase their external connections, and establish an expectation of teaching as an evolving, not static, practice. She realigned the professional development budget to focus on these priorities.

As this transition process unfolded, the Winsor faculty took on big discussions that would ultimately lead to a restatement of learning priorities. They created a forward-leaning vision and began to realign their resources to that vision by shifting the faculty evaluation, compensation, and workload profiles. Rachel created a key new group, the Teaching and Learning Committee (TLC), which is a critical part of their work and success. The charge of the TLC is to investigate and bring to Winsor best innovative instructional practices and to create mechanisms for these to be adopted by every member of the faculty. Participation in the TLC changes every year, with the goal that the number of thought leaders in the community increases all the time and those thought leaders can spread knowledge and resources in support of the overall mission. The TLC provides a home and locus of responsibility for teaching and learning priorities, which is critical to a sustainable effort.

While private schools can self-organize new groups to manage and promote change, most public schools have a built-in team that plays a critical role in organizational change: the teachers' union. Poway Unified superintendent John Collins says that developing a relationship of trust with the union is perhaps the most critical key to enabling real organizational change: "We have been working closely with the union for a dozen years, getting them to see that there may be a different way of 'doing' school. With our huge budget cuts in the last half-decade we have had unsustainable increases in teaching loads. So we are looking at different staffing models and pushing the limits of the state education code. If we did not have this trust relationship with the union, we would be forced to turn schools towards the charter model. We would rather not do that, so we find mutual 'wins' where the union can help support changes that we know are going to improve educational outcomes, even if they involve very different ways of structuring our learning environments."

Developing a relationship of trust with the teachers' union is perhaps the most critical key to enabling real organizational change.

Alyssa Gallagher is the director of strategic initiatives and community partnerships in the Los Altos School District, a K–8 district with 4,500 students and nine schools. The district is in the heart of Silicon Valley, so there is a fairly affluent, knowledgeable parent base, but up until a few years ago, Alyssa says the schools were completely traditional. With the influx of new leadership in 2010, they asked themselves, "Can't we do better?" Alyssa said their focus for two years has been on developing a culture of ongoing learning in the schools: "Our teachers felt unempowered; that they did not have permission to change." The district was introduced to Khan Academy two years ago. Alyssa says, "Khan was a great tool to give our teachers something tangible to work with, to start moving away from the assembly-line model and build a blended learning experience. It helped us all to build the rationale that we need to 'do' learning in a very different way."

This toe in the water led to a focus on in-house professional development. Alyssa wrote grants, found some money, worked with the teachers' union, and began to offer small stipends to teachers who would work on something new and then share it with district colleagues. School leaders even created a small performance-based stipend award system for teachers who were effective at creating these nuclei of innovation teams in their respective schools. In 2012, they started offering a wide range of professional development options to teachers in the afternoons. They offered design thinking, STEM development, and a whole host of new teaching ideas, some related to technology but many rooted in how to rethink what takes place in a classroom. Teachers volunteered to attend on their own time; 40 percent of the district teachers came to at least one offering, and the facilitators found they were kicking teachers out the door at 5:15 PM! Alyssa says their teachers "naturally want to gather, to learn, to advance their skills and keep up with what is happening in other educational settings. We just had to find a way to allow them to make those connections."

Innovation teams track emerging trends from outside the organization and generate ideas that are practical, feasible, and potentially impactful inside the organization. They use their combined skills to identify, model, test, and promote a wide range of new ideas that can create or enhance value. In the schools I visited, I saw this work focusing on adaptive learning technologies, restructuring of school calendar and daily schedules, shifting learning responsibility from teachers to students, rethinking the age-dependent structures of grade and subject, reallocating the student-to-teacher ratio, dissolving subject boundaries, and more. Members of these teams comprised teachers, administrators, students, parents, and community members with particular areas of expertise.

Innovation teams track emerging trends from outside the organization and generate ideas that are practical, feasible, and potentially impactful inside the organization.

Networks and teams often coalesce around natural leaders, employees who tend to command authority regardless of corporate hierarchy. They command authority not because of their superior position of responsibility, but by force of personality and experience. They are effective at laying out a plan of action and ensuring outcomes that are meaningful beyond their own narrow scope of interests. They command an audience within the organization that is out of scale with their position in the hierarchy, and they are particularly effective at the kind of nimble and creative leaps that foster innovation. In a school setting, natural leaders might be teachers with a particular magnetism or reputation among students, or a teacher or nonacademic employee who regularly crosses departmental and divisional lines to create connections in the pursuit of creating new value for the school. Natural leaders are the nucleating agents at the center of effective innovation teams and networks.

Like student-learners, natural leaders are most effective at developing nodes of innovation if they are provided the time, space, and autonomy to do so. In schools, unlike in more capital-intensive endeavors, money is not usually the limiting factor. Natural leaders embody passion and are willing to put in large amounts of "sweat equity" to achieve their goals. They stay after school, work on weekends, serve on committees, and build informal consensus for their work. At schools where innovation is percolating more rapidly, natural leaders are publicly recognized for their work. Senior school administrators look to them as models of performance expectations, not exceptions.

Overcoming Organizational Fear of Risk

Organizations, like individuals, learn from taking risks and assessing both successes and failures. Gino and Pisano (2011) identify three potential hazards to learning from risk taking that are particularly relevant to schools. First is the inclination to make fundamental attribution errors. When we succeed we overstate the value, talent, or skill that produced the success, and when we fail we overstate or blame external causes. Second is a bias toward confidence, even in the face of risks that are outside of our normal comfort zone. Success increases this bias, and continuing success results in overconfidence that may be unwarranted. Third, organizations fail to ask why something becomes successful. Lacking this investigation or objective analysis, the default is to assume that the organization is good at taking measured risks, which also contributes to overconfidence.

Schools are starting to embrace design thinking as a way to overcome these obstacles to effective innovation and to frame risk and failure as terms in the innovation equation. Diego Rodriguez (Rodriguez & Jacoby, 2007) is one of a growing number of design thinking provocateurs who preach a proactive approach to innovation, defining risk as just one of many variables in a good design model. In trying new things there is the risk that the program will fail to meet its objectives, with no return on the investment of time and resources spent to build it. Schools are increasingly recognizing the other risk: in *not* trying a new program, they may have rejected something that could add real value to the organization.

> *Schools are increasingly recognizing that along with the risk of failure there is another risk: in* not *trying a new program, they may have rejected something that could add real value to the organization.*

Rodriguez offers two ways to mitigate the risk of failure that apply to knowledge-based organizations and certainly to schools. One is to gather feedback quickly and early in the process to allow corrections in the program while the investment is still essentially in test mode. This feedback should include the customer's viewpoint (perhaps a survey of students and parents before and after a trial of the program) in order to combine the process of innovation with a true measure of value. Many now refer to this process of rapid iteration as "failing fast and failing forward". A second way to mitigate risk is to think big and boldly about opportunities for truly value-laden innovations, but to start small and scale up based on hard data. Frequently schools evaluate major program shifts over very long periods of time and move forward only after lengthy assessments have appeared to prove an increase in student outcomes. Such a process may mitigate the risk of being wrong about a particular program adoption, but it eliminates quick feedback that may either kill the project or suggest important major changes to make it successful.

Organizations that do not have a great deal of experience with taking risk need to establish a risk tolerance profile. They develop a common language and approach to risk taking, so the decision to take a risk in changing the learning experience, for example, can be made at the class-room level. Schools often see risk in terms of threats to the health or safety of their students or employees, rather than as opportunities to improve the value of their learning experience. Schools do not generally risk sig-nificant human and intellectual capital if the perception is that the risk is likely to fail. Yet this is exactly what the experience of other successful knowledge-based organizations tells us is required. Slotnick and Schulten (2012) outline a series of questions that organizations should address in considering the downside of failure, the upside of success, and the down-side of not taking risks at all: What is failure and who defines it? How is failure useful? How will we recover from failure? What are some examples of past organizational failure?

Introducing the element of choice into decision equations can eliminate much of the fear associated with taking a risk. John Collins of the Poway district told me, "Choice is huge. Our new Design 39 Campus school, where we will be doing things *very* differently, will be a choice school: Parents can choose to send their kids there, and we will make very sure that they know what they are getting into. They will know that this is not what they, the parents, are familiar with. They will know ahead of time that we may not have a traditional Halloween carnival every year. It will also be a choice school for teachers. Not all teachers are comfortable in a setting without fifty-minute periods or their own classrooms or few textbooks. That's fine. We want the teachers who are comfortable with taking these risks, who choose to be there. We will build that community around people who *choose* to 'do school' differently."

Speeding the Rate of Change

The pace of program evolution is another opportunity to structurally align innovation with changing goals of learning. Significant programmatic changes in public schools, like creation and adoption of the Common Core State Standards, may evolve over a period of five to fifteen years. Private schools that do not have to run the same gauntlet of review and approval as the public schools operate largely on the basis of five-year strategic planning cycles. Both of these time frames are long relative to changes in the external environment. Outside of education, it would be hard or impossible to find a successful knowledge-based company that operates on a five-year plan, let alone change models that require more than a decade to implement. Educators will remember that in 2009 online learning was just starting to receive recognition as a scalable learning model, and no one had ever heard of an iPad. If schools are to keep pace with this type of external innovation, large, slow-to-turn structures have to yield to flatter organizations that can accelerate design, workflow, and feedback.

In most schools, ideas take a long time to percolate up the Management 1.0 ladder, and decisions take a long time to descend back down. Administrators at many of the schools I visited told me they are more comfortable with small nodes of innovation that have slow or isolated impact. Most schools do not have a mechanism to take those small nodes and place them in an overall context that leads to intentional, system-wide change. There are exceptions. When a major change is imposed from the outside, like the change in statewide standards, schools have no choice but to retool and react. Similarly, I found a number of schools where charismatic leaders required their schools to act quickly on major changes.

John Collins of Poway shared some concrete examples of dramatic change in a public school over a five-year period. "We took one of our lowest-performing schools, with a high percentage of free and reduced lunch students and a very high percentage of ESL students, and turned it into one of our most high-performing schools in just five years. This was Los Penasquitos School, the origin of Damen Lopez's 'No Excuses University,' which is now being used in hundreds of schools around the country. It started with some small pilots at the school, which we were able to quickly ramp up to the all-school level." John said that the unusually fast rate of change was due to a highly intentional focus on rapid innovation that broke with previous conventions; school leaders intentionally decided to *not* allow change to occur at an organic pace.

Innovating quickly requires more than just generating new ideas and waiting to see what works. Chris Lehmann at Science Leadership Academy says, "We iterate fast and we are not afraid of ideas. But we also 'problematize' well. We consider the worst and negative consequences of our best ideas, and we do all of this quickly. When people have an idea, be that a student or adult, they generally bring it to me and I immediately put it out to someone with the positional authority to move it forward, to make a decision. I trust those people to make good decisions wisely and well. I always tell people 'when in doubt, cc me on an e-mail.' We have the tools now to keep each other in the know, to share ideas and process. We don't have to meet on every detail. I may even forget I was in the decision loop, and that is OK."

Chris also says that adults have to break their perceptions and habit of yielding authority for innovation to senior administrators. "When we have someone new to the school, we often have to coach them up to this level of decisional empowerment, so they will just go and make things happen. Teachers are like anyone else; they bring the ghosts of every past experience with them. They have an expectation of me as 'the principal' that I am going to act in a certain way. I have to break them of that; I tell them, 'You are here now, I want you to come bother me if you have an idea.'"

> "When we have someone new to the school, we often have to coach them up to this level of decisional empowerment, so they will just go and make things happen."

What Do Innovative School Structures Look Like?

Creating a culture accepting of real change at a school requires adopting strategies that allow people within the organization to dream, try, pilot, imagine, test, fail, succeed, and share—not in response to an order from the boss but because that is how the organization best meets its mission. I am not a fan of checklists, but in combining research on organizational innovation with examples from schools, I find the following structures and processes to be particularly effective:

- *Structures that promote innovation are based on shared interest*, rather than on a vertical system of departmental authority (Zaninni, Folk-Williams, & Komori, 2011). Innovation teams include people from a variety of departments, with a range of expertise, and with a diversity of attributes required for innovation to succeed. These teams are given time and resources, develop clear goals, and make decisions themselves for what is in the shared best interest of their goals, not what is in the best interest of a department or existing program. By their nature, innovation teams, or networks, burst traditional silos of isolated work. While membership may be fluid, successful innovation teams have owners, some person or group tasked with the activity and success of the team.

- *Superintendents, heads of school, and principals require their employees to think strategically*, not just tactically. Senior management provides training in strategic thinking and provides team-based opportunities for putting it into practice. Natural leaders in the organization who may have heretofore been left on the sidelines are placed in positions where they can strongly impact innovation and attract others into the process.

- *Innovation teams create real autonomy of decision making* for activities related to their work at division and lower levels. Senior management sits back and lets these groups work. Sometimes the teams fail; they miss deadlines; their ideas are unrealistic; their proposed innovations are flashes-in-the-pan that do not bring real value to the school. Management does *not* step in and direct the team to reach a different solution. The basic job of management with respect to enhancing innovation as an organizational imperative is to hire good people, give them resources, set broad goals, get out of the way, and when failure does occur, help the team to repair, rebuild, and be more effective in the next iteration.

- *The school adopts an organization-wide ethos that encourages, and even demands, willingness to change*—what Rowan Gibson (in Kelley, 2010) calls a "deeply embedded capability." Adults in all roles look for opportunities to improve their teaching and administrative functions, and to engage colleagues on a regular basis as symbiotic parts of a learning ecosystem. Schools increase what Gibson calls the "demand side" of innovation. Innovation is visibly and tangibly rewarded and recognized along with teaching excellence, cost containment, and other operating performance criteria. Trustees and the community hold senior management accountable for prioritizing innovation best practices.

- *Leaders realign resources to provide people, time, places, and budgets for innovation*, allowing innovation teams to meet, work, and launch the process of innovation with faith in real outcomes and real change.

Committees and reporting structures that impede change are discarded, even when this is uncomfortable and counter to tradition.

- *Innovation teams develop goals that align broadly with the school's vision* but have latitude to explore truly creative pathways that test foundational assumptions. For example, school innovation teams might work on ways to leverage the use of technology to enhance learning, create a new program that will attract higher admissions demand, find efficiencies in how classes are conducted, or partner with community organizations or corporations to offer new curricula.

- *Finally, the teams get to work, creating and evaluating ideas*—assessing, gathering support from management and testing customer reactions, tweaking and revising, and ultimately selecting opportunities that can be scaled up to full strength. Perhaps most critically, the teams provide rapid, perhaps even real-time, feedback to management. Many if not most ideas either die in committee or fail to scale in sufficient magnitude to create real new value for the organization. While this process can be frustrating, an effective innovation team has alternatives and other ideas in the pipeline, and other teams also have ideas in process.

REFLECTION

Change is not hard relative to other tests in life, but it can be messy, complicated, and uncomfortable. Change can also be energizing and empowering, giving us vistas of opportunity for growth that fire the imagination and a new reason to get out of bed in the morning. The impassioned faculty that I met along my journey would not be transferring those passions for learning on to their students if they did not have the carrot of change, the opportunity to create, to find a better way, always dangling out in front of them. Doris Korda, assistant head at the Hawken School, summed up the process of organizational change for a school: "Anyone who thinks you can go get the future in a package or in a can or subscribe to it is wrong; it is about putting yourself out there, in the mix. Be prepared; you will mess up. Start small, you don't have to start with the whole answer, but get started. You are going to mess up and then you are going to pick yourself up."

We are not used to scaling up an idea until we have completed full assessment of its impact on teaching and learning. But the rate of change in the world has increased, and we don't have the latitude to take years to make change when those same adjustments in the external world are happening in months. The good news is that other knowledge-based organizations have pioneered this process for us, and as we have seen, we merely need to translate their experiences and successes into the language of education.

It may seem to be an overwhelming challenge to change the culture and skill set of a large organization populated by employees who are valuable and valued for their expertise, passion, and dedication, but who may not be hard-wired for rapid changes in their work environment. As I look back over my log of comments on the obstacles these schools face, there they are—leaders of schools of every type telling me, "It is like trying to turn an aircraft carrier; it just can't be done very quickly"—and then, in nearly the same breath, "But we don't have the luxury of time. Change is already happening, whether we like it or not."

CHAPTER FIVE

More Bumps in the Road
The Next Five Obstacles
to Innovation

Hotel chains may sell themselves as different and better, but once you step out of the elevator in a Comfort Inn, Hilton Garden, or Holiday Inn Express and walk down the hallway, they are pretty much the same: carpeted floors, keycard, bed on one wall, TV on the other, window over the parking lot, small bottles of shampoo and conditioner in the same spot by the same sink, and pillows you would never buy at home. Every night a different hotel; every night the same hotel, but in a different city. After a few nights on the road I remembered to consciously look at my room number, remember it as different from the room number the night before, and it worked, all the way until I got to Norfolk, Virginia, checked into the cookie-cutter hotel on a late afternoon with just enough time to quickly change into my walking shoes for a short jog around town, skipped down to the lobby . . . and realized I had no idea what room I had just left.

Traveling alone, it is the little things that can jumble together and cause headaches. Bad weather, a late meeting, traffic on the road, no restaurant open late at night, Wi-Fi shaky in the room. I quickly learned to keep a small box of PowerBars and juice boxes stocked in the car for that late-night dinner in the hotel lobby. I learned to set two alarms after one night when the hotel alarm failed. After my tire pressure indicator light came on halfway from Boston to Manchester, I checked the pressure every few days when filling my gas tank. After my iPhone died in North Carolina, leaving me without GPS guidance, I saved maps to my laptop as a backup.

Sometimes it is not the one big thing, but the snowballing of other things that can cause the bumps in the road, and when you are on your own, you have no one other than yourself to map your way out of that maze.

In the preceding four chapters I have discussed what I found to be the largest and most frequent obstacles to school innovation and how some schools and leaders are overcoming those hurdles. As I logged hundreds of comments about why school change is complex and problematic, another group of five common themes recurred more than others. While they do not provide the existential challenges that we find with the use of time, for example, these five hurdles are difficult enough to constrain progress for well-intentioned change leaders who fail to surface and deal with them.

The Students Are Changing

Teachers at many schools I visited told me that students today are wired differently for learning than they were in the past, in many ways. Attention spans are shorter; we are all used to getting immediate results when we turn on our computer and enter a few words into Google. Young people are increasingly conditioned to take in short pieces of knowledge at a rapid pace. They are comfortable at multitasking, taking risks, and seeking work-arounds in ways that adults are not. Some teachers believe that students have shorter memory spans and worse retention; students are used to finding information on their phones that we adults had to keep in our own memory banks. Students today feel more empowered and want to shape the world more than previous generations, and they feel that that is a very real possibility. They are not comfortable just being led down an intellectual path; they want to help design the path.

Students today feel more empowered and want to shape the world more than previous generations.

Students increasingly interact socially and academically online, and some groups of both teachers and students I met with feel they need less "face time" with teachers and peers. It is unclear whether this shift will have negative long-term social impacts, but online interaction is very different from the way many adults *want* them to interact in school. The interface between students and their world for the school portion of the day is dramatically different from the rest of the day. Social media are blocked by school firewalls, and student-owned mobile devices are often banned in the classroom at the same time that the school is debating which mobile device to buy for all their students. The goals of collaboration have become increasingly blurred with the rules against cheating. Teachers struggle with how to interact with students who work online outside the normal school hours; who access, create, and manage knowledge without ever touching a piece of paper that they can turn in to the teacher; who work comfortably in groups where it is difficult to track progress with worksheets and quizzes.

In the past decade, neuroscientists have made extraordinary leaps in understanding how the brain actually works, primarily through increasingly sophisticated use of magnetic resonance imaging, or MRI. Unfortunately, most schools and educators have largely ignored this research and continue to deliver content to students along traditional pathways rather than changing those pathways to best fit our state-of-the-art understanding. One school I visited is pioneering the opposite approach: restructuring virtually everything they do in the classroom to align with the latest research in how the brain *actually* works and how people *actually* learn.

St. Andrew's Episcopal School (SAES) is an independent K–12 school in Potomac, Maryland. SAES has developed a unique partnership with the department of neuroscience at Johns Hopkins University and established the Center for Transformative Teaching and Learning (CTTL) with the goals of bringing access to cutting-edge research to the SAES faculty and creating a public-private forum for advancing teaching and learning. Glenn Whitman, the Center's director, says, "This is really a brain research-focused effort. We get access to the latest in the field of brain research, and are working with university scientists to pilot how to put the research into immediate practice. If you are not using this knowledge and research, it is hard to see how you can see yourself as serving the needs of twenty-first-century learning. The CTTL is a game-changer for SAES. We let our families know the value that we are adding with these new teaching and learning strategies." Glenn says that modern neuroscience helps us understand how to create and enhance student engagement and performance, design authentic assessment tools that students under-stand, and forge an environment where students see themselves as "able agents of their own learning."

Teachers at St. Andrew's don't just read the latest research and wait to see what takes hold. School leaders have created a constant improvement cycle that keeps track of a neurodevelopmental analysis regarding the strengths and weaknesses of each student, so they know how each student learns best. Their teachers are developing teaching and learning strategies that focus on conversations and reflection instead of lecture, as research proves that students will retain knowledge longer if they have a chance to digest and embed it in their brains, rather than just memorizing facts. The CTTL shares what they are learning with other educators in both pub-lic and private schools through an increasingly robust set of professional development tools and meetings.

Effectively innovating schools speed up their cycles of profes-sional development to keep teach-ers and administrators astride, rather than behind, these changes. These schools recognize inevitable shifts that impact students out-side of school and more quickly embrace, channel, and filter them, rather than resisting them. Resources are targeted at exposing adults to new interactive technologies and platforms. We may never become as com-fortable with them as our students, but at least they are familiar and less frightening to us. Some schools create opportunities for students, either as volunteers or for pay, to work with adults in training and program development embracing new interactive technologies. Schools that visibly adopt the "teacher as co-learner" model find that both teachers and stu-dents embrace and enjoy this new relationship.

Effectively innovating schools speed up their cycles of professional development to keep teachers and administrators astride, rather than behind, these changes.

Inertia

Fear and inertia are often cited as two of the most powerful forces act-ing to retard organizational innovation. We have already talked about the problem of fear; inertia is even more powerful, particularly at an organizational level. In my school visits I frequently heard, "This is the way we have always done it." At many schools, the arguments about a better model have insufficient weight to overcome this inertia. Since schools tend to be risk averse, trying something that is unproven is almost always seen as a more difficult option than sticking with what we know has worked in the past.

Since schools tend to be risk averse, trying something that is unproven is almost always seen as a more difficult option than sticking with what we know has worked in the past.

I found two main causes of paralyzing inertia at the schools I visited. First, success in the past is a powerful driver of inertia; schools and systems that have been the most successful may have the least incentive to innovate. Not only can they say, "This is the way we have always done it," but they can correctly add "and we are darn good at what we do." The schools that do well by current objective measures have the most to lose if they move from a proven to an unproven model. Significantly, many of these very successful schools are actually leaders in innovation; they are successful because they have both the resources and culture to recognize and act on the need to change. Many of the leaders I cite in this book work at highly successful schools, and they are smart enough to know they will not continue to be successful if they try to stand pat while the world around them is rapidly changing.

Second, regardless of whether a school has high school students, schools are driven more by the needs and results of graduating seniors than by any other grade-level consideration. Program and curriculum flow down from the needs of graduating seniors. The powerful forces of college acceptance drive what high schools offer, which drives what is expected of middle schools, and to a lesser extent what is expected of elementary schools. Schools are most willing to innovate and try new things at lower grade levels, and that willingness is frequently present up through eighth grade. At the K–12 Rowland Hall School in Salt Lake City, after a day working with a

The powerful forces of college acceptance drive what high schools offer, which drives what is expected of middle schools, and to a lesser extent what is expected of elementary schools.

mixed division faculty leadership team, teachers from the high school turned to the teachers in the elementary division and told them, with real surprise, "You guys have been teaching creativity all along!" Trustees at one highly reputable school in Pasadena told me, "We want to change our program, and it is easy to make these changes in the lower grade levels, but we are just afraid of changing what has worked for getting our kids into top colleges in the past."

As the challenge of college admissions gets closer in time, a rigid mind-set takes hold, and for schools that have developed a strong reputation for good college entrance results, willingness to change becomes increasingly rare in grades 9–12. In both public and private schools, the most obvious manifestation of this has to do with the reverence we pay to SAT and ACT scores and AP courses. There is a growing narrative from many colleges and universities that standardized test scores are decreasingly important in the admissions process. Many college admissions officers publicly claim they are looking for students who are independent, creative thinkers. Despite those claims, many colleges still tend to select students with the highest test scores. Put simply, the College Board directs what we teach in much of our K–12 system of education. No one likes it, but the inertia is overwhelming.

Schools that are effectively tackling inertia share some common strategies. They recognize that they cannot rely on past results to indicate future success when the boundary conditions are changing so quickly. These schools ask questions that open the future to new ways of thinking, rather than basing strategy on a refinement of what they have done in the past. They are willing to challenge foundational elements of the school organization and traditions. These schools seek a balance between standardized tests and deeper learning, and focus resources on communicating how their nontraditional classes and programs actually improve student performance. Schools willing to doggedly challenge both internal and external measures of performance are able to overcome these major forces of inertia.

Organizational inertia often plays out as a desire, either overt or subliminal, to protect the status quo. Steve Blank of Stanford University (in one of his 2012 blogs) says, "Committees protect the status quo. Everyone who has a reason to say 'no' is represented. New market problems call for visionary founders, not consensus committee members." For institutions like schools that either are, or want to be, highly democratic and transparent, large committees are standard fixtures. When dealing with complex, highly disruptive, and ambiguous futures, these structures more frequently act to prevent innovation than promote it.

In contrast to the committee mentality, Dave Monaco at Parish Episcopal highlights Seth Godin's emphasis on "shipping" a product. "Once you have germinated some ideas and created a structure replete with people who buy the vision and want to get after it, you have to be courageous enough to advance. We launched six signature innovations in 2010, unsure which would ultimately gain. Ideas don't have to be baked perfectly to roll it out. In fact, small wins gained in early implementation generate enthusiasm among your pioneers and eventual innovation stewards. It becomes a self-perpetuating feedback loop in which the very act of shipping builds the momentum and enthusiasm necessary to propel the implementation to a more finished form. Whether you refer to it as shipping or 'failing forward,' to use the design term, an innovative culture must include a willingness to forge ahead into the unknown with the confidence that you will figure out what needs to be figured out along the way."

> "An innovative culture must include a willingness to forge ahead into the unknown with the confidence that you will figure out what needs to be figured out along the way."

Inward Focus

For millennia, schools have been a physical space dedicated to learning, often a cloistered set of buildings with tall walls and locks on the doors. Educators kept the keys of knowledge to themselves, holding them apart from an ignorant world. Over the past decade, that reality has been completely upset by almost universal access to content knowledge via the Internet, yet the insularity remains. Schools are having a hard time adapting to the concept that learning takes place in a connected world anytime, anywhere, with anyone.

Few formal school activities involve interactions with the community where students and families live—or if they do, these interactions are occasional and shallow, perhaps a service project to pick up trash on Volunteer Day, a field trip to the zoo, or opportunities for high school students to help at the local soup kitchen. Schools largely exist apart from communities packed with knowledge-based companies and organizations like universities, museums, laboratories, libraries, and not-for-profits. Our communities embody the streets, people, and natural systems we want our students to prepare for, yet we largely keep our students, teachers, and their learning removed from all of it, teaching inside our four walls.

Schools are mentally as well as physically isolated. Few teachers visit other schools or collaborate frequently with teachers or administrators from other schools or with the many knowledge creators and managers in the community. Few teachers make lasting connections with colleagues in other parts of the world. Few teachers are familiar with the latest research, for example, in how the brain works during the learning process. They don't read scholarly journals. Most don't follow educational blogs or engage in professional development via social media, which make knowledge and research highly accessible. Teachers almost always try new technologies *after* their students have become proficient with them. When it comes time, then, for a discussion among the adults in the school community about how the organization might or must change, those having the discussion are ill equipped for it. The majority is forced to yield through ignorance to the suggestions of those who have been exposed to fresh ideas.

These are some of the easiest obstacles for schools to overcome, as we recognize that schools are increasingly connected to the outside world. Educators find that their communities are rich learning environments that can be accessed within just a few steps or miles of campus. Educators can plan for and mitigate the risks associated with leaving the secure campus, realizing that teaching students how to balance risk and reward is an essential life skill. These educators embed off-campus learning deeply into core curricula rather than setting it aside as an after-school extra or one-time experience.

All over the world, teachers, students, and administrators are finding new opportunities for frequent, inexpensive or free collaboration with colleagues and peers they would never have met in the past. During my trip, several New Jersey public school educators contacted me after following my blog and tweets. They are exemplars of edu-

All over the world, teachers, students, and administrators are finding new opportunities for frequent, inexpensive or free collaboration with colleagues and peers.

cators around the country who are rapidly increasing an outward-looking perspective on their profession. Though I did not have time to redirect my Prius to include visits with them, we chatted on Skype. Danielle Hartman is a teacher and technology integration specialist at Burlington County Institute of Technology; Elissa Malespina is a librarian and technology specialist at South Orange Middle School; and Bill Krakower is a teacher and technology specialist at Beatrice Gillmore Elementary in Woodland Park. All three told me that they are driven and sustained by informal connections and professional development based on nothing more than the desire of teachers to do what they know will enhance learning for their students. As in other parts of the country, dozens, sometimes hundreds, of New Jersey teachers from all kinds of schools and districts meet with colleagues from around the state at physical events like EdCamps and virtual meetings like the weekly #Satchat on Twitter. They participate to meet and develop new ideas, usually on their own time and often not even receiving professional growth credits for doing so. All three told me a version of the following: "Twitter is the most powerful tool I have in my professional growth. I routinely meet up with educators from the region and all over the world to share ideas and resources."

As the world is increasingly connected, educators are rapidly expanding their professional networks beyond their own school. Educators don't have to plan far ahead, make a long trip, or take an entire day to visit and learn from colleagues. Collaborative professional environments on simple-to-use social media like Twitter and a rapidly proliferating spread of free or inexpensive online courses bring the world directly to our desktops and sofas at home. Connected co-learners share resources, lesson plans, what works and what does not, new ideas and frustrations. Educators can rapidly expand their own professional networks and have a real-time participatory voice in evolving best practices, research, and commentary. Teachers make time in their busy days for frequent short bursts of professional connections, rather than waiting for the traditional annual conference.

Communicating the Value Proposition

There are many specific definitions of an organization's value proposition. The definition that I think most closely reflects the needs of schools is this: Your school's value proposition is the difference between what you say you are going to do and what you actually do, as viewed through the eyes of your customer. A school's value proposition is different from its mission or vision. The mission and vision define the foundational principles against which we measure our program and ourselves. The value proposition is the reason parents decide to send their children to our particular school rather than educate them via a growing number of public, private, and virtual alternatives.

On most of my school visits, I met with the site leader or the leadership team. We talked about the vision and values of the school and how those are changing. I asked many of them the same questions: "If I walked down the halls and randomly asked teachers what the school's vision is, would I get the same answer that your senior leadership team gave me? Would I get the same answers at all, or a mixed bag? Would I get blank stares?" At the majority of schools I visited, the leaders predicted that the results would be mixed at best and that there would also be a lot of blank stares. They recognize that communicating a common vision throughout a diverse school organization is difficult but that without that shared vision, establishing a clear value proposition is impossible.

Communicating a common vision throughout a diverse school organization is difficult, but without that shared vision, establishing a clear value proposition is impossible.

School organizations have not studied value in the past. Laws that require children to attend some form of school have, until the past two decades, largely protected public schools. Private schools have focused some of their attention on value as they seek to convince potential clients that the education their school offers is worth a fee and that their services are better than those offered by competing private schools. Both public and private schools, though, have been driven much more by their stated mission of getting students ready for college and the workplace than by the need to demonstrate differentiated value relative to other educational options that a family might have.

That is changing rapidly. A decade ago, few families had any real school choice. The alternatives to the neighborhood public school were private schools (expensive), home schooling (detached from key social experiences), or charter schools (untested and not available in many places). Online learning was a developing infant. Today, the options are multiplying rapidly, and each option offers a range of value to a diversified client population. Many public school districts allow families to apply to a range of choice and magnet schools within the district. Data collected by the National Association of Independent Schools show that over the past decade, private schools are, on the whole, seeing fewer applications for admission and are increasingly discounting their tuition to fill seats. Home schooling continues to attract increasing numbers of families as online access to quality education explodes. The number and quality of charter schools continue to expand in many urban areas, offering pro-grams tailored to specific client demand. Blended hybrid schools that combine online learning with a physical campus and qualified teaching and mentoring staff are attracting growing numbers of families. Students are taking college MOOCs (massive open online courses) or other online offerings for credit, which decreases their reliance on the formal K–12 school system.

Schools that I visited highlighted some very specific measures of value that parents are increasingly demanding. Those most commonly men-tioned consist of these:

• Student access to, and comfort with, an increasingly global network of interactions—parents recognize that their children need to be comfort-able working with other cultures and in other parts of the world.

• Access to the latest technologies that they use in their homes and that parents use in their own workplaces.

• Balance—while demanding technology, parents hope that school is a place where students can "unplug" and that the value of sending their children to a physical school rather than just taking online courses lies in the personal interactions they have with adults and with their peers.

• Exposure to a core set of character values that a generation ago were viewed strictly as the responsibility of parents to imbue in their children.

• Preparation for acceptance to colleges that still rely heavily on objective, content-based exams, even as the schools are moving away from teaching strict content in favor of a more balanced, contextual curriculum.

However a school or district chooses to focus and articulate its vision, those that are successful at change communicate so effectively that all members of their community—teachers, students, parents, potential families, community stakeholders—understand the value of what actually happens each day at the school. Communication strategies change almost as fast as we can develop them. School communities are a hive of full-time connectivity, and aligning key organizational messages with the vision and mission requires a level of coordination that most schools are struggling to develop. Parents today want to know what is going on at school all the time, and if they either don't get that information or do not like what they see and hear, they can quickly move their children to competing educational environments.

Working the Problem Ourselves

Adults in schools are used to a top-down management structure, with someone in authority telling them what to do. Adults in our schools are as hooked on "teacher-provided" knowledge as are our students. When a new idea or educational direction comes along, when authoritative researchers or pundits who write best sellers tell us what to do, when a new textbook is published and delivered to the classroom, most educators are comfortable with accepting the new doctrine and turning it into classroom lessons. The pyramid of decision making is incredibly steep, with a small group who make decisions and a very broad base of front-line educators on the receiving end of those decisions.

The story of the assembly lines at Toyota has been told many times. In the old days of supremacy of the Big Three Detroit automakers, the assembly line could be stopped only by a very few people. If a mistake was made in putting some part on a car, the line continued to move, with the result that a lot of cars built in Detroit had defects. Toyota came up with a different approach. Every person working on the assembly line had the authority and ability to stop the entire line. Production slowed down, but the cars had many fewer defects. Over time, Toyota learned how to avoid numerous line stoppages and still build cars with fewer defects. Toyota required their rank-and-file employees to "work the problem"; they did not leave it up to an oligarchy. We know that when we are engaged in finding and solving problems we take a stake in the outcome. And yet schools have become largely dependent on outsiders to tell us what and how to teach.

School leaders at many of the schools I visited described this inability to work the problem as a real obstacle to making significant change. Their teachers and administrators insist on having a model to follow, rather than creating one themselves. In some systems, site educators are allowed virtually no autonomy to create or adapt learning for their own group of students. Front-line educators are often not used to asking fundamental questions that entertain the possibility of major organizational changes. They are uncomfortable stating their own visions and assembling the resources to pursue them. Small ideas emerge, but few are willing to put in the time and sweat to pursue those ideas unless they are sure ahead of time that they are on track with some greater paradigm that is being developed by the oligarchy. The rank and file have been burned in the past: ideas may be good at a local level but are then trumped by "the next good thing" or the next approved textbook, and all of that hard work and thinking must be tossed aside because those at the top of the pyramid made a decision about what and how we teach.

Effective leaders at the schools I visited are breaking down this cultural reliance on oligarchical decision making by insisting that their employees "work the problem" themselves. This insistence does not mean that leaders forgo access to outside expertise; in fact, with massive connectivity and the free sharing of knowledge across the Internet, ideas and information flow in from a growingly diverse set of experts in near real time. Nor are successful leaders giving up their responsibility to manage effective implementation of changes. Effective leaders, however, inculcate a culture of questioning, imagination, prototyping in place, authentic reflection, and tweaking, as opposed to seeking or accepting a cookbook solution. Creating and pursuing new ideas becomes part of job descriptions all around the school. One-size-fits-all thinking is easier, but it is utterly antithetical to breaking away from assembly-line thinking—for our students as well as for us.

Mike Davis, head of Colorado Academy, says that building this internal capacity was a key to the school's rapid transition to a more innovative culture: "While we have brought in outside experts to talk about important education trends, we have tried to get faculty involved in continuing efforts of retraining and supporting their colleagues. While an outside thinker can be effective in opening a teacher's mind to a new approach, working alongside their peers and learning from peers boosts confidence and creates more opportunity for successful implementation."

REFLECTION

When I started my journey of school visits I had no idea that this wide variety of schools, public and private, wealthy and poor, urban and rural, early childhood to secondary, would share a discrete number of obstacles on their paths to innovation. In the abstract, change can seem overwhelming, but when broken down into tangible pieces we see that not only are the pieces manageable, but other schools have already managed to turn those same obstacles into opportunities, often in ways that enhance their public value proposition. There are schools all over America that have already solved the problems that are tripping up the rest of us.

That is great news, and the even better news is that educators are almost always willing to freely share their successes. In most industries, companies are reluctant to share what works, to let go of a competitive advantage. In this way schools were part of a cooperative, "open-source" world long before that term was invented. Schools have always shared what works, and now we have the ability to do that in real time on a massive scale. We just have to get out and see what those successes look like, and then bring the templates back to our own schools. And the "we" can't just be principals or department chairs. Many of the educators I met rightly expressed jealousy at the trip I took. I am convinced that if our school systems not only allowed but demanded that many others have this same opportunity, on a smaller scale, change would be rapid and far easier to accomplish. Of course few schools and districts have the funds to pay teachers to travel the country visiting other schools. But schools do have resources that, realigned, can dramatically increase the degree of connectivity and exposure that can scale change. On professional development days that are already funded, teachers can visit colleagues in nearby districts. Teachers from private, public, and charter schools can connect more frequently, sharing what works in all of their environments rather than focusing on the obvious differences. In just a few minutes a week, teachers and administrators across the country can post and share resources or meet up in video hangouts.

To complete this metaphor, then: We have all seen roadbuilding crews working in the summer sun, grading out bumps, removing big rocks, and laying down a smooth layer of fresh asphalt. It is long, hot, sweaty work. But it works!

———————————————————————————

PART TWO

Blazing the Trail: What Does Transformative Learning Look Like?

I VISITED SIXTY-FOUR SCHOOLS IN THREE MONTHS. THE SHORTEST VISIT WAS about two hours, the longest a day and a half. The majority were half-day visits, either in the morning followed by a mad dash across town to another school, or in the afternoon followed by a drive to the next hotel in the next town down the road. Ten days into the trip I found myself in a hotel staring at the wall and imagining nearly three more months of the crazy calendar I had set. I called my wife and told her that there was no way I could maintain the pace for another eleven weeks. But by the time I crossed the Mississippi, with the long drives of the West and Midwest behind me, I had built a routine of fourteen-hour days: one or two school visits, find a hotel, catch up on blog posts, upload video, update my log of key takeaways, load GPS coordinates for the next day, and try to sleep.

I viewed my role on this journey as an observer, questioner, and recorder. The schools I visited showed me what *they* wanted to show me. I could poke and prod with the growing knowledge of what I had seen at other schools, but for the most part I saw what this somewhat-random group of schools thought of as their most innovative programs. When I got home at the end of the trip I started to sort through the pieces, looking for common elements in the hundreds of interviews and dozens of classrooms. I read and reread my pads of notes and lists of key takeaways, watched and transcribed dozens of video clips, turned them into decks of cards, and started pinning the cards onto bulletin boards, sorting and resorting, moving them around until I saw the common threads fall into groups and patterns. I kept coming back to a central question: "What are the common elements of innovative learning in these schools?"

After much sorting and shifting of all those cards, I believe the common elements of innovation fit into five "buckets" that I will describe over the next five chapters. The chapters are full of stories from these schools. It was painful to select a few such stories for each chapter because it meant leaving so many more untold in this book. But that does not mean the stories are lost! During the trip I wrote something like 120,000 words in my blog posts, and while I certainly did not have time to review and edit those posts along the way, they hold a wealth of additional examples of school innovation and points of connection with colleagues who are willing to share their stories (the interested reader can search my blog, *The Learning Pond*, www.learningpond.wordpress.com, for entries from September through December 2012).

In naming these five areas of change, I struggled to find just the right words. Every day at every school I saw or heard something new, students and teachers excited about how they were breaking ground in some class or grade level at their school or following a decades-old tradition that now seems like innovation to the rest of us, not because they wanted to fit into some new learning paradigm but because they felt the driving energy and passion of creating their own new learning experience. The labels I place on these "buckets" of innovation are not perfect and are not meant as ingredients for some cookbook recipe that will result in the perfectly innovative school. I did not visit a single school that consciously constructed such a recipe using all of these ingredients. Hopefully the names of these buckets, the titles of the next five chapters, are broad and flexible enough to describe the exciting changes to learning that I saw. But the reader should not get bogged down in semantics if you disagree with the words I found to describe these evolving elements of learning.

As I wrote these chapters, I realized just how fluid and nonlinear these descriptive terms are. The difficulty in parsing these drivers of the learning process, of course, is what leads me, in the following section, to describe learning as a natural ecosystem, not an assembly line. It is hard to find the right word to describe *exactly* how learning is evolving in schools, just as it is hard to put one's foot on the *exact* boundary between a meadow and a forest. The real world has few rigid lines; that is the nature of ecosystems, and we are starting to realize that great learning looks like a natural ecosystem.

After that one night of doubt about ten days into the trip I got into my routine and found a source of remarkable energy flowing out of the schools and people I met. Tired and brain-dead at the end of each day, worn out from driving and writing and eating another salad at another one of the chain restaurants that always seem to sit across the street from clusters of chain hotels, I would get out of bed and visit another school the next day. For people at each school, it was just one visit, and they had a half-day to show me what was most exciting and innovative in the life of their school. I don't drink much caffeine, but now I know what a big shot of Red Bull feels like! Teachers eager to share, lively students excited about a messy new collaboration, classrooms with desks pushed aside and question-laced Post-it notes covering the walls, robots in the corner, proud stories—noisy, active, engaged—each day I got a jolt of what learn-ing *can* be, and the fatigue would just melt away in the raw optimism that school *can* be a place all of us look forward to every day.

CHAPTER SIX

Schools Are More Dynamic
Mess, Noise, and Chaos

How American poetry would suffer
without the bounty of autumn colors!

We Southern Californians pay a price for our perpetual summer, our spring in February and balmy Thanksgivings. We never get to see the blazing fire of autumn's last gasp as it ripples across the deciduous belts of the Northeast, the Mid-Atlantic, and the South. The locals there yawn at the early days of the annual classic, waiting for that week of high color when the reds are brighter than blood and the yellows chase away the pedantic greens of summer, and then they are gone, blown across old byways, cold streams, and rocky hillsides by the first stiff winter winds.

My timing was perfect. I drove through the wild, rich variety of high color for almost six weeks, following the tide from central Massachusetts down through Washington, D.C., south across the Virginia battlefields, crisscrossing the Carolinas, angling through Georgia, clipping the northern edge of the Mississippi Delta, and ending in Memphis where the yellow leaves on downtown streets in mid-November were just as bright as the hills of Deerfield in October. Like the surf-gods who follow the mythical endless summer, I lived each day for more than a month wrapped in the thoughtful lessons of autumn.

Every weekend, after logging video interviews, writing my blogs, filing my notes, and calling home, I found some trail or mountain park, trying to snap the perfect picture of blazing colors and fading lights, before shoving my camera phone deeper into my pocket and just enjoying the path.

Can you walk through the New England fall and not ponder two roads diverging in a yellow wood around every turn? Can you sit on a log in the North Carolina backwoods without seeing a wild turkey skitter through the leafy downfall, even if it is not really there? Can you drive down a potholed two-lane in the steep defiles where Georgia fades into Tennessee, with the wind blowing clouds of leaves across the road, and not liken it to a flurry of snow, if only snow had color and the hardwood's promise of renewal? We spend too much time in the places of man where time is measured in years and generations. It is good to spend time in the places where cycles of life ebb and flow in ways beyond our ken.

Listen to the Students

If we want to know how schools are changing, all we really have to do is listen to the students. During the trip I had lunch or group interview time with students at more than a dozen schools. I asked them, simply, "How has school changed for you in the last five years?" and "What skills do you need to succeed in your future?" One high school student told me, "Teaching and learning styles are changing because people are breaking away from the traditional ways of doing things and creating their own versions of what benefits their students. Our teachers have learned new techniques that really engage students." Another reflected, "Instead of teachers talking at students, they are starting conversations. Students are able to process and respond. Students look at each other and talk, instead of just listening." And a third summed up a radically different learning system than when they had entered elementary school, just a few years before: "We think of teachers really as the lead learners. While we are learning, we find things that the teachers have never learned, or they look at things from our perspective. We feel we are a learning community. Students get the chance to be the lead learner in the group. It gives all of us—students and teachers—the opportunity to look at things from different perspectives."

At three schools in the Dallas area, I asked high school seniors what skills they needed to be successful and happy in their futures, and in just a few minutes they created what I use as my master list of the "Essential Qualities of a High School Graduate":

- Persistence
- Confidence
- Resilience
- Patience
- Openness
- Creativity
- Adaptability
- Courage
- Perspective
- Empathy
- Self-control

We could discuss and argue whether this is or is not *the* definitive list, but it would be an argument at the margins. I have shared the list with hundreds of educators and not a single one has suggested that they disagree to any significant degree. And I *love* this list, because it came from the kids.

Why Do We Go to School?

Our schools are becoming vastly more dynamic learning environments. Neat rows of desks with students sitting in various states of inattention are vanishing, giving way to noise, messiness, and controlled chaos. A high school student at Science Leadership Academy told me that the students are responsible for deciding where the curriculum will take them, and it is up to the teachers to keep pace. A sixth grader at Brecknock Elementary in Pennsylvania told me that technology means the jobs of tomorrow will be different from the ones her teacher prepared for in the past. These students see and understand this fundamental change in education: the retooling of the foundational relationship between student, teacher, and knowledge; the reframing that has its roots in Socrates and its modern expression in Dewey; the understanding that good teachers are guides, not gods.

At the heart of this retooling is the knowledge, and perhaps memory, that how each of us learns cannot be captured within a single box of time, space, and subject matter. The lodestar of mass-production in the industrial age is that one size fits all, and in education that is simply not true. It has never been true. One size tends to the mean, which results in average education. Statistically, half the students in a class are being held back, while the other half are falling further behind. Uniformity kills passion and enthusiasm, which are the drivers that lift the bottom up and blow the top off the high end. We know better. We know what creates enthusiasm in students and how to tap into the variety of learning modalities that speak to the diversity of learners in the room. Schools that are truly preparing their students for their own futures are cutting loose from the rigidity of desks in rows, Bloom's taxonomy, and the assembly line.

The lodestar of mass-production in the industrial age is that one size fits all, and in education that is simply not true.

I introduced you to Pam Moran and the Albemarle County District, west of Richmond, Virginia, in the first chapter of the book. I met with Pam and her leadership team during one of their weekly sessions as they were preparing for a critical board meeting. They shared with me their simple argument that is leading Albemarle to redesign the nature of learning. In addition to the traditional balance of teaching content and providing context to students, they insist that learning include the third dimension of *relevance*, of providing students that critical opportunity to engage with why they are at school.

In her blog series, Pam explains that the district's Design 2015 plan is not just a set of isolated pilot programs, but a redirection of learning in every school. "We are implementing Design 2015 projects in every school to support experiences that engage, challenge, and encourage questions and curiosity. Our educators want children to acquire, use and synthesize knowledge. We want to inspire our young people to work well together and find value in working with people who bring different skills and ideas to teams. When our current preschoolers graduate in 2027, we want them to be ready for a world that will be different from the one we know today. In order to do all of this we need to be intentional. All of our site leaders are asking questions like, 'What will your school look like a year from now? How will it sound? What choices will students have inside and outside the classroom that they do not have now? What will you and your teachers let go of in order to embrace this new vision? How will classroom management and assessment be different?'"

In order to implement this redesign, Albemarle has defined seven areas of concentration. While some are familiar, like a focus on interactive technologies and project-based learning, others are more unusual. Rather than using one standard curriculum, the district asks teachers to use alternative representations of information, multiple tools, and a variety of instructional strategies to provide access for all learners to acquire lifelong learning competencies, knowledge, and skills that are specified in curricular standards. The district has a fast-growing "maker" curriculum that amplifies the process of imagining, creating, designing, building, engineering, evaluating, and communicating learning. Teachers are encouraged to allow students to engage in both physical and virtual learning networks with peers in the school and anywhere else in the world in order to learn with demographically diverse colleagues and communities.

Karen Heathcock is a third-grade teacher at Broadus Wood Elementary School in the Albemarle district who has latched onto this latitude and authority to reimagine learning for her students. "In the midst of lots of professional reading and exploration, it hit me," writes Karen in her blog. "These were principles that were not going to *in*form my teaching, they were going to *trans*form my teaching." Karen's third graders are blogging with students at a school in Australia and two schools in the United Kingdom. They are Skyping with other third-grade classrooms around the United States to learn about maps, questioning skills, and regional diversity. The students are connecting to experts and finding peers around the world via Twitter. Every Friday, they do an engineering design challenge that allows the students to "collaborate, create, think, test, tweak, and troubleshoot." So far, the students have designed hovercrafts, NASA-inspired Mars Rover landers, and twelve-inch newspaper tables that can hold the weight of a textbook.

Karen writes that she has "committed to ensuring that every time my third-grade students walk into the classroom, they are going to feel like they are walking into their future, not into my past. It doesn't matter how I've taught something before, or how I learned it myself, or what I happen to have in my filing cabinet. I am going to provide my students with the experiences, the knowledge, the tools, and the confidence to master state standards, of course; but more importantly, to pursue what interests them."

Students Own the Learning

Sabot at Stony Point, a pre-K–8 independent school with 178 students, is housed in the old home of a Virginia tobacco baron on the west side of Richmond, bounded by one hundred acres of designated open space forest that the school uses as a playground and outdoor lab. The school follows the Reggio Emilia model for early childhood education, which was developed after World War II in Italy and which focuses on the interests of each child through development of a self-directed curriculum.

There are few, if any, rigid lines at Sabot, either in how the classroom works or how the students learn. Teachers use guiding questions, not to cover a detailed map of content area within quantum packets of time, but to allow students to investigate fewer themes more deeply. They have a list of "habits of the mind" that guide curriculum more than content, including taking risks with ideas, conversation, project design, and flexibility. Head Irene Carney says, "We certainly accommodate the individual, but we also pay a lot of attention to how the group works together, how students help each other and learn from each other." As I heard from a number of early childhood educators on my visits, even the young students are highly metacognitive. "Bloom and Piaget were wrong," says Irene. "We tend to go high on the taxonomy at an early age and just see what happens. Even

"We certainly accommodate the individual, but we also pay a lot of attention to how the group works together, how students help each other and learn from each other."

the young students interweave writing, drawing, conversation, and music all within the same topic or question." That was not just propaganda. I had the chance to sit down with several students. A boy *in sixth grade* volunteered, "Our teachers asked us to think about Bloom's taxonomy and why it is always drawn as a triangle or pyramid. I thought it would be more accurate as a circle, and then I realized I was wrong and drew it as a spiral." Probably looking a bit unhinged, I asked the boy how he even *knew* about Bloom's taxonomy, much less had the understanding to analyze it. "Oh, we have been talking about it since kindergarten; that's when our teachers started talking to us about how we learn and know things."

The flow of the day at Sabot at Stony Point is certainly more chaotic than in most schools. Teachers listen more and talk less; they inquire more and tell less. Teachers don't plan ahead in detail; they have a general plan for the day, the week, and the term, but they adjust after observing the students and tweak their detailed plan from day to day to meet the students where they are. One teacher told me, "Students essentially figure out the learning. I am quieter and other children will finish each other's thoughts or sentences themselves. Students will naturally go over and work with someone who is struggling a bit. And of course we know that helping to teach is the best way to learn." Irene adds, "If students actually own their learning as they do here from an early age, more students per teacher in the older grades is not a problem at all. We focus on the social and emotional skills at the younger ages so by the time they get up to about third grade they are really owning their own learning pathway."

I asked what kind of teacher is successful in this environment and how they find new staff. "We find smart people who really want to teach this way," says Irene, "and then we have our own learning specialists who work with faculty to be successful in this framework. The critical piece is that new teachers have to share the idea that students come to school with powerful ideas, and then they can learn the rest. It might take a year or so to get comfortable with this student-teacher relationship, but then the teachers just keep getting better at it."

Does this kind of learning come with a high price tag? No. While the adult-to-student ratio is certainly lower than at most public schools, the tuition at Sabot is on par with what many states provide as the annual per student stipend to their public schools. I found that to be the case at many of the schools I visited. *Some of the most innovative* Private schools in America charge *schools I visited had the fewest* a wide range of tuitions, from less *resources and large class sizes,* than $10,000 a year to well over *while some of the wealthiest private* $40,000 a year. There is similarly *schools with the smallest class sizes* a wide range in the levels of pub- *were the least change-oriented.* lic support for public and charter schools. The main cost driver in all school systems is the ratio of students to adults. Some of the most innovative schools I visited had the fewest resources and large class sizes, while some of the wealthiest private schools with the smallest class sizes were the least change-oriented.

Blending Content and Skills

The existential issue in education of our time, particularly in the public sector, is the tension between "teaching to the test" and teaching the skills that students will actually need in their futures. It takes a dynamic mix to find that sweet spot where the students master heavy doses of content *through the use* of what we call twenty-first-century skills. In chapter 1, I introduced Brecknock Elementary, a public K–6 school in rural Lancaster County, Pennsylvania. Brecknock has about 480 students and all of the pressures of a public elementary school. The educators at Brecknock are caught in the tension that faces many of their colleagues around the country: Their jobs depend on teaching to an objective standard, while their educational experience and expertise drive them to prepare their students to live in a dynamic future. Rather than just wringing their hands, they are effectively innovating to make the most of both imperatives.

When I visited Brecknock, then principal Lyn Hilt and her team told me that they needed to use new standards-focused programs, even though they find many to be overly teacher-directed and focused on "drill and kill." The solution of several of the grade-level groups is to meet frequently, parse upcoming units, and see where they can tweak actual classroom activities to cover the required content, but in much more student-focused and project-based ways. The grade-level groups are making these adjustments on a weekly basis; teachers who share grade levels use much of their allotted professional development time to look ahead at upcoming units in the published curriculum and then build in the skills component, almost on the fly.

Stephanie Ciabatinni, a third-grade teacher, described how the team meets once a week, takes a "have to do" from the proscribed program, and breaks it down to insert higher-order projects and skill work. Teachers build class units around four goals beyond the mastery of standards: work should be student directed; include a heavy emphasis on student collaboration; develop students as independent learners; and keep students actively engaged during class time. The teachers need time in their busy day to self-create these lesson plans, so Lyn figured out how to carve out forty-five minutes of common time for every grade-level team *every day*. This daily interaction reduces decision cycles to days or sometimes even hours.

What actually happens in the classroom looks very different from the experiences of most "drill and kill" systems, and these teachers are doing it with large class sizes. I visited every classroom in the school. Most had about twenty-eight students, but in every class the students were calmly and quietly working away at creatively designed learning stations, comfortable reading corners, and the like. In every room, groups of five or six students worked hard at each station and then self-rotated through to other areas. The school doesn't have a computer for every student, but in every classroom there was a group of students doing independent work on a set of aging desktops. I did not see a single room where the students sat in their rows answering to a teacher standing at the front of the class. And test scores? They have increased every year since Lyn took over and the team developed this fluid hybrid approach.

Reaching Every Student, Every Day

If there were a single Holy Grail of a reimagined learning experience (and there is not), it would look something like this: a combination of time, place, and teachers who all provide a supportive environment in which each child develops both understanding and passion in exactly the way that they can best participate in their own learning. This Holy Grail is mythical in most schools, because our mass-production system does not allocate resources in support of this tailored approach.

There is nothing new about the concept of differentiated learning. We know that people all learn in different ways and at different rates. As long as we limit our model to one teacher standing in front of fifteen or twenty-five or thirty-five students, we can never attend to the needs of each child. But we now have the technology to offer a remarkable level of differentiation, to actually tailor the learning experience to each child. It requires that we keep track of large amounts of data on each student on a daily basis. As Khan Academy founder Sal Khan reminds us, keeping track of large amounts of data "is what computers are really good at," and almost all schools have increasing access to computers.

Educators at Presbyterian Day School (PDS), a pre-K–6 boys school in Memphis with 630 students, have figured that out. Lee Burns was head of school at PDS for thirteen years, and just about everyone who knows him talks about his combination of vision and humility. Lee says, "Change comes slowly, but we are building an ethos and culture of growth, of teachers as lifelong learners. We pose provocative questions to ourselves as a community on subjects both within and outside of the specific field of education." A few years ago, Lee laid out their overarching vision questions: "Can we provide a customized learning journey for each student? Can we create a curriculum every day to match just what each student needs?"

Lee and his leadership team tackled these questions and started working on a completely new learning flow for the school. Faculty visited the d.school at Stanford University. They visited innovative schools in New York and Silicon Valley, and over the past few years almost all of the PDS faculty have attended Harvard's Project Zero program, where they started mapping out critical learning paths and tossing out curricula that no longer fit.

The guiding question for every teacher in every class has shifted from "What are you teaching?" to "What is the learning outcome today for both the student and the teacher?"

The teachers have discarded most of their textbooks. According to Assistant Head Susan Droke, their guiding question for every teacher in every class has shifted from "What are you teaching?" to "What is the learning outcome today for both the student and the teacher?" Susan, Chief Information Officer Cathy Kyle, and math teacher Windy May built an entirely new vision of how to teach math. Windy says it started with a simple question: "If one of my students has already mastered order of operations, why should his class time be wasted on that when he is ready for a more advanced concept that day?" The team "reviewed and curated hundreds of different math activities related to different skills" and created a digital resource base of activities and projects for a broad range of basic and accelerated skills. Because it is understood that students learn in different ways, the activities and projects cover a variety of learning pathways.

Math is now built around a series of eight-day units. The start of each unit is a video podcast that the students watch at home, which gives them an overview and context. The first three days center on fairly traditional teacher-led instruction. Short assessments reflect how each student is progressing with the material. After three days each student can opt to take a test to assess mastery of the unit. Those who pass at a high level then spend the next four days in either individual or group projects to explore math-related topics of their choice in what they call a "Guided Challenge." Windy meets with each of the students to help design their Challenge, including an assessment of the learning the student has set out to achieve. The Challenges may include math at a level up to what is traditionally assumed to be a ninth-grade level (for fifth-grade students).

There are a number of novel stops in the Guided Challenge and learning circuit, but none more so than the Learning Studio, an open room where groups of students splay out on beanbag chairs, work in groups at barstools and on a variety of flexible furniture, link to off-site tutors, and work problems together on an idea wall. Three learning coaches roam the space, answering questions and providing guidance. These adults are not there just to assist the project work; they are also wired into the same database as the classroom teacher, so they can quantitatively assess how each student is progressing through his or her work. Feedback is in real time and specific to each individual learning need. The students are constantly moving when they need to; the teachers are there when they are needed and on the side when they are not.

Students who do not choose to take the test or do not pass with a high score after three days enter a four-day "learning circuit." The circuit reminds me of a strength program designed for varsity athletes. Small groups of students move from room to room depending on their individual needs. Learning coaches at each station approach the unit material from a variety of different viewpoints and approaches that target instruction to the particular skills that each individual child needs. At the end of these four days, the students take the assessment test. The goal is for each student to master each unit, through whatever means works best. The early results, as we might imagine given this tailored approach, is that test scores have increased across the board.

PDS teaching coach Abbie Fowler told me that they are using real-time feedback to "break it down": "This system allows students to work at their own level. We group students according to ability, and within that group they may be on the same level but they may have different strengths and weaknesses. They are all in their own learning zone, but they are all together in terms of social space."

Will truly differentiated learning become common for private schools along the old laboratory school model, but rare or slow to evolve in the public sector? Hopefully not. The cost of computing drops every year, and software that allows differentiated or adaptive learning profiles is evolving rapidly. The program at PDS is being achieved with no increase in cost or the number of adults required. California public schools operate with less funding than most schools in the country, and class sizes have exploded as a result. Yet the Poway Unified School District near San Diego will open the new K–8 Design 39 Campus in 2014 that will encompass much of the same differentiated learning model with a baseline ratio of up to thirty-five students per teacher. District Superintendent John Collins has given the new school team a nearly blank slate to question every assumption upon which the current system is founded. "We need to provide a system where every child can be successful to the limits of their ability. We don't do that today. The current system is tremendously inefficient. If a teacher is

"If a teacher is standing in front of a class and some of the students already understand what she is teaching, that is just a wasted resource."

standing in front of a class and some of the students already understand what she is teaching, that is just a wasted resource. An adaptive learning model will reduce or eliminate that waste and rechannel the resource to where deficiencies remain." Founding principal of the new school Sonya Wrisley says that the adaptive model that the team is building will "disrupt the old system in ways that do not allow us to go back to the old system. There is so much inertia in our schools that if people feel that this is another 'flavor of the month' they will actively resist, and rightly so. We are burning our ships. There needs to be no going back."

REFLECTION

After I finished my trip, I talked to a teacher whom I have known for years, an excellent and perhaps even iconic teacher at his school. He was frustrated that his juniors and seniors in high school struggled with owning their own learning, with pursuing learning purely because they wanted to. They kept asking him, "What do you want me to do?" These are bright, motivated kids, but, I told him, since the age of five or six, they have been rewarded for doing what the teacher or parent asked, and then moving on to the next unit, paper, play date, after-school activity, or grade level. Can we blame them, should we be surprised or disappointed when, at age seventeen or eighteen, they are not suddenly ready, willing, eager, and prepared to grab the reins of learning on their own?

This journey allowed me to observe the reimagination of learning. Students and teachers are testing the fundamental model of "one size fits all" in the classroom through the use of new technologies, but more significantly through the breaking and reforming of relationships and traditions that have served well in the past but restrict students from learning how to take ownership of their own learning process. Many educators are worried that we don't have long-term studies demonstrating that students will learn standard content better with this transformation. In response, I would point to schools that never forgot what John Dewey and the other giants of the Progressive

Era taught us—that students learn better when they are engaged through experience to find their passion, the relevance of education. For those of you who have yet to watch this engagement unfold in a classroom or lab, an art studio or a visit to a stream or farm, it is a beautiful thing to see!

CHAPTER SEVEN

Schools Are More Adaptable
Changing with the World

Visitors rarely drive in New York City; to out-of-towners, driving in the city can feel like mental suicide. Traffic is legendary, parking is impossible, drivers and pedestrians ignore all signs of control. Driving in the bottom of skyscraper canyons, the only landmarks are rivers and tidelands. Wrong exits lead to tunnels and bridges to places like New Jersey. Uncertainty is a sign of fear. California license plates are just another excuse for irritated honks and angry gestures.

I could not have made my trip around the country without modern technology. I could not have survived the Cross Bronx Expressway on a clear, peaceful Sunday morning without my GPS—even with it, I was sweating out each voice-directed update that might come a fraction of a minute too late, a vital lane switch the difference between a clear path and someplace I had only imagined in Pacino movies and HBO crime shows. The Cross Bronx Expressway was one long maze of potholes, forgotten construction, and detours. Readers from New York are laughing. I sweated in my air-conditioned Prius, turned off the music, and drove as slowly as the local traffic would bear, praying the GPS would find its guiding satellites through tall buildings, tunnels, and overpass steel and concrete. I made it, but did not stop until I was thirty miles down the New Jersey Turnpike and knew for sure I had not made a wrong turn back across the Hudson.

I can read a map as well as anyone and better than most. Put me in the mountains with a topographic map and compass and I can navigate without breaking stride. You laughing New Yorkers want to join me and see who sweats then? But you can't read a map and drive at the same time, not when the traffic is fast or angry, when the landscape is all new, and the off ramps fly by at freeway speeds. No, I could never have made this trip alone, not safely and with a hotel reservation each night, a place to eat a late-night snack, and on time at every visit I had scheduled months in advance, without modern technology: GPS, cell phone, laptop, MapQuest, and iTunes playlists to keep me awake on the long drives. I didn't panic when the car died in the middle of the endless Kansas plains as rain pelted and darkness descended; I had my cell phone. No, the only moment of the trip I panicked was driving hard through rush hour in the Raleigh–Durham–Chapel Hill Triangle, with no printed map in the car, destinations plugged into the GPS on my phone, when the phone went blank—just stopped, no life in the battery. Without it I might as well have been a blind hiker on an unknown peak, not knowing whether the next turn would take me downstream to salvation or deeper into the starvation wilderness.

Adapting to a Changing World

The world is indeed changing at a dramatic rate, and outside of school, in the natural and business worlds, problems and opportunities are not neatly diced into quantum packets of subject and time. Responding to change involves understanding and working with complex matrices of questions, problems, and cross-disciplinary systems. Innovative schools are adapting to these external changes and demands. These schools are taking a hammer to the rigid framework that has defined the industrial assembly line of education. The world no longer fits into a tight map of seven or eight academic subject tracks. Adaptation means that school starts to look more like the real world.

Nearly every school I visited showed me a new course, a new collaboration, a capstone-learning project, or a department that did not exist three years ago.

At nearly every school I visited, the teachers and programs touted as "our most innovative" were adapting to promote connections, not separations, and to allow students to follow personal passions rather than a rigid course outline. Nearly every school I visited showed me a new course, a new collaboration, a capstone-learning project, or a department that did not exist three years ago. In each, I found teachers and students excited not only because they were breaking with convention but because the flexible boundaries of evolving courses of study allowed both adults and children to follow their own passions.

Schools are adapting to their local physical conditions rather than shoehorning canned curriculum into the school regardless of where it is located. Schools in New York City showed me how they use Central Park and the Hudson River as outdoor laboratories, as one might expect. Schools in cities like New York, Boston, Cleveland, Dallas, and Washington, D.C., also access the rich variety of museums, nonprofit organizations, and government offices in their areas as practical laboratories for learning. Students study issues of homelessness and interview people who live on the streets, or visit the offices of the subway or bus system to study how mass transportation actually works. Schools in rural areas take advantage of nearby farms and ranches to study the economics, biology, and sociology of food, health, and nutrition.

There are common threads to these adaptations, and the good news is that they are extremely easy to promote and follow. School leaders give adults the latitude to think outside the traditional constraints of subject-defined roles. Teachers take on the mantle of co-learner or lead learner rather than purveyor of information to students. Teachers undertake a flexible approach to curriculum development and deployments, knowing that each year will see new twists, tangents, and trials. Teachers who are keen to adapt often say that the first step is to throw away the syllabus at the end of each year. Others start each year by having the students in a class or a grade level develop and vote on major themes for the year, and then both students and teachers study subject material through the lens of those big, all-school themes. Teachers may work within a set of common standards, but they see those as the floor, not the ceiling of what they and their students intend to achieve. Perhaps most important, teachers reach across the silos that have separated them in the past. They collaborate on developing and teaching new units or entire courses with other teachers whose strengths complement their own.

I also saw similarities among the students who participate in these adaptive and evolving courses of study. Students sit and listen less; they are active participants in both the design and implementation of courses. Students make informed choices about which projects and problems to pursue and often create these themselves. They lead class discussions and teach and learn from each other as well as from the adult in the room. Students ask questions as well as find and provide answers. The courses allow them to make connections across areas of study that were previously separated in their minds. Students may pursue an area of inquiry in more than one class or for more than one semester or year. In my many classroom visits where I had been told "You really need to go see this class," I found students more excited, engaged, and able to articulate both what they were learning and why compared with students in traditional classes.

Improvising Learning

Early in my journey I sat in on one of the most dramatic (to use a pun) examples of adaptive learning I would see. Dr. Joe Figlino is a veteran middle school science teacher at St. Anne's Episcopal School in Denver. Joe has twenty-seven years of teaching in his rearview mirror. Jason Lemire is a young, energetic drama teacher with a special love of improvisation. Why not combine efforts? Over lunch one day they started thinking about that, and the result was a crucible of learning that I had never imagined. Once a week the seventh-grade science classes meet in a room off the gym, nothing but blank concrete floor, tall walls, and tumbling mats stacked in the corner. The day I visited the students sat in groups of four or five on the floor. Cartoons and questions about cell biology were projected across a wall. Jason paced through the students urging them on. "Rather than answering this question in maybe a more traditional way in which one or two people are giving input and twenty people are sitting there waiting to see what happens, let's try 'yes-anding' it. Two cycles in each group, two cycles in each group. Go!" And with that the students exploded into noisy shouting of ideas and follow-on, three minutes of crowd-sourcing creativity with each student riffing off of the comments of another. Then the students quietly summarized their ideas for the rest of the groups and went on to the next improvisation.

Afterward, Joe and Jason sat down with me. The veteran, Joe, explained, "This takes us back to the days of da Vinci, the combination of art and science. Today the students are strengthening their understanding of hypothesis with

The students exploded into noisy shouting of ideas and follow-on, three minutes of crowd-sourcing creativity with each student riffing off of the comments of another.

the 'yes-and' technique. One person puts forward an idea, and the next carries it to the next level, just as we do in experimental science. We are using it today so the students can design a cell to get the best form and function for the cell. The groups are given the functions of a specific type of cell, and they are imagining what the form of this cell might be. We are taking advantage of the group share approach so everyone feels included, that they have something to bring to the discussion."

Jason continued by explaining why we need to create these kinds of flexible learning experiences: "More and more, these kids' lives are structured, and they are results-oriented structures. When I was in middle school, we got off the bus and went and played touch football for hours, and it didn't seem to matter if you won or lost each day. It was a volume-based experience. Today each experience these kids have is pressure packed. They feel like 'I don't know if I am going to get to do this again,' before they are off to the next thing. If you are just playing football with your buddies and you get creamed on Friday, you have another chance to win on Saturday. The way our classes are set up now is the opposite. In a traditional class you might raise your hand and get called on once or twice in a forty-five-minute session and you have that one shot to say something serviceable, and if you get it wrong, that is it. Not only might the teacher lose that kid for the hour or the day, you might have lost him for the week or the month. That is why something like the 'yes-and' technique makes so much sense. You know that even if you say something silly or stupid, thirty seconds later you know you get to contribute again, to dust yourself off."

Changing Perspectives

Most of us assume that "school" is a fixed condition—that "school" is where learning takes place. But what if legacy concepts of school stand between students, their teachers, and real learning?

When I visited the inner-city public Design Lab School in Cleveland, Principal Eric Juli had created a completely new learning environment for his students across the street at the local community college. As we have seen, Design Lab serves students from some of the poorest areas of Cleveland, and many come into ninth grade with test scores two to four years below grade level. Eric has his hands full just meeting students' basic needs and getting them working at grade level. Yet he has adapted the course flow for the students to cross the street and take classes in engineering and rocketry at the community college. Eric says that innovation means something very different for this school from what it might mean at most of the other schools I visited: "We have to rein-

"Here they are in a brand-new environment that challenges their very concept of what school is. For the first time they are seeing what learning can be, because we are offering new ideas in new settings."

vent every norm, every structure, every routine that is typically associated with school. We have a bunch of kids who are used to passively receiving information. But when they come to these labs, they become doers."

For many students who did not grow up with Legos, model airplanes, or Easy Bake Ovens in their homes, this lab is the first time they have ever built a working model of anything, the first time they tried to follow a plan or work together on a project that did not have a predetermined outcome. The same students—who, an hour earlier in their traditional classroom, were either sitting with their heads on their desk or arguing flippantly with their teachers—were riveted to the work on the lab bench. Eric said the reason is simple. "They don't feel like they are in school. School for them is a place to just come and get along and get moved to the next grade, to do the minimum. Here they are in a brand-new environment that challenges their very concept of what school is. For the first time they are seeing what learning can be, because we are offering new ideas in new settings."

Breaking Silos of Subject Matter

Most schools have developed a rigid orientation around teaching the six or seven standard subjects that have framed liberal arts education for decades or centuries. School time, space, and people are organized around these subjects, which have little practical relationship to the transdisciplinary or nondisciplinary systems in the world outside of school walls. Breaking these silos of "subject-centric" learning is beginning to happen at schools everywhere, but on my trip I found better examples among private and charter schools than public schools.

When Berkeley Carroll School in Brooklyn took a risk and decided to move away from Advanced Placement courses, it freed up space and time for a wealth of new elective courses designed around what teachers *want* to teach and what students *want* to study. The high school science department started offering courses in optics, bioethics, and a science writing collaboration with the English department. Science Chair Scott Rubin and his team also untracked the core science curriculum: "We should not segregate students in tracks; we can meet them where they are and it makes for better learning." They allowed modest increases in class size, which Scott insists is a positive. "If you are truly student-centric and using student collaboration and project-based learning, having more students is often a powerful positive. I would not want to get classes too large, but we have seen good things happen when we go from 15 or 18 students up to about 22 or 24 in a class."

Students at Berkeley Carroll meet or exceed all of the standards while pursuing individual passions instead of following one set curriculum. The new multiyear Science Research and Design program combines independent research and experimentation, peer review of research and products, and ultimately a published paper and major presentation of the students' work in front of hundreds of community members. Some of the students don't even intend to pursue science in college but elected to take the sequence—"because I get to dictate my own learning," and "I got interested in a topic and needed three years to look into it." I interviewed students who had designed their own projects on post-traumatic stress disorder related to HIV in rural Rwanda, the quantum physics of time, and biodiversity in the Hudson River.

Two Berkeley Carroll high school teachers created an Art and Engineering lab based on "curiosity, questions, asking why things are the way they are." Students take things apart to see how they work and what they are made of. Then they take the pieces and create a piece of "kinetic sculpture" artwork out of them. The English and social studies departments have adopted a combined American Studies course model, which gives them a double block of time all year, sometimes as much as 125 minutes in a day. Six teachers write the course, and they teach in teams of two. When I interviewed the students, they had just finished a three-week experiential game in which students adopted roles related to New York City in 1775. The students told me that the game focused on developing their skills in "persuasion, oratory, appealing to others, thinking on your feet, and resilience. We were pretty much consumed by the game. At one point people are shouting at you and not letting you speak, acting like a mob would act, and the teacher told the mob they weren't being tough enough! Some people got really emotional."

This interdisciplinary collaboration has started to break the divisions of class and department at Berkeley Carroll. Untracking all the classes broke the silos of "smart" and "not-so-smart" kids and forced teachers to think about leveraging the power of differentiated learning, rather than sticking to one type of teaching based on a more homogenous student group in each class. English teacher Chris Moses-Jenkins says, "Collaboration is hard, but anything we don't deal with as adults we put on to the kids. We owe it to them to model collaboration if we expect them to do it."

"Collaboration is hard, but anything we don't deal with as adults we put on to the kids. We owe it to them to model collaboration if we expect them to do it."

Another place where teachers are breaking through the silos is the Asheville School, a coed boarding and day school in Asheville, North Carolina, with 270 students, big rocking chairs on the veranda, and an explosion of fall colors in the trees on the day before Halloween. Over a day and a half at Asheville I sat in on a number of classes, mostly in their four-year humanities sequence, which is a tapestry of interdisciplinary renaissance learning. The courses breach so many disciplinary boundaries that, as a visitor, I did not know whether I was attending a class on history, music, philosophy, literature, or art.

In the European Studies class, the students paired as cocurators of a mini art and architecture show. They used the artwork to lead a discussion of time, place, and context. The teacher urged the other students in the class to "ask pushing questions, not just about the thesis" of the presenters. He told them that "as observers you need to be critical analysts, turn questions back on themselves to promote deeper understanding." The discussion kept coming back to the way that art and architecture are not only reflective of a time but also predictive of things to come in history.

In Pre-Calculus, pairs of students presented analyses on sets of United Nations data about historical population trends in various countries, considering various best-fit models and predicting future trends. Students had done some quick research into the social and economic histories of those countries and offered ideas to explain population increases and declines. The students had worked the problem outside of class and used the class time to present and discuss with their classmates. The teacher sat in the back of the class for the entire section.

And finally, after seven weeks of my own hectic journey around the country, I sat in on World History, where the teacher read several short poems from the Tung dynasty to get the students into frame and then dismissed them to go outside, find a spot—alone as was the habit of poet monks from this period— and write some poetry in the style of one of their favorite ancient Chinese authors. I went out, sat on the porch, reflected for a few minutes, and then shut my eyes and took a nap.

Teachers don't lead; they herd. The goal of this learning experience is not mastery of knowledge by the end of the day or week, but mastery of understanding by the end of four years.

In classes like this students co-create threads of art, writing, literature, and broad historical themes. Teachers don't lead; they herd. The goal of this learning experience is not mastery of knowledge by the end of the day or week, but mastery of understanding by the end of four years. At the end of my day at Asheville, I had the chance to sit and talk with students and teachers about this style of learning. One student told me, "You can take a test and if you don't take the time to think about *how what you know* is all connected, two weeks later it is gone. Reintroducing yourself to something helps get it right in your mind, and you won't make that same mistake again. We learn best when the teachers give us a project and tell us to find out how this works and what it means. Teachers here are really good about letting us go through trial and error." Another summed up my entire three months of investigation: "Innovation is finding a new way to solve an old problem, or finding a new problem to solve."

The teachers were equally eloquent in explaining their approach: "We all learn better through experience, and we are creating that experience for the students. There is the constant tension around assessment and the justification of grades. Parents want to know what the students are learning and that they are making progress. We know they are, but our style of learning is less focused on these short-term results. It starts with team teaching and collaboration. When we are forced to collaborate we have to think about why we are doing this, what is our purpose. It has made me a lot better teacher. Every year I am surrendering a little more control. It is hard. I need to think. It makes me grow as a professional."

Starting with Interests, Not Standards

Some public schools *are* finding ways to allow students to breach the bounds of subject-centric learning. In chapter 1, we saw how Don Wettrick and his Innovations class at Franklin Community High School adapted the "Google 20 percent time" model to their daily class schedule. Students in this semester elective come up with their own ideas of projects to pursue and then use social media to connect to resources outside of the school, in the community, the region, or anywhere in the world, to meet their project goals. As part of their project development, the *students themselves* figure out how their project will apply to Common Core standards and what credit they can achieve in math or social studies or art by researching the standards and designing the projects to

> *The* students themselves *figure out how their project will apply to Common Core standards.*

meet them. Each is different, but the project does not go forward if it does not also meet some state standards for which students will receive credit.

A year after I first talked to Don about his class, he reported both successes and failures. His students continue to create and develop an impressive array of projects that connect them with experts and colleagues outside of school in ways that they never would have done in a traditional subject-focused classroom setting. But the traditional routine of exams and homework from other classes often crowds out the "Google time" students had set aside for creativity. Other teachers and administrators are reluctant to recognize the value of the Innovations class when it might impact their own time and space, and Don has not seen the level of percolation and support that he thought would take place given the enthusiastic response of his students to the program.

Meridian Academy in Boston is the smallest school I visited on my trip, just forty-three students in grades 6–12 on the third floor of a brick building on Beacon Street. It was founded by Josh Abrams, and it is about as progressive a learning setting as you are going to find. Many will be tempted to dismiss the lessons from such a school as not applicable to their own issues and opportunities, but I think they would be wrong. Meridian combines all of math, science, and engineering into a sequence of multiyear, thematic courses, and the humanities into another blended track. Language and art get some of their own designations, but they are both woven into the other courses as well. I sat in all of the school's classes and talked to all of the teachers and a number of the students. On my trip this was the closest I saw a school come to mimicking how the rest of the world actually works.

The students learn content when they need it for a problem they are working on, not at some time determined by their biological or school clock. All of their assessment is based on preparing projects and presenting them to an internal and external audience three times a year, and since they are presenting their own work, they want it to be good. Both the teachers and students told me that it is typical for students to *want* to rewrite a paper or poem eight or ten times before being satisfied they have done their best.

By the time the students graduate they have been through a year each of high school biology, chemistry, physics, and statistics; math up to at least pre-calculus; seven years of art and Spanish; and a rich mix of humanities. Sometimes teachers lecture at the front of the class if that is what is needed; other times they set up a range of tasks and the students take over. There are no grades. The transcript submitted to colleges consists of a one-page summary of research and projects by the student and a one-page summary of student work by the teachers. Josh says that college admissions officers are very happy with what they provide, with its inclusive "story to tell, one that stands out from all of the high GPAs and AP scores on all the other transcripts." The colleges recognize that these students have learned to research, design, experiment, think, learn, analyze, and, most important, Josh says, "how to get unstuck if they are stuck. Our students are really good at problem solving, but more importantly at problem posing. That is what we do here."

One Meridian sophomore told me, "You don't have to switch from your math brain to your Spanish brain during the school day. It is one brain all the time. Students here don't have just one thing they are trying to learn." A senior reflected: "Our classes are microcosms for learning. Our conversations connect from one class to another and from one year to another."

> *"You don't have to switch from your math brain to your Spanish brain during the school day. It is one brain all the time."*

In the sixth- and seventh-grade math class, students told me how triangles relate to the shape of tree leaves and how ratios could be applied to the size of a tree and the reach of its branches. They told me how they learned estimating by working out the number of hot dogs consumed at Fenway Park in a year and the number of likely piano tuners in Boston, all questions that the students posed for themselves. In the high school algebra-biology-stats class they learn to set up their own problems, define questions, and "simplify, represent, and interpret." Students recently thought up and solved: how to eat a Reese's Peanut Butter Cup with the same portions of chocolate and peanut butter in each bite; how to harvest lobsters without a population crash; how to reduce tension at a meeting of the United Nations; how to design and build a pendulum clock.

At the end of the visit, I asked Josh what he thinks is truly transferable or scalable from their model to other, larger schools. Among other things, he pointed out the "fluidity of learning created by truly interdisciplinary courses. Many schools have cross-departmental classes but most still try to get through the traditional quantum of material by the end of the year. The Meridian approach is to create opportunities for student engagement and use 'just in time' content provision. Teachers and students develop a mindset of co-learning and adapting to current interests. Teachers don't necessarily change their course material every year, but they will when they want to and, more importantly, if the students self-direct into new tangents of interest."

Hacking School

These few stories represent a small fraction of the new approaches to course development and changing student-teacher roles I saw on my trip. When I visited these schools, I did not ask educators to talk about or show me the courses I have described in this chapter; I only asked to be shown what *they* felt was their most innovative or exciting program, and every school I visited had something to show. These are the pilot projects that leaders at each school believe hold the keys to their evolving future. Nearly every school I visited is adapting course descriptions, testing the bounds of subject, and starting to place student engagement at the core of the academic program. Courses of study are evolving to embrace the life skills that even children recognize are more critical to their future success than a specific body of content knowledge. Schools are remembering the power of passion, both in adults and students, unleashing energy by allowing students and teachers as co-learners to follow those passions and through them achieve both foundational and extraordinary learning outcomes.

A few months after I arrived back in California, a social media contact told me, "I know you are checking out how K–12 education is evolving to link interest to learning; you have to check out this kid." "This kid" turned out to be then

Whether a learner is writing, speaking, studying physics, interning at a local clothing design company, or learning wilderness survival skills, the motivation of studying what he is passionate about speeds up the learning process.

thirteen-year-old Logan LaPlante, who gave a TEDx talk at the University of Nevada in February 2013 that, at the time I am writing this, had crossed over 4.7 million views.

Logan's parents pulled him out of the traditional school system when he was nine years old, and he explains in his talk how he and they have developed the mindset that education, like pretty much anything else now, can be effectively "hacked" without participating in a traditional school institution. Partly on his own and partly in connection with the Squaw Valley Kids Institute, Logan says he spends his days learning, but on his own terms. He studies a lot of traditional subject material, but often through the lens of his first love, skiing. He says that whether he is writing, speaking, studying physics, interning at a local clothing design company, or learning wilderness survival skills, the motivation of studying what he is passionate about speeds up the learning process.

Logan says that when adults ask kids, "What do you want to be when you grow up?" the adults generally assume the answer will include a profession. Logan says that adults largely anticipate that happiness occurs as a function of doing well in school, going to college, and getting a good job. Kids, Logan says, pretty much just want to be happy, and he asks why education does not prioritize the practices of being healthy and happy. The lack of that practice is what drove him and his parents to try hacking school on their own.

"Hackers are innovators who challenge and change systems to make them work differently, work better," says Logan in his talk. "Everything is up for being hacked. I don't use any one particular curriculum or stick with any particular approach. I hack my education by taking advantage of opportunities in my community to experience what I am learning" (LaPlante, 2013).

No doubt Logan comes from a family with supportive parents who value education and have the time and resources to pay attention to these needs. He is bright and articulate and would likely succeed at any school. But he chooses not to attend and succeed at a traditional school for the remarkably simple reason that schools do not prioritize the skills that even a thirteen-year-old knows will lead to a happy and healthy life.

REFLECTION

We often think that technology is what changes most quickly in the world around us, and that may be true. But once we understand that, in education, technology is an enabling tool and not a goal, we see that the world beyond technology is just becoming a more complex place than it was a century or a generation or a decade ago. A hundred years ago, adults could correctly assume that the skills and knowledge that their children would need in their lifetimes would largely mirror the past. This is just no longer the case, and learning systems therefore have to adapt to future changes or become increasingly irrelevant.

Some educators jump to the conclusion that new transdisciplinary arcs of study are required, and they are right: STEM is born. Others recognize the natural affinity of the arts to the creative nature of science, technology, engineering, and mathematics, and STEAM is born. In my opinion, these are short-term turnouts on the road to understanding how students need to develop their learning capacity. The world is just a vastly more systemically integrated place than our traditional schools allow.

Once out of school, young adults are faced with social, economic, moral, technical, and political challenges that cross all boundaries of academic subjects. Most will go on to a job that demands cross-subject knowledge as well as collaboration with people and other cross-disciplinary responsibilities. We know that most people who succeed in these environments are those who can work across boundaries, not just within them. I am not sure we always want school to look just like the world beyond the boundaries of a campus; in many communities, school is a refuge from a hard, painful life. But school needs to *function* like the outside world, a world that is not shrink-wrapped into packets of pre-assembled recipes that rarely change. Schools can take a big first step by simply asking, "Are we teaching our students to become great chefs, or are we teaching them how to eat ready-made meals?"

CHAPTER EIGHT

Schools Are More Permeable
Where We Meet, Not Where We Learn

Sunrise, five miles west of Salina, open road but for a few early morning long-haul truck-ers, bottomland rich in ripe alfalfa bounded by rising buttes of banded red and white, Neil Young's "Helpless" the first song of the day. A morning like this will buckle your knees, driving or not. It is high summer here, yellow flowers trace the highway, stubby pines dark dots of green, and even the sage is more olive than gray. Quaking aspen choke every low draw and creek. Over one hundred million years these mountains raised their deep-sea sediments, bruised upward by forces as far away as Mexico and the Pacific Rim. For ten thousand years this must have been Eden for Native Americans—bounty and wealth in the summer; hidden, deep valleys protected from brutal winters. Then came fur fever, Manifest Destiny, and smallpox and now it is another Eden, small ranchers holding tight to the bottomland.

It is a day like this that makes me want to smash every digital device in school and home and scream, "It's all right here!" That would be rash and intemperate; each tool has its place. But I tell you what: If I had seen a family van driving alongside of me today with kids glued to a Disney flick on the in-car DVD player, it would have been a knife to my heart and soul.

Give me students and time to walk down just five miles of these hills, plunging down through the history of the earth, asking why that plant grows there and how water and soil and bugs and air all create high summer in one range and not in another. Of course these five miles are a metaphor, and we want each student to find their own "five miles of Rockies heaven" that will stir some question or passion in them. It might be a community service center, a lab, a volleyball court, a musical score, a train station—we don't care. But I know this: If any student takes the time to deeply understand just "five miles" of their choosing, the "how" and "why" and "what if" of just those five miles, they are set for life, and we have done our jobs.

Any time I have the honor of being with students, I try to find a time to turn them loose in some slightly unfamiliar setting: a forest or creek bed, an airport or dirt road, a village in the hills of the developing world—and ask them to go off alone for a few minutes and find something that is new to them, some question to which they don't know the answer, something they care about, and report it back to the group or note it in a journal. That is the start.

Back in the day we had a saying: "This is your movie, man!" Well, it is a good saying. If we make the movie for our students, it will always be our movie, not theirs. We have to give them a place and time to create their own movie. I added a scene to mine this morning, thanks to a God who was kind enough to wake me for the sunrise, and splash Her bounty for me to see down this winding road.

Where We Learn

School is no longer where we learn. It is where we meet. The physical identity of schools is undergoing a radical transformation as educators realize that learning should, and can, take place anytime and anywhere. Much of the focus of this transformation has been on connectivity made possible through the use of new technologies. But schools are also expanding the learning space into surrounding communities, regions, and around the world. Schools have reimagined the boundary of the physical school, searched for and found value in authentic learning within the surrounding community, and become increasingly

Most nontraditional learning settings do not entail significant additional costs, and in some cases schools actually spend less money by leveraging community resources for free.

connected both locally and globally with other learning communities. Most of these nontraditional settings do not entail significant additional costs, and in some cases schools actually spend less money by leveraging community resources for free. Most or all seem eminently exportable to other schools, if we just unburden ourselves of the concept of "school" as a set of buildings where we go to work.

Learning is no longer constrained within a physical boundary. Access to knowledge is becoming universal at a remarkable rate; whatever statistic I write today about the number of Internet-accessible smartphones on the planet will be out of date before I finish the sentence. We accept the fact that essentially all students and teachers in the developed world already have real-time access to knowledge, and the developing world is close behind. The methods of accessing that knowledge are also growing at a staggering pace: online courses, self-directed learning, hybrid learning, free massive open online courses (MOOCs), iTunes-U, open-source knowledge bases, "socialstructed" start-ups, interest-based virtual collaborations, and people just sharing with other people via the social media that permeate the lives of a majority of youth and many of us older folks as well. All of that is a given.

"If school is meant to prepare our students for the world, why do school and the world look and act so differently?"

There is enormous value to meeting, to personal interactions, that no human can get on their own or through an LED screen. But as much as we may revel in the warm dream that schools were *built* to nurture those magic moments of interpersonal connection, it is largely a myth; those connections are wonderful by-products. Schools were built to create an efficient transfer of knowledge from one generation to the next, and that purpose is no longer valid. School communities that truly understand this are meeting at school, but learning in the world. They are reaching out to the world and bringing it in to the school setting, and sending their students and teachers out to operate in and interact with the world off campus. Some of this reaching out and bringing in is done on computers, with no actual human interaction. Some is done by video chat and teleconferencing. And some is done the old-fashioned way: getting up and walking or driving or flying somewhere.

Some fear that learning will become impersonal, that breaking the boundaries of the traditional school leads to rows of students with headphones gazing at computer screens, logging in to virtual classes with teachers they will never meet. But distance and online learning are just one facet of the permeable school. Students and teachers are actually becoming *more* intimate with people, not less. They are quickly and deeply engaging with the communities in which they live, just outside the school walls. They recognize the powerful learning resources and opportunities that our communities hold, and the passion for learning that emerges when students and teachers engage with the real world, not a world filtered through textbooks, computers, whiteboards, and static lesson plans. Students and teachers are breaking the walls, both physical and mental, that we have built between our schools and the world outside of school. They are answering the question that Bo Adams often asks: "If school is meant to prepare our students for the world, why do school and the world look and act so differently?"

The Classroom Across the Street

Schools reflect their communities. While the neighborhood school is less typical as more students enroll in charter, choice, magnet, and other public and private school options, schools are still a strong manifestation of who we are and where we come from. Some school leaders are realizing that their students can engage in powerful learning experiences literally right across the street from campus, if they will just open the doors.

We have already been introduced to the public Maplewood Richmond Heights Middle School (MRHMS) in St. Louis, one of a growing group that call themselves "expeditionary" schools. Students and teachers spend up to 30 percent of their time off campus, embedded in the community, using the world as their classroom. It is impossible to list all the ways this happens; we would have to download the daily schedule. Students work with an urban design group on a major urban renewal project as an elective class, learning to prototype, produce and present alongside professionals. There are working gardens across the street and down the block; a lettuce-growing pilot using a fish tank for fertilizer; a huge beekeeping project; a chicken and egg production pilot; farm-to-restaurant relationships—all worked by students and families and percolating out into the community. The school keeps a database of all the families in the community who raise chickens! All of these authentic, hands-on experiences come back into the classroom in terms of content in math, economics, science, social studies, art, and more.

Some of the learning takes place right across the street from the main campus in a series of home-based food gardens. Some require a ten-minute walk out into the community to take a survey of shopkeepers or to participate in a census of homeless people in the neighborhoods. Sometimes students pile into a bus and head out of town to research the health of a river system. One teacher told me, "It helps to have an understanding family at home. Sometimes we decide within a matter of hours or days that we need to go and learn somewhere else, and I throw a sleeping bag in the bus and go."

"Students start to look at teachers as friends and mentors, not just the person who hands out worksheets in class."

The teachers at MRHMS believe that students who may struggle for a range of reasons in the classroom can find their way or their voice in off-campus projects, including just working and learning in the garden. For some students with diagnosed attention disorders, their fidgeting fades away as they focus on the bees in the hive or learn plant biology while digging in the dirt. Expeditions allow students and teachers to forge deep relationships. In a world where many children spend more than six hours a day looking at some form of electronic screen, longer exposure to adults and the wisdom they can bring in a nonclassroom environment is a powerful experience. Former MRHMS "principal learner" Bob Dillon says, "In a permeable classroom, schools use their community and beyond to learn by using the resources, inspiration, and environment beyond the walls of the classroom to generate learning experiences that can't be replicated in the school house. This larger space of learning provides opportunities for passion-based learning, systems thinking, and much more. When we leave campus, either for an hour or a day or several days, students and adults encounter real-world problems and have to rely on each other. They get to know and trust each other. Students start to look at teachers as friends and mentors, not just the person who hands out worksheets in class."

On the other side of St. Louis, the small early childhood–sixth-grade College School has put together a remarkable bouquet of outdoor, community, and experiential learning around the ideas of environmental sustainability. This broad context ingrains real-world systems thinking in the students, even at the youngest grade levels. Several years ago the school built an on-site greenhouse, garden, and large-scale model stream and pond that the students learn in every day. Each year they orchestrate a neighborhood giveaway of 2,500 native and drought-tolerant plants to the community. The garden includes butterfly-attractive plants, making it a stop on the monarch butterfly migration flyway. Fifth graders tag the monarchs and share their data with nearby Weber University scientists. Fourth graders manage the water cisterns, a row of linked fifty-five-gallon plastic containers that capture rainfall alongside the garden and greenhouse. Students paint the cisterns and take them home at the end of each year, bringing what they learn about sustainability and water use back to their parents and neighborhoods.

The school's links to the community go far beyond the greenhouse and garden. Every year third graders go into underserviced St. Louis communities and survey people about their community structure, services, and needs. The students bring the survey data back to school and work with an urban planner to design model cities based around the concept of a barter economy. Rather than taking a test on what they have learned, the students create a multiday presentation of their city designs and invite the community to take part in the event.

> "Students are learning at least 30 percent more efficiently outside the classroom than they were inside the classroom."

Students at the College School spend about 30 percent of their time off campus. They don't take standardized tests until the sixth grade, yet their students go on to perform very well at all of the area public and private high schools. Despite spending so much time on projects and off-campus experiences, students effectively cover almost all core standards. I asked one teacher how he thinks the students manage to do so well on standardized tests, even though the students are spending 30 percent less time in the classroom, learning the material they will be tested on. He patiently explained the obvious to me: "They are learning at least 30 percent more efficiently outside the classroom than they were inside the classroom."

While many schools think of field trips and learning beyond school walls as an extra expense, Josh Abrams at Meridian Academy in Boston is saving money every time his students leave campus. He has found learning resources throughout the community and is unabashed about seeking free learning experiences for the students. "Librarians love the fact that we want to send them a group of students, not just for a field trip, but to really spend a day or two learning about how the library works and using it as a resource. The same with local museums. Local high-tech firms are always looking for ways to bring students in and expose them to the latest research and use their educational labs. We just take advantage of all of that and figure out how to turn it into a serious part of our course work. We learn music by attending free dress rehearsals at the opera and we learn art history in the museums. And it is all free; I don't have to hire an extra teacher."

The Virtual Classroom

Online learning takes many forms, and those forms are evolving at an incredible pace. It would be a waste of words to try to summarize in detail how online learning is being implemented at schools across the country; as soon as these words are typed they are out of date. In a few years we will look back at the evolution of online learning the same way we do now with the use of computers in the classroom a decade ago. Online learning will be tightly woven into the fabric of everyday education; it will be a natural and seamless extension of the physical classroom.

Many of the schools I visited are testing or mainstreaming some form of online learning. Some allow students to take university courses online, either for credit or just because a student wants to. Others have joined large consortia where the school or student pays a fee to take a class created and hosted by another school or by a private vendor. The entire state of Florida requires public school students to take at least one online class in order to graduate from high school. Some schools have developed online courses for their own students, offered by an off-site teacher. Some of these are free and others cost a lot of money. Some provide students with one-on-one face time with a remote teacher and others, like the MOOCs being created at a number of colleges, are open to people from around the world with few or any filters.

While the options are many and multiplying every day, it is the process of adapting the learning experience to include some form of online learning that is important. The Barstow School in Kansas City recognizes that the school charges a lot of money in a market with public schools that are considered top quality, and therefore Barstow has to offer something extra. Sarah Hofstra is the "director of hybrid learning" at Barstow, a title that most schools have yet to even imagine. Head of School Shane Foster has given her free rein to design and implement a truly impressive distance and hybrid-learning program. The goals of the program are to offer fully online courses; increase collaboration with distant partners, including universities and industry; increase flexibility in the daily schedule; increase course opportunities; and prepare students in the lower grade levels to become familiar with the blended learning model.

Schools like Barstow that are willing to take risks before a guarantee of success recognize that "analysis paralysis" is a threat to their future. Thirty years ago, Peters and Waterman, in *In Search of Excellence* (1982), showed that high-performing organizations innovated more rapidly than their competitors, a theme reinforced in education more recently by Michael Fullan, in his book *Motion Leadership* (2010). Successful organizations take calculated risks before the picture of success is clear and therefore are able to test potential breakthrough pathways while others are bound to traditional methods. The Barstow School went from concept to decision to training to development and implementation of their own customized online learning program in just nine months. "Yes, we are designing the plane while flying," says Sarah, who easily convinces me that this approach is not only possible, but *right*. "We didn't try to create it and then launch it. Our leaders were just willing to step on that edge and take the leap, and we really could not imagine that it could get off the ground so successfully. We're doing blended learning, we're implementing fully online courses, and it is that blend of those, the willingness to take a risk and the freedom and opportunity to grow and change, that is so critical. If we are not educating our students to have that mindset, we can't grow that way as a culture. We're showing our students ways to connect with schools and other students around the community and around the world, with companies, with partners in the community wherever that opportunity is. In some ways we have a traditional curriculum; the courses are just online. Our teachers are bringing that human connection, the human quality of having the students asking a question, but literally having the world to go to find answers, not just in our own four walls."

Sarah thinks that a key for schools making this transition to a more permeable relationship with the outside world is the sense of ownership of the learning process. "I think educators, and maybe even Americans in general, have a hard time letting go of the ownership of anything, including knowledge. In the future, we are going to increasingly share knowledge because it benefits all who participate. It will not be about 'my' course, but a much more fluid exchange."

The Regional Classroom

There is no doubt that some off-campus programs cost a lot of money, and private schools or public schools serving a more affluent demographic can offer overseas trips that are out of range for many families. But sometimes the transformational experience is across town, in another section of the city, or across the state, and affordable for anyone. American communities and the schools that serve them remain segregated by race, ethnicity, and economics, so in order to find divergent points of view or experience, some schools are creating opportunities for their students to cross those community divides. The Baylor School in Chattanooga, Tennessee, has the resources to send students around the world on experiential learning courses, but they choose their own community as the launchpad for the most sustainable commitment to off-campus learning that I encountered on my trip.

Housed in her office in the student center, Director of Community Learning Joli Anderson tells me about the program she started more than seventeen years ago. "If we want to change the world, we need to live that change; that is what Gandhi taught us. We need to introduce kids to a world beyond their own, remove the blinders, and increase our vision." For seventeen years, Baylor students have gone into some of the least served areas of Chattanooga *every day*, to areas of high crime, poverty, gangs, and "wonderful people." Students tutor youngsters in partnership with other community nonprofits. In 2012, about 20 percent of the entire high school student body participated, tutoring at five sites. Joli says she "wanted to go where others won't; people won't even deliver pizza to these places, but we can go there because we go every day. Yes, we are helping the children in these neighborhoods academically, but the most important thing is that we are building relationships and experiences that will last a lifetime. It is not a matter of us helping them; they help us by allowing our students to share with them. This is the only way our students are going to understand some of these critical issues." Joli goes on police ride-alongs and is in touch with the police gang unit. Baylor students organized what is now an annual cookout in the neighborhood, attended by families and police, because those two groups were not talking to each other. When issues arise before the City Council that impact the neighbors they serve, Baylor students attend and speak out.

Joli teaches the students how to write foundation grants; they can apply for internal seed funding and then go out to external sources if their ideas take root. The students have to research, write, present, and compete for resources, just like in the real world. Students run the service learning board, meeting around the Baylor board

"It works because the school has gone all-in with our commitment to community, and we need to embed ourselves in that community if we want our students to grow up with any degree of comfort in settings that are different from their own."

table and learning what it takes to run a large, complex organization. Student leaders run the daily sites in downtown Chattanooga, meet with parents of their client children, track progress, and set learning guidelines. Joli believes these programs are highly exportable to schools with budget constraints and in all kinds of settings. "The costs of the local and regional programs are minimal, and the impact on the students is enormous. It is long-term and sustainable, not dependent on one group of students who want to 'do good' their senior year. It works because the school has gone all-in with our commitment to community, and we need to embed ourselves in that community if we want our students to grow up with any degree of comfort in settings that are different from their own."

The World Classroom

The world has gotten much smaller in the past decade as people connect in real time via social media. Students are able to easily video chat with people who live a life vastly different from their own. Students and teachers routinely carry on Skype conversations with peers in other schools around the world. I found many schools routinely hold international Skype sessions with students as young as the early elementary grades. They practice their language skills, share homework assignments, collaborate on projects in their respective classrooms, and just hang out and chat about the many interests that young people everywhere share.

Still, a video chat will not replace the full experience of living as others live, even if it is for a short period of time. Leaving the security of a campus and traveling to places in the world they would otherwise probably never see has transformed some of my own students. For six years I have taken high school students on two-week trips to the Philippines. My goal is to give them just the slightest understanding of the more than three billion people on the planet who live on less than two dollars a day. Students spend six days in rural villages living with families and in homes where the shower is likely a bucket of water and bed is a mat on the floor or maybe a thin mattress on a wooden platform. Students help cook food, wash their clothes in the stream out back, maybe kill a chicken for the first time in their lives. And for long hours of the day with no cell phones and scarce computers, they sit with young strangers who over just a few days become close friends. In 2011, after just those few days, my students refused to get on the van we sent to pick them up; they did not want to leave, to go back to their air-conditioned homes, full refrigerators, cell phones, and big cars. When the students finally shared their last goodbyes and rejoined their classmates, they struggled to understand why they were crying over a way of life that, until a few days before, they never realized even existed.

"For the first few days," one girl managed through her tears, "I didn't even know who were the children of my host family. We sat down for dinner and anyone from the village who came in the door would just join us and eat. I mean, my own family at home, we don't even eat dinner together. One morning we all got up before dawn to go sing Happy Birthday to a girl who lived a few houses down. The whole village was there, and then we went back to bed or made breakfast. Why don't we do things like that for our friends at home?"

A boy joined in: "I have lived in the same house for years and I don't even know the name of my next door neighbor. We call him 'the guy with the noisy air conditioner.' I met more people in that village and knew more of them by name in the first day than I have for years at home."

And another girl stared at her own reflection of the days in her village: "The whole village shares, like, one soccer ball and one basketball. They don't have anything. They make up games with a few sticks. They sing the same songs over and over. But they are happy. They are happier than we are with all the stuff we have." And then she broke down crying again.

> "The whole village shares, like, one soccer ball and one basketball. They don't have anything. They make up games with a few sticks. They sing the same songs over and over. But they are happy. They are happier than we are with all the stuff we have."

Sometimes breaking the traditional school walls does not even require the students to leave the campus; schools leverage the world experience of teachers and other adults who can bring a picture of the world to class with them. I met Terry deBardelaben as I randomly walked the halls of the St. Stephens and St. Agnes Episcopal School in Washington, D.C. Her classroom is a chaotic art studio filled with paintings, drawings, and an elaborate metal sculpture growing from the middle of the floor. I asked her how her teaching and the experience of art for students have evolved over the last few years. She started to bubble with excitement as she gave me a mini-tutorial on how to draw the world into a classroom, how to help students paint a picture for themselves of viewpoints that they might never get to experience firsthand. "I got a grant to create a book about the pottery traditions in Ghana, and I brought those ideas and information back to the students, and they were so *thrilled* and *fascinated* about the lives of young people in the village and what age do they marry and how do they use the pottery in the villages and in their lives. We got a chance to discuss all those things! It's about creativity and knowing that these things happen in different places in different ways. Students need to be flexible and resourceful and go beyond the boundaries of their experience, and that happens when you expose them to other ways of doing things that are practiced by other people in very different ways."

Making New Friends

Everywhere I went, students who had the opportunity to connect with peers from different cultures told me it was the most formative experience in their entire school career. Students at the Collegiate School in Richmond host a congress of fellow students from all over the world each year for two weeks. The students manage the entire program. They identify major environmental issues facing the developing world and work in international collaborations to design, research, and propose solutions. On the day I visited Collegiate, the high school was out of session, but the students who organized the second annual Emerging Leaders Conference came in just to see me and rightfully boast about the power of this two-week highlight of their long school careers. All of these students are college-bound, all taking a host of AP courses and packing their personal schedules with resume-enhancing extracurriculars. But they ditched all of that for two weeks during the conference.

"I thought we would have a lot of differences in how we would look at a problem, and I was shocked how quickly we all got over that."

One senior girl summarized their experience: "When you first meet these groups and tackle these problems there is an initial barrier and you don't really know each other and you don't really understand each other. But the more you are forced to work together you realize that you are all students and all kids. You realize how easily you can become friends, and once you begin to have fun with the work, the problems are easy to solve." I asked the students how this sort of experience would help them in their futures. They looked at me as if I was the child and they had to clearly explain an obvious truth to me. "We know we can collaborate with our own friends here at school, but we found out just how quickly we could get past cultural differences with people from very different places and work well with them. I thought we would have a lot of differences in how we would look at a problem, and I was shocked how quickly we all got over that."

REFLECTION

I found that the ability of schools to expand learning beyond their own physical walls requires several things. Leaders must be willing to take some degree of risk and learn to mitigate risk as students and teachers both physically and virtually leave the relative security of campus. Leaders understand that learning in the absence of risk is often a sterile experience. Forward-leaning educators break down their own mental barriers that separate learning in school from real-world experiences and see the community as a classroom, often with resources that can reduce costs. Perhaps most important, educators understand that students are no longer constrained to learning in the hours and days they spend at school. Students are denizens of a naturally occurring ecosystem of connected knowledge that operates completely independently of any organizational limits that schools try to impose. Schools need to find ways to link what they are doing to that ecosystem, not avoid it.

Lessons that students and teachers learn outside the school walls amplify content knowledge, so students do better on standardized exams because they have a personal connection to knowledge. The natural learning environment for this and future generations is a connected knowledge space that is open and available via technology any time and anywhere, and students are increasingly comfortable exploring and living in this space. Schools will increasingly become a point of contact, a collection zone, a mother ship where students and adults can share their accumulating store of global knowledge and experiences.

CHAPTER NINE

Schools Are More Creative
Knowledge Is Not Just for Consumption

Toward the end of the first month of my trip, an administrator at a boarding school in upstate Connecticut called me a "Johnny Appleseed," and I could not have been more proud! What a wonderful way to expand a journey: to gather seeds and spread them along the path. One of those seeds found its way into my teacher's imagination at the Latin School of Chicago.

The Latin School built an incredible new science center with a video wall, new labs, and the exploratory feel of a children's discovery museum. Lord only knows what the new center cost, but what impressed me most were not the flashy screens and displays. The real game changer, the seed that I then spread to every school I visited for the rest of the trip, was this: every vertical surface in every lab—every wall, cabinet door, and backsplash—is "writable." Walls are not places to post up pictures of the past; they are places to work the problems of today, of the moment, to create and share ideas in real time. There is no front to the room where a teacher perches and talks at students because, well, there is no front to the room. Across one lab wall, a student had sketched a long, arcing red dragon with its mouth ready to swallow a line of beakers on the counter. That dragon had nothing to do with chemistry, but it had a lot to do with a student adding something playful to a science lab.

Idea walls are nothing new; they have been staples of high-tech offices for years. And yet I helped design and build an entire new school campus, and none of us ever pushed the idea of simply painting classroom walls with erasable paint so students and teachers can create and share on the most visible, accessible feature of every classroom. Idea walls are a technology that connects people faster and more cheaply than any computer network, that allows students and teachers to collaborate visibly. It forces us to ask, "Why do students sit in rows and raise their hands to answer questions, one at a time, when they could all be up at the walls, all answering all the questions all the time?" For the rest of the trip I saw classrooms and entire school buildings through a completely different set of eyes. I saw every wall, hall, stairwell, office, desk, table, and cabinet as a place for easy, cheap, collaborative creation.

Creativity

Of the many skills we recognize as critical to the future success of students in an increasingly competitive world, creativity is the one that is most difficult to outsource, to send offshore, to replace by less expensive competition that threatens to overwhelm us. Computers, robots, and cheap labor can replace many of the jobs of the industrial and information ages, but so far at least, there is no cheap replacement for the individual or group of individuals who come up with a great new idea that adds value to our lives. In a world that is changing so quickly in so many ways, the incredible value of a creative mind seems to remain constant.

In a world that is changing so quickly in so many ways, the incredible value of a creative mind seems to remain constant.

Forward-leaning educators see creativity not as a by-product of education, but as a core part of what students learn. In most schools if you ask to see an example of creativity you are immediately led to the arts studio—if budget cuts have not killed the arts program. As school leaders step back and assess the skills we want for our students, they are increasingly bringing creativity out of the shadows and the art studios and on to center stage. They recognize that creativity is a sort of nuclear reactor of learning that feeds new energy into the system and creates a whole array of untapped learning opportunities. Creativity changes learning from a system that is largely about *consuming* knowledge and ideas to one that is also about *generating* knowledge and ideas.

The writable surfaces I found in the Latin School science center are a visual manifestation of the latent creativity that lies in every classroom, with every group of students and teachers. At Trinity School in Atlanta, first graders draw and share outlines of the human body on the Idea Wall, helping each other to name the parts in a wild mash-up of art and science. Design 39 Campus, the new public K–8 school in Poway, California, will have writable walls, movable whiteboards, and tables with writable surfaces that roll around the room to form flexible niches and caves of creative sharing. Students at Science Leadership Academy create art or post ideas on the hallway walls. The Lovett School in Atlanta gutted a high school English classroom so the teacher could use the walls as a collaborative learning space to get students out of their desks and "actively interacting," not just once in a while but as a habit. The libraries at Maplewood Richmond Heights Middle School in St. Louis and Cushing Academy in Massachusetts and the learning labs at Christ Church Episcopal in Greenville and Collegiate in Richmond all have rooms where wall writing is encouraged, as they transition from the old concept of a library as a place to shut up and study to a communal learning space where learning means sharing, working, and creating.

Creational Thinking

In my first book, *The Falconer*, I wrote that the goal of learning, what I really wanted for all of my students, was for them to become "creational thinkers." Everything else we focus on in education—problem solving, critical thinking, collaboration, communication, questioning, content, synthesis—all of it leads up to what we really want, for each student to have their own "aha" moment of discovery, to find some new passion or new idea or new twist to an old idea that powers them on to the next idea and the next, to find a reason to come to school full of optimism, not dreading the toil.

My metaphorical teacher, Mr. Usher, advised his students on the scaffold of creativity:

> *Seek and secure interdisciplinary relationships.* Most people are good at one or two things. They may understand math or plumbing or music or art or science or accounting. A creational thinker needs to understand and use the layering of disparate fields of knowledge to create new links, new bridges, new relationships, and new ways of thinking new thoughts. Consider the first chef who placed an edible flower petal in a salad, the first engineer who encoded ones and zeros on a silicon wafer, the first military consultant who integrated the Tao into a battle plan. These are the creational thinkers. Build bridges of information.
>
> *Find opportunities in the voids.* Just because we don't hear or see or know that something *is* there does not mean *nothing* is there. Maybe we just haven't seen or heard or thought it yet. The first musician who left a hard-driving four-four rhythm for a half beat of syncopated silence created jazz! Physicists who study the universe find more answers in what we cannot see or detect than in what we can. Voids are the frontiers, the realm of the under-explored, the under-created, the fertile ground for creation. (Lichtman, 2008, p. 148)

Synergy

One of the most dramatically creative learning experiences I have encountered is Synergy 8, developed a few years ago at the Westminster Schools in Atlanta by coteachers Bo Adams and Jill Gough. The class is an opportunity for eighth graders to move beyond the traditional boundaries of subject, which Bo describes as "a transdisciplinary, community issues, problem-solving class. We considered ourselves to be part of every department in the school, because the issues we were dealing with were real-life issues where those disciplines are integrated and we can look at them holistically. The backbone of the class was our practice of observation journaling. We took time for the students to observe and record the world around them, and then upload those reflections to a pooled site. After accumulating hundreds of those observations, the students mined the data for areas of interest they were recognizing in their school and community."

Bo and Jill amplified what I heard repeatedly on my journey: that the key to learning for any student or adult is that the learner actively participates in designing the

The key to learning for any student or adult is that the learner actively participates in designing the learning experience.

learning experience. The role of the teacher is to set up opportunities for students and provide them a skill set to engage fully in the learning design process. Jill says, "We want students to experience real problem solving where the students can find content to serve the problems and not the other way around." They tell the story of a day, a few weeks into the class, when they both just sat quietly and waited to see if the students could and would solve the problem of self-organizing themselves as a working community. Bo remembers: "We had spent time working on how people organize to make decisions and take action as a community. The students had mined their observation journals and now it was time for them to decide what problems to focus on. Jill and I came into the room one day and just sat at the back. It was really uncomfortable at first. The students looked at us for direction; some just talked and played around, but we did not step in. Finally, after about ten minutes, one girl stood up and started suggesting ways to move the group forward, reminding them of the skills they had already learned. Within a few minutes they had organized groups and assigned tasks and were working on the problem-finding task. We had not said a word."

Is this kind of student-led creativity replicable in other classes at other schools? Absolutely, says Bo. "We have to blur the boundaries between school and real life. If school is meant to prepare students for real life, why does it look so different? The real world is driven by curiosity and exploration, not based on a lecture." Jill described how students developed projects that could have been applied to any other subject area. One group of students got interested in food deserts in the city. At first they thought a community garden was the solution, but as they interviewed members of the community, students found that the community needed jobs, not gardens. The students staged a job fair; the first one failed completely, but they repeated it three weeks later. Ten people came and two left with jobs. Bo says their job as teachers was merely to show those students that in this case, 20 percent success was huge. Bo says that the students "not only learned to overcome and learn from real failure, they learned about persuasive writing, statistics, sociology, communication, and the history and economics of unemployment."

I asked Jill and Bo how they would advise other teachers who want to develop a truly student-led creative learning experience. Jill said that the most important element, which is replicable in any class, is to "be a learner too. See if you can narrow the authority gap in your classroom. It's fine to tell kids, 'We are going to learn this together.' Be brave enough to take the risk of finding your curriculum in the interest of the students." Bo added, "Incorporate elements of design thinking that hinge on the common characteristics of empathy, listening, discovering, practicing innovation, observing, and questioning. When the questions are the students', so are the answers. Curiosity should be the taproot of all that happens in the classroom."

> *"When the questions are the students', so are the answers. Curiosity should be the taproot of all that happens in the classroom."*

Design Thinking

Many educators are becoming increasingly aware of the field of design thinking, which combines empathy for *why* we want to create with a method to stimulate, analyze, systematize, and communicate creative thought. Design thinking is a way of organizing the thinking process that increases the generation of ideas and breaks new ground or the old ground in some new way. Design thinking is a set of tools that is naturally familiar to young students, because it aligns with how they think and allows them to put their ideas into test and practice.

What educators like Bo and Jill pioneered a few years ago (and John Dewey and others more than one hundred years ago) is now percolating rapidly through schools across the country. I visited a number of schools that are actively incorporating design thinking at both the institutional and classroom levels, and more schools are adopting this approach every day. Schools practice design thinking to help restructure their management practices and embed design thinking in the curriculum as a way to encourage creativity in all classes. Rarely a week now goes by that I do not read about an example of design thinking in the classroom on my blog or Twitter feed. (As of this writing there is an extremely active weekly Twitter chat on design thinking in schools; any teacher or administrator can instantly, and for free, connect with an extraordinary network of creative educators and get usable program ideas using the Twitter hashtag #DTK12Chat.) By explicitly teaching better ways to approach problems and come up with creative, value-laden solutions, these schools are exposing their teachers and students to the tools that help them to become self-evolving, self-correcting learners.

David Kelley, the godfather of design thinking and founder of the Stanford d.school and the huge design thinking firm IDEO, links the goals of creativity with the process of design thinking in his latest best seller *Creative Confidence*. Simply, Kelley says, "Belief in your creative capacity lies at the heart of innovation" (Kelley & Kelley, 2013). The design thinking process is a set of steps to help individuals and groups to unlock their native creative capacities. "We don't have to generate creativity from scratch. . . The real value of creativity doesn't emerge until you are brave enough to act on those ideas" (Kelley & Kelley, 2013). What Kelley and others have developed at the center of the design think-

"Belief in your creative capacity lies at the heart of innovation."

ing methodology is a profoundly human-centered focus on problem solving that is applicable in any school setting. "Being human-centered is at the core of the innovation process. Deep empathy for people makes our observations powerful sources of inspiration. We aim to understand why people do what they currently do, with the goal of understanding what they might do in the future" (Kelley & Kelley, 2013).

If there was one moment on my journey when I knew I saw the future of learning, it was in a fifteen-minute visit with teachers and students in the Design Lab at Mount Vernon Presbyterian School in Atlanta. Teacher Mary Cantwell brought me into the converted classroom with writable walls, boxes of stuff to build things, and a messy arrangement of little tables and chairs. A seemingly post-apocalyptic raincoat hung in a corner of the Lab. Mary told me that the elementary school students had seen a video of an African village in a rainstorm. They noticed that there was a lot of trash in the village, so they came up with the idea of turning the trash into affordable rain gear. They designed and built a raincoat out of candy wrappers and tape that costs about two dollars. Mary introduced me to a second-grade student. He and I perched on those tiny plastic little-kid chairs and I asked him what he and his fellow students do when they come into this room. He stared back at me for a moment, collecting his thoughts, and then matter-of-factly said, "We ideate, prototype, design, build stuff, and see what works. We fail fast and fail forward." Later, I watched a YouTube video of Mount Vernon first-grade students and teachers on a walking field trip to look at a corner bus stop. They reimagined bus stops: what they should be, how they might be built, how they can best meet the needs of riders. These student-creators are never going back into the box of assembly-line learning. They are being given the keys to the learning kingdom—or perhaps more accurately, the keys are not being taken from them.

Los Altos School District (LASD) is a K–8 school district on the edge of Silicon Valley with nine schools. Alyssa Gallagher, director of strategic initiatives and community partnerships, told me that three years ago leaders decided they needed to "revolutionize learning for all students. While we have been doing some incredible work, it started to become apparent that we were missing a critical voice in the room. We started to ask how we could engage students in a meaningful way. Like many schools and districts we had ways for students to be involved, like student government or a focus group or an advisory board, but those felt really limited. So we asked how we could really engage a group of students in a meaningful way to rethink learning during the school day. We recognized that we would have to help them think beyond what they already know, to push their thinking beyond what they have thought of as 'school.'"

Borrowing ideas from Big Ideas Fest, a conference that brings together adult thought leaders to collaborate creatively using the tools of design thinking, LASD created their own "Student EdCon," a three-day, student-centered design thinking conference that included attendees from the entire school community. Alyssa says that they first "exposed the students to thought leaders who would resonate with them and their interests. Then they learned about the design process, and had a chance to develop solutions they had created for different ways to approach learning. Nine different student teams pitched prototype ideas to our broader community, comprising their parents, our school board, superintendent, teachers, and administrators. We ultimately selected three of those, and we are working on how to have the students involved in implementing those in the year ahead. We don't want this to be something where the students come up with the idea and then the adults run with it."

"We spend 180 days a year with our students and we don't know that they are capable of so much more. It was a real 'aha' moment for us."

I asked Alyssa what benefit, other than some practical ideas for innovation, the teachers and professional staff got from going through this experience. "We wanted teachers to have an experience of just what students are capable of. I am not sure who learned more in those three days, the students or the adults. At the end of the first day one of our veteran teachers said, 'I am just struck by how creative our students are, by how many great ideas they have.' On one hand it was great to hear that revelation from that teacher and on the other hand it was pretty frightening. We spend 180 days a year with our students and we don't know that they are capable of so much more. It was a real 'aha' moment for us. We had to ask ourselves, 'What about our current system is not allowing our teachers to get that in-depth knowledge about their students?'"

Is this something that requires large resources? Alyssa emphatically says no: "I think this could be effective at either a district or school level. We did it on an extremely limited budget; we actually had teachers volunteering to participate. The work was really in thinking about it ahead of time. Financially it didn't cost us much of anything."

Alyssa said the conference had a real impact on how the district thinks about the whole process of creating change. "The real impact was that we could just jump in and stop talking about doing it. It wasn't perfect. It was a prototype for us; we will hold Student EdCon every year, and every year we will iterate and improve the process. My best advice is to just jump in and identify the issues you want to engage the students with. For us, the big topic was the use of the school day, but we envision down the road that you can use this process to get students to understand that they don't have to wait until they are adults to act. You don't have to wait to have a college degree to do something that matters. What you do today matters; you have a voice; you have a way to positively impact the world around you; and the adults around you care about what you have to say."

Design thinking has taken firm root at Colorado Academy, where it is viewed as an essential element of the learning paradigm, and all teachers are expected to develop teaching units around the core ideas of a thinking laboratory. Over the next few years, they will have restructured their entire curriculum to focus on the development of contextual thinking rather than specific content. Paul Kim developed a new ninth-grade class on design thinking that "uses an inquiry-based model of learning that allows students to explore some of the ideas that inform the modern world and work toward solving a problem in a twenty-first-century global context. As they work toward this project, students will learn the design thinking process to develop more generative and expansive insight into human experience." Paul says that students recognize that iteration and prototyping yields stronger results than the old "write it and turn it in" approach.

"It really screws me up in other classes where there are black-and-white answers."

I interviewed some of the students in Paul's class to find out what *they* thought about the goals and outcomes of the course. These are ninth graders who had only been in the course for about two months prior to this interview:

- "We have been doing history our whole school career by learning about the sequence of events. Now we are looking at it by how people think."
- "History is normally written from a certain perspective; in this class we are getting multiple perspectives."
- "Mr. Kim does not give us specific instructions. He gives us a general outline or direction. What is important in this class is the thought process, and we don't try to make an exact replica of another project."

- "I am learning to think for myself. We learn to not just go to Google for the answers but to look in other places."

And this priceless testimony, one of those student comments that makes a teacher's life worthwhile:

- "It really screws me up in other classes where there are black-and-white answers."

Building from Ideas

If there is an exploding trend in learning today, it is the "maker" movement. Maker studios packed with tools, materials, open spaces, workbenches, and 3D printing capability have cropped up in schools and cities around the country, places where people of diverse ages and interest can go and imagine and build. Maker Faire is a series of events initiated by Maker Media publishers, which the founders describe as "all-ages gatherings of tech enthusiasts, crafters, educators, tinkerers, hobbyists, engineers, science clubs, authors, artists, students, and commercial exhibitors." Schools are rapidly entering this learning space, which is, of course, a throwback to a largely forgotten past when students and apprentices of all ages shared ideas with, and learned from, master craftsmen in the trades of building, design, and commerce.

Just when many schools had converted their auto shop, home economics program, or welding benches into computer animation studios, some are reconverting to build makerspaces filled with a combination of manual tools and high-tech, computer-driven accessories. 3D printers have become a link between creative minds and rapid building. Limited to big industry just a few years ago, affordable 3D printers may be the poster image of distributed creative capability. The possibilities are as limitless as the imagination. At the Marymount School in New York City, I talked to elementary students who had imagined ways to improve on toothbrushes, particularly for disabled and elderly users. They surveyed, questioned, drew up ideas, discussed in groups, drew some more, and then programmed the printer to bring their mad assortment of Dr. Seuss–like toothbrushes to life. At The School at Columbia University in New York, the 3D printer sits in the library, redefining the space as one where knowledge is created as well as discovered and consumed. A tenth-grade student at Colorado Academy showed me the working robotic hand he had printed out on the school's 3D printer, not as part of any class, but "because I was interested in how it would work. It was great to have this at school," he told me, "because the makerspace I was going to in the city cost me sixty dollars an hour, and here I can try things over and over and mess up and then get it right."

"Making" is an obvious manifestation of the creative process, and many schools view it as a natural fit in STEAM courses. But if creativity is a critical skill, where does it fit in a history, English, or foreign language class? More important, how can a focus on creativity help to break our subject-centric organization of learning? At Presbyterian Day School in Memphis, students and teachers go through Post-it notes like water. Want to analyze a short story? Students gather in groups, brainstorm, categorize their thoughts, post notes on the walls, "gallery walk" to see what the other groups have come up with . . . and *then* they write their essays. Want to solve the problem of food waste in the cafeteria for a science project? The students generate entire walls of Post-it notes, self-direct to the Internet to research ideas, seamlessly move around and work across areas of thought . . . and *then* focus on one or more possible solutions. Creating a theme related to civil rights for sixth-grade social studies? The students lie on the floor or drape themselves over their chairs, sort historical photos on the carpet, draw affinity maps of the ideas represented in the photos, imagine the different viewpoints of the people in the photos . . . and *then* think about developing a project outline.

Design thinking leader Shelley Paul and others took over an unused classroom at the Woodward Academy in Atlanta and turned it into a "beta version design lab," with multiple writing walls, a rack full of dry-erase markers, sticky notes, game-play pieces, and a wall of windows open to a well-frequented walkway. Student-teacher paired design teams worked on issues related to "building a stronger school community." The students told me that the process involves setting goals, interviews, analysis, ideating, mapping ideas, selecting priorities, and prototyping. One group came up with the idea to start a "student-teacher speed dating opportunity" so the two groups would have closer connections with shared passions for learning. Another group of students and faculty are focusing on environmental

sustainability issues around the school. They identified the issue of dispos-
able plastic eating utensils on campus and built a prototype dispenser to
reduce waste: "We looked at the issue from the point of view of the user who
wants just one utensil but also
wants to make sure it is clean." The
students were so fired up about the
design process, they proposed
teaching an initial session in design
thinking for interested members
of the Woodward faculty.

*In all of these classrooms and
studios, there is a powerful common theme: gaining comfort with
the uncertainty of an ambiguous
future.*

In all of these classrooms and studios, there is a powerful common
theme: gaining comfort with the uncertainty of an ambiguous future.
Young students are less fearful of not knowing the outcome; older students and adults have been conditioned to shy away from the possibility
that we don't know the answer to a problem. If there is a skill our students
need to develop to be successful in a world that changes in real time, it is
this comfort with ambiguity and uncertainty. They have to know how to
ask questions; they have to know how to find and parse problems; they
have to know how to sort through complex data and multiple, cross-
disciplinary inputs. The most forward-leaning educators I have met understand that practicing these skills can occur in every classroom, every day.

Creating Content and Textbooks

Schools that are serious about enhancing creativity are making the leap
from students and teachers as consumers to creators of knowledge, and
one prime target lies in alternatives to traditional textbooks. The cycle
of curriculum development in traditional schools takes years or even
decades. Textbooks are written, evaluated, and undergo lengthy qualifi-
cation, rewrites, and political battles at the state level. During that time
of development, the state of knowledge may have changed dramatically.
Several years ago, the University of Virginia School of Medicine conducted
an internal study of their teaching practices and content and found that
roughly 50 percent of what a first-year student learned would be either
irrelevant or wrong by the end of five years.

In contrast to the outdated modes of content creation and management of the past, we have access to real-time content updates via the Internet. Accessing, filtering, and using that knowledge base takes a different set of skills than just picking up a textbook and believing it holds the truth. But school is a place to learn skills; that is what we are good at. We are on the very leading edge of a dramatic shift in how we access knowledge in our schools, moving away from a one-size-fits-all, politically validated consumption model based on industry-driven textbooks and teacher training. The new model demands that teachers and students become effective creators, curators, and filters of knowledge that is accessible in real or near-real time, possibly without ever seeing the same paper book in use by a classroom next door or across the country.

One major player in this field of content creation and customization is the nonprofit CK–12 Foundation, started in the mid-2000s to provide free, open-source tools and technology that allow teachers and students to make that leap from being consumers to being creators of knowledge. Using privately raised funds, CK–12 generates high-quality curriculum units for K–12 schools, primarily in STEM subjects. The foundation pays experienced, qualified educators to write content that meets a range of state and national standards and then goes through substantial peer review and editing. The foundation has generated thousands of units, *and it is all completely free.*

"So far, education has been 'one size fits all.' Now teachers can customize content to meet their own needs."

The foundation has not built the content library just to shorten content delivery times or bypass publishers. Cofounder and Executive Director Neeru Khosla told me that the real driver is that allowing teachers and students the flexibility to design, create, add to, and edit their own learning materials changes the entire pedagogy of the classroom. "So far, education has been 'one size fits all.' Now teachers can customize content to meet their own needs. We are not going to be successful unless and until we treat everyone as an individual." Neeru told me that the tools allow teachers to create curriculum that suits their own students, meeting them where they are in language, culture, and ability level.

Now that the CK–12 Foundation has built a library of seed units, the foundation has added another layer that allows students and teachers to design their own text materials and to add, edit, and customize their own books. "What happens," says Neeru, "is that it is not just about creating the text. Students go out from their classroom and ask a question like, 'Why are the trees dying, why is there no water here, why is it not raining?' and they can add video, photos, and their own text and links to the materials. It adds a level of extraordinary contextualization."

This kind of access is amplified by technology, but the benefits are transferable even where students don't have full access to computers. Neeru told me that CK–12 is working with a school in Utah where "the students don't have their own computers, so the teachers took our content library, created only what they needed, and gave that to the students in hard copy. They told the students, 'in a normal published textbook we can't ask you or let you write on it or change it or whatever,' but with these tools they created an entire text for $4.60 a copy, so they could tell the students 'write in the book, use it, own it.'"

Back in the Design Lab at Mount Vernon Presbyterian in Atlanta, a ninth-grade student told me, "In history class we were assigned a chapter in the history textbook and we redesigned the chapter, thinking about how it might be changed to be better. We talked about what we liked and didn't like. We wrote our own chapters in a more useful and creative way that we think we can learn the material better. We created it in a Google doc. We've added pictures and websites to link to and are going to present that all to the class. In English class, instead of taking a vocab quiz, we *made* the quiz, and I think I am learning the words a lot better because I learned to use and apply the words in a lot of situations. It brings you back to why you are doing it, thinking about a new way to apply the facts you learn, and you can always go back to those and focus. It reminds me about why I am learning this and how I might be able to apply them later in life. It reminds me of why I am going to school."

This shift from consumer to creator is really just beginning to percolate beyond the initial pilot stage at many schools I visited, but the rate of adoption appears to be rapid. Some teachers or departments have decided to create their own teaching materials or a combination of e-books and material curated from accredited open sources. Other teachers recognize the latitude this approach brings to their courses and, for schools with significant budget constraints, the potential cost savings (not to mention the reduction in weight in student backpacks). As more schools implement 1:1 computer programs and the number of students across socioeconomic categories who own a mobile computing device continues to increase rapidly, the natural platform for access to the knowledge base will irrevocably shift away from mass-published books, in either print or digital form.

REFLECTION

We are not all born with equal amounts of natural creativity. But neither are we born devoid of it. As many authors and educators have pointed out, young children express confidence in their own artistic abilities up until a certain age, and then begin to pull back with the sense that they are not "good" at drawing or music. Traditional school does not reward creativity; it rewards repetition and duplication. Yet creativity is a set of teachable skills, a learnable set of habits. Student-led creative exploration lies at the very heart of Dewey-inspired learning. For all the reasons we have discussed and that I will share in the rest of this book, we, the adults who constructed the education system, have decided to withhold the lessons of creativity from our students. We have decided that those lessons and skills are not a priority.

This is the most profound change taking place in K–12 education today, and perhaps what differentiates those who are contributing to a transformed learning experience from those who are holding fast to the industrial age model. Some of our "best" teachers—those known in the school to demand that their students think for themselves and answer big, relevant, bold questions—still do not yield the keys to creativity to their students. They create their own lesson plans, decide where and what the students will learn, repeating successes from past years, laying out the playing field in such remarkable detail for their students that we applaud them as the hardest workers—the best. And yet they are teaching as we, ourselves, learned, in a setting of known answers and predetermined, unambiguous outcomes, a setting that is utterly unlike the world their students will inhabit. The rising tide of forward-leaning educators who see the world as a fluid, rapidly changing environment are willingly sacrificing the known for the unknown, embedding the actual skills of learned creativity in everything they and their students do.

CHAPTER TEN

Schools Are Self-Correcting
Empathy, Mindfulness, and Reflection

High desert, low desert, sand dunes, stone cliffs, saguaro wash, cholla hell. If you want to taste the true soul of the desert, not a place on the map with a Hollywood name, but the grand reach of dry land that covers a third of North America, then you must leave the places of people behind. The desert sun will split rocks and boil blood, bleach a Coors can white in two desperate months. Canyon wall echoes are swallowed in sandy washes and evaporate on the endless flats. Most days, other than wind and maybe one raptor's cry, the desert is deaf.

Rattlesnakes don't bother to coil and strike. Unless you step on them, they just don't care. In the desert the bad things you have done perch beside you, waiting quietly like a hawk above a rabbit hole to see if you will honestly atone.

Where there is a hint of green, birds chirp warnings. When there is a hint of springtime, sun teases out wildflower splashes, exploding blooms of buttery yucca, red-flamed ocotillo tips, chubby, pulpy prickly pear, and the earth-bound smell of rock-ground sage. But the hint is just a hint, never a promise. An oasis is a rumor. A creek is a myth. An artesian spring is God.

Visitors are like flash floods to this endless land: violent monsoon thunderstorms, wayward drunken miners, crazed new-age pilgrims, brazen narco-soldiers, rapid auto tourists, dusty two-car towns, asphalt slashes, disappearing tracks. All of these transients are as inconsequential to the great Western desert as a pinprick supernova in the infinite sky.

I am no shaman, no priest, but I remember one Sedona day when I thought I saw the Great Kachina carved in a red sandstone cliff, and the wispy tails of cirrus cloud stallions chased by puffy gray wolves across a cobalt sky. These are visions that avoid the world of water and the lands of life. And one Death Valley night, long on baked-in heat and short on friends, I climbed a scree-covered hill, sat alone, and watched a full moon cast white ghost-light across a stillness so deep that even the howls of coyotes on their midnight hunt fell short of heaven.

Desert mind is Buddha mind: no us and them; no here and there; no this and that. There is just desiccated space where imagined angels raise the light and sing a vaulting and a tortured hallelujah.

The Busy Day

Schools rarely build in time for either adults or students to stop and reflect with any significant frequency. Teachers may be asked to think and comment on how they progressed toward their goals once a year. Administrators adjourn for a pre-year retreat and set aside an hour or two to think about the connective tissues of their organization. If adults at school have time for a cup of tea in the afternoon it is rushed, and if they take that long walk where a great new idea might surface, it is on their time, not the school's. Students walk quickly from one class to the next. Teachers ask them to hurry up, take their predetermined seats, and get ready to ingest the quantum of knowledge required for that day or week or month. Entire districts focus on the importance of "bell-to-bell" instruction. High school English students may take the time to write reflective essays, but when was the last time a math or physics teacher asked the same of students?

We know the value that time for reflection and authentic mindfulness brings, and we want that time and skill set for our students.

One of the most frequent comments I heard at schools around the country is that schools—students, adults, and the organization—need to take more time and opportunities to stop, reflect, self-assess, and re-calibrate their goals, resources, and purpose. We *know* that these are necessary good habits of creative minds, of fulfilled lives. We *know* the value that time for reflection and authentic mindfulness brings, and we want that time and skill set for our students. We *know* that they will benefit in their futures if they have the skill and wisdom to step back, be still, and reflect outside of whatever daily pressures they might face.

Yet few schools are acting on this deeply held imperative. Schools are just beginning to either develop homegrown programs that focus on skills like mindfulness, empathy, and reflection, or are bringing in outsiders to train students and faculty in their use. The beginnings are there and the benefits appear too great to ignore. My sense is that this is a true growth opportunity for schools, a way to offer differentiated value in the future. Benefits that might have been viewed just a few years ago (and even today by some skeptics) as "fluff" are increasingly verified by brain research and empirical observation. And, importantly, taking just a few minutes a day to learn and develop good, life-long habits, does not cost much, if anything at all.

Empathy

The story of John Hunter and the World Peace Game would have fit into any chapter in this book. I chose to put it here because, of all the life skills that John's young students learn, he says he is most proud of their focus on empathy, and he says he got there by reflecting on himself and his work as a teacher.

John may be the iconic teacher of our generation in America. If you are one of the few who has *not* seen the award-winning *World Peace Movie* or read John's book, *World Peace and Other Fourth Grade Achievements* (Hunter, 2013), search them out, as it is a story impossible to adequately summarize here. Over almost three decades, John, a teacher in Virginia's Albemarle County Schools, has developed an experiential game-play simulation for and with fourth-grade students. The game is played out over a period of about eight weeks on a three-dimensional Plexiglas cube, four feet on a side, a piece of the real world replete with people, environments, politics, weather, and war. The students run four countries, and the only way to win the game is for all four countries to encounter and overcome obstacles of conflict, economy, environmental stress, and chance. There are rules, but the students must interpret the rules. The students must make difficult choices; they encounter tremendous and real opportunities for failure. There is the real chance that one group of students will "annihilate" another group, and they have that choice. John does not teach the students or make decisions for them. He gives them the opportunity to live the game for themselves, and the results are the stuff of educators' dreams.

I first met John at a conference where I, along with about four thousand other educators, gave him a long standing ovation following his talk and a view of the movie trailer. Later that evening I found him sitting alone in a hotel lobby. John uses *The Art of War*, not a text normally taught in fourth-grade classes. In my first book, *The Falconer*, I also make the lessons of this signature text accessible to very young students. We shared a few minutes of conversation, and I told John if there were ever a chance I could get on a plane and fly somewhere and spend a few hours with him, just talking about the art of teaching, I would relish the opportunity. (I didn't know then that, through our mutual association with the Martin Institute for Teaching Excellence, I would be privileged to spend many such hours with him in the future.) Anyone who

> *"The outcome that I most appreciate and desire is that students actually learn how to be more compassionate human beings."*

knows John knows he is one of the most humble, self-effacing people on the planet. He said how much he appreciated that and somehow got me talking about my work instead of his!

When I interviewed John in depth about the goals of the World Peace Game, he had just returned from taking his fourth graders to the Pentagon, where they showed the game to a room full of generals who were fascinated that kids could find legitimate ways through the most realistic, complex problems, to arrive at peace. I asked John what does he set as his highest goals, among all the skills that the students develop through this remarkable experience. "I used to think that I wanted students to gain academic outcomes from the game," John told me, "to learn more about math, science, and the rest. But what the students have shown me, the outcome that I most appreciate and desire is that they actually learn how to be more compassionate human beings and that they actually learn to help others reduce suffering in their own lives. And this is borne out as students come back after twenty or thirty years and tell me how their lives have been, about how their lives have been more compassionate, about them caring more for other people; I think that is the greatest reward I can have. For the students to become good people I think is at least on par with their becoming good at science or math or other academic achievements."

I asked John how he sees the remarkable experience and success of the game fitting in with other, more traditional teaching, what lessons other educators can take away as they try to embed lessons of empathy or compassion in their academic subjects. "Of course there is no blanket answer and I always try to avoid giving advice because I don't know anybody's particular situation, but I can say in my own practice, what I have found most helpful in being more creative than I might have been is first, a practice of introspection, of reflecting on my own strengths and weaknesses and fears because as a human being I bring baggage to my profession. I have prejudices and biases that are not helpful. If I don't know what those are, I bring them in and put them on my students or in the way of their learning. That work of trying to clear that space, of not being an obstacle to myself, has been the first step. On the other hand, on the part of the students, if you have so much compassion for them, that you listen to who they are and find out from them what is their deepest concern, their deepest wish, their deepest passion, what they love, what they are interested in, if you can find that out, or that can be revealed to you, then you can begin to build curriculum, to tailor curriculum specifically for that person. In doing so, they can see my effort as a teacher to do things for them with them in mind. They see the love and faith you have in each one of them and recognize that you must care about them to some degree."

How often do we get to interact with colleagues in unscripted time and space where none of the parties have a pre-set agenda or an intended outcome? One of those gems of unplanned outcomes was my short meeting with Ayeola Elias, director of diversity and multicultural affairs at the Charlotte Latin School in North Carolina. Ayeola was a part-time teacher just a year ago and now is a passionately articulate leader helping other teachers to embed a wider range of viewpoints into their curriculum. At the time of my visit she was working on an all-school initiative to bring the concept of empathy into focus for teachers, students, and parents as a core interpersonal skill. They are developing lessons within the advisory program that include media literacy and a series of lessons and events for both students and parents that deal with media filtering. Teachers are working to present their subjects through the eyes of whomever is being studied instead of through the eyes of the historian or the textbook author.

Ayeola told me, "We want physics students to see the material through the eyes of Einstein, and we want our students to understand the Civil War from the viewpoint of both a slave and a Confederate soldier. Empathy is the one thing that is really going to help our children grow. We can give them all of the math, science, and history we want, but empathy is what is going to help them to become genuinely good people.

Trust between the teacher and the student is what prompts students to take a risk in their own learning.

And to do that when we teach our subjects, we need to allow our students to see those subjects through the eyes of 'the other.' When you can do that you can force the student, in a very comfortable way, to let go of who he or she *is*, and somehow connect on a higher level with who he or she can *become*. I ask students to 'know that when we are studying this subject, let go of who you are for just a moment, and know that in that moment I am doing the same thing for you.'"

Like John Hunter, Ayeola believes that trust between the teacher and the student is what prompts students to take a risk in their own learning, to try something and possibly fail, knowing that the teacher and the system will not be overly critical of a reasonable risk. "Know that you can count on me because my focus is what is best for you, and through that I grow as a teacher. We build that trust that their teachers and their peers have their back, we can all let go, sink our teeth into a subject that maybe we are not confident in, but through that, by letting go of who we are at that moment, the kids are amazed at how they grow in that moment."

Mindfulness

Lorraine Hobbs is a psychotherapist and senior teacher with the Center for Mindfulness at the University of California, San Diego. She and her partners have developed programs to teach mindfulness to preteens and teenagers and are beginning to implement the programs in local schools. I asked Lorraine what lies at the core of mindfulness training. She quoted Stanford researcher Philip Golden: "Parents and teachers tell students a hundred times a day to pay attention, but without teaching them how." Lorraine says, "We know from neuroscience that the amygdala, the part of the brain that controls mechanical responses, develops in humans at a younger age than does the prefrontal cortex, where cognition and reasoning takes place. Stress can block relationships from developing between the two, so it actively impacts the slower-developing, thinking portions of the brain. We are teaching students to actively pay attention to and manage the stress in their lives, to drop into a practice of mindfulness the minute they identify that something is stressful. This gives them a sense of control over their emotions and behavior. We work with them to recognize and be able to move from their thinking mind, where we all live most of our busy and hectic lives, to their sensing mind, where they can be connected to the world and the moment."

Mindfulness training helps to strengthen the parts of the brain that increase focus and attention and decrease the natural wandering that derails that focus. Lorraine says that where she has had access to students over a period of six or eight months, even for just a half hour or an hour a week, they see real results. "I have had students tell me that they can quickly adjust their breathing and lower their stress level on the tennis court or before a test or when they are in an argument with their parents. These are lifelong skills that have real mental, social, and physiological impacts on people's lives."

"Mindfulness addresses a wide range of issues that are not addressed through pure academic learning. It prepares the mind to learn, and it addresses the social and emotional side of learning and of life."

While immersive programs that highlight reflection, empathy, and mindfulness are by no means mainstream in schools, they are starting to reach an increasing number of students. Just one example is Mindful Schools, an outreach organization in the San Francisco Bay Area that has worked with more than 11,000 students in more than forty, mostly public schools, many of them serving traditionally underperforming student populations, in the past four years. Meg Cowan with Mindful Schools says that, in general, they see "increased ability to pay attention in class, improved self-awareness, which leads to impulse control, which is probably the most appealing entry point for education. Mindfulness addresses a wide range of issues that are not addressed through pure academic learning. It prepares the mind to learn, and it addresses the social and emotional side of learning and of life. One should not be neglected at the expense of the other; they both serve each other."

Dan Siegel, a child, adolescent, and adult psychologist at UCLA and the Mindsight Institute in Los Angeles cites research that shows that

> adults who focus their attention in a mindful way in a training period of about eight weeks can actually change the way their brain functions. That finding, along with some amazing research in neuroscience that shows that the brain continues to change throughout the lifespan, have gotten people really interested in how to use the mind to change the structure and function of the brain. In children we are interested in seeing if education can develop parts of the brain that develop early on, the pre-frontal areas, that give you, for example, the ability to pause before you act or have empathy for others. At this point, education, which for the most part is focusing on things like reading, writing, and arithmetic, is not helping the pre-frontal cortex develop directly. We need to add the process of reflection. Reflective skills help young people develop these pre-frontal abilities, what we call executive functions. (Siegel, 2013)

Like the practitioners I spoke with, Dan goes on to say that research has shown that children who have had training in mindfulness are able to calm themselves down in what could otherwise turn into very volatile situations.

Stopping

During my visit at Christ Church Episcopal School in Greenville, South Carolina, my guides took me outside on a windy, chilly morning to see elementary students quietly walking around a flat maze of paving stones set into a grassy knoll. It is a weekly ritual for all students at the school. One at a time the students start on the path, making their way silently to the stones at the center, where they sit and wait for all of their classmates to arrive. The process takes twenty minutes or so. Then they retreat to benches to share their thoughts. Where did they find time for this in a busy schedule? It is a form of recess.

At Alexandria Country Day School in Alexandria, Virginia, I visited a class of fifth graders, just arrived in the early morning, as they started their day. The students and teachers stood together in a close circle, and took turns introducing each other by name. They do this every morning. Of course they all know each other, but it was a wonderful moment of quiet, and then Assistant Head of School Nishant Mehta told me it is "a way for every child to be recognized by his or her peers at the start of the day." The teacher read a few sentences out of a book; the students shared a minute or two of reflections, and then it was on to the day. Even I felt calmer when I left the room!

Some teachers start or end their classes each day with just a minute or two of quiet "centering time" to help focus students on the moment.

Quaker Friends schools gather as a community at least once a week for as much as an hour for meeting time, most of which is spent in silence, allowing each in the gathering to pursue his or her own thoughts. At Sidwell Friends School in Washington, D.C., the entire middle school shares a few minutes of silence in the cafeteria at the end of lunch before going back to class. Some teachers start or end their classes each day with just a minute or two of quiet "centering time" to help focus students on the moment. Bruce Stewart, retired head at Sidwell Friends, helped me understand the role that meeting times play in the life of the school: "These periods of quiet during the day teach students the powerful tools that deep thinking gives us for both understanding our own lives and in developing empathy for those around us."

In their book *Tuning In: Mindfulness in Teaching and Learning* (2009), Irene McHenry and Richard Brady have compiled stories from teachers who share specific ideas for how to use quiet and reflection as an aid to learning and how to develop these skills in students, starting as young as kindergarten. The authors describe how small pieces of time devoted to mindfulness and reflection can have a powerful cumulative impact on student learning. These teachers might take one or two minutes at the start of each class period, ring a small bell, and ask the students to focus on the moment, the present, to center themselves for learning. Over time, students build up a powerful life skill that will be vastly more helpful to them in their future personal and professional lives than almost any bit of content knowledge they may acquire in school, and it takes just minutes a day.

Finding Time

Shelly Sowell is a counselor and mental health professional who works with schools on mindfulness development. I asked her how schools are becoming more intentional about teaching the skills of mindfulness and reflection as part of everyday curriculum. She told me that many schools just toss out their old Health and Fitness class and put in its place a "healthy living and don't-do-drugs class": "Students listen and then many blow it off, as it has no meaning in most of their lives."

"What has changed," says Shelly, is that children now have "fewer guiding lights in their lives. Many come from single-parent homes; fewer attend church or have a family-based spiritual focus. They are trying to figure it all out on their own. We just need to help kids slow down and connect in a meta-awareness way. With just a little exposure and context they get it and start to apply it in so many ways to their lives and decisions."

I asked Shelly what success looks like in a school that creates a serious and intentional focus on mindfulness. "The school must have a strong support statement about student and community health from the administration. Kids watch adults, and adults need to model health and mindfulness in very visible ways for students to buy in. The kids don't care what you call it—mindfulness, meditation, reflection—but they have to know that it is important and not just something else being tossed at them. When the administration encourages and supports the model, when they check in with people to see how they are really doing, we start to see a dramatic change in the classroom. As a whole school, we see very positive outcomes when about 50 percent of the teachers are integrating some aspect of mindfulness training once a week in classroom. It does not have to take a lot of time; the real key is just a bit each day or each week, not the big speaker coming in once and then leaving."

I also talked with Susan Kaiser-Greenland, a former lawyer who has been working on implementing mindfulness education for more than ten years. In her book *The Mindful Child* (2010) and in our interview, Susan says that mindfulness should "not be in the head"; it needs to shift away from the "thinking mind" to the "feeling, or sensory mind." True mindfulness generates a physical response or set of sensations that we can recognize as it takes place. Once we understand that sensory response, that steadying of heart and breath, we are then ready to delve into the skills that help us use our mind more clearly.

Susan mostly works with pre-kindergarten through seventh-grade students, but she is building a K–12 scope and sequence manual with the intent that mindfulness practice can become a full-fledged part of the curriculum. "The field is young and we are not there yet. There are a lot of different ideas about what mindfulness is, which causes confusion but also creates the upside of opportunity for good discussion. We are trying to train teachers in classic secular mindfulness, including an age-appropriate scope and sequence." Susan says that she gets the normal push-back and initial reaction from many teachers that this is another fad that will go away. But mindfulness education is also gaining converts, teachers who begin to integrate the skills of mindfulness into what they are already doing. "The goal is to teach teachers the basic pedagogy so they can use the tools at different times when needed and appropriate. This is not just ringing a bell and getting kids to sit still once a day. It is about a teacher being able to pull something out of their toolkit when a class or a student really needs it."

REFLECTION

Late on a gorgeous fall day, I sat and talked for an uninterrupted hour with five high school students at the Asheville School in Asheville, North Carolina. One told me, "You get caught up in your life and your work and your activities, and you don't really get time to just sit with yourself and get to know who you truly are and how you truly feel." Another student added, "We spent some time outside today observing our surroundings and reading some poetry. I just think we don't take the time to do that enough." It reminded me of what I had learned coming across the vast Western desert.

It is clear that many schools recognize the importance of inserting skill development in mindfulness, empathy, and reflection into their students' lives, but most schools are struggling to bring it along from a tangent to the mainstream. Many adults and students mentioned it as a top priority, yet few have increased exposure from the pilot to the systemic level. Most that do are faith-based schools, or schools with a historic background in faith-based traditions. Those schools have time set aside for chapel and all-school meetings, some of which are convenient community gatherings and some more contemplative and reflective. Individual teachers ask their students to keep a journal, but most of those are in English class; I did not encounter any science or math teachers who recognized how this would help their students. I have yet to meet an educator who argues that students learn *less efficiently* if they have time to reflect on their learning, yet most schools are just beginning, if at all, to provide the time, space, or training to implement time for reflection.

Few schools I visited have prioritized these behaviors at an organizational level. The busy day defeats most attempts to increase time and frequency for adults to stop, either alone or in groups, to authentically reflect on what they and the school are doing. Weekly or monthly departmental and staff meetings are overwhelmingly about "stuff." Deeper thinking is relegated to infrequent retreats or time-limited meetings. We tell ourselves, "Now is the time to think deeply," which of course is not the best way to think deeply! Creative knowledge-based companies have learned that the investment in time to think and reflect is rewarded many times over; there are very good reasons that Google allows employees to spend 20 percent of the company's time in this mode. Innovative schools will start to see the same benefits from emphasizing the same organizational self-correcting mechanisms we are starting to bring to our students.

PART THREE

The Road Ahead: How Do We Get There from Here?

IN THE INTRODUCTION I SAID THAT CHANGE IS NOT HARD, BUT IT IS OFTEN uncomfortable. Well, this is the section that may make readers squirm, and squirming is not a bad thing. I think one of our school mottoes, for students and adults alike, should be something like, "If we're not squirming, we're not learning."

I started my visits to schools with a simple central question: *What does innovation mean to you?* Teachers, administrators and students helped me see the answer through their eyes. Most said that schools need to provide learning opportunities that are centered on a set of skills and abilities that have less to do with *what we know* than with *how to manage* a dynamic and unknowable future. Many other authors and educators have argued that schools need to change. In the following chapters I lay out a roadmap to actually get there. I identify a different type of strategic approach that is in line with both the rate and magnitude of change that is occurring in the world outside of school.

The innovations that will reshape education will take place in response to changes that many of us see, and other changes that many of us probably do not recognize yet. In chapter 11, I will introduce you to four voices from outside education, experts who see profound patterns in the world around us that will have equally profound impacts on our schools and our patterns of learning. These are the existential challenges and questions that compel us to envision a very different learning system.

In response to the increasingly unknowable future, we want our students and teachers to become self-evolving learners, and they cannot do so on an assembly line.

In chapters 12 and 13, we will see how the model of education has to fundamentally shift in order to align with our vision of what we *want* it to be. Our current educational system is an assembly line designed and maintained by a process of social engineering. In response to the increasingly unknowable future, we want our students and teachers to become self-evolving learners, and they cannot do so on an assembly line. Evolution takes place in natural ecosystems, and the drivers of a natural ecosystem are fundamentally different from those of an engineered system. I am not the first one to propose that schools act more like ecosystems or that teachers behave more like farmers than assembly-line workers (Thomas & Seeley Brown, 2011). But I am going to dig deeper to show what this really means, and I argue that we can't go part way. We cannot tweak the assembly line and hope it will operate like a natural ecosystem; that is foundationally a square-peg-and-round-hole problem. We have to reimagine learning as an evolving natural ecosystem and then allow ecosystem-like processes to take over what is now a rigid, highly controlled, repetitive, creativity-killing assembly line.

Successful process engineering did not start with Henry Ford. The world around us is full of great examples of engineering and the thought processes that engineers go through. Our framework of society would not exist without this system of thinking. When small groups of villagers first started planting crops thousands of years ago, their increasing yields were based on fine-tuning an engineered process. When builders built pyramids, smithies forged bronze, shepherds raised herds, or writers printed books, they followed a developing science that we can summarize in the language of the engineer. In fact, as Margaret Wheatley reminds us in *Leadership and the New Science* (1999), the way we have thought about our world for centuries is based on a successful Newtonian view of the universe as constructed of discrete, measurable bits of matter that act in highly predictable ways. We have used these idealized building blocks to get closer to an understanding of our universe, but we now have to leave them behind. We know that the physical universe is comprised of probabilities, processes, and relationships, with hard-wired uncertainty beyond our control. We can't prepare our students for a future based purely on Newtonian building block thinking. That future does not exist. The world around us and certainly the future are less knowable and more ambiguous than at any point in human history.

Ecosystems are profoundly different from engineered processes. In part two of this book, I showed that the main characteristics of this new learning system are dynamism, adaptability, permeability, creativity, and self-correction. These are not the sole drivers of natural ecosystems, but they are more ecosystem-like than they are engineered. It is important to remember how I arrived at those characteristics. I asked educators and learners at the schools that I visited to share with me what they felt was driving their future ideas of learning. In most schools, these ideas are viewed as innovative pilot programs. It is only when we step back, distill, and synthesize the common elements that we see that collectively they accurately describe an evolving natural ecosystem.

This book is about building capacity and comfort with change within a school organization. In chapter 14, I describe how a school can accelerate on the road to building that capacity and comfort. Talk is just talk if it does not result in action. The primary reason I left my well-paying school job and undertook this journey was that we have a gap between, on the one hand, great educators who know a lot about how students learn but not about organizational change and, on the other, great change agents who know a lot about successful innovation but have never spent time working in schools. We can and must bridge that gap. Along with both formal and informal colleagues around the country, I believe we are developing a new set of strategic-level thinking and processes that all members of the school community can use to quickly and effectively begin to move schools off the assembly line and into a sustainable, self-evolving, ecosystem.

The final chapter sets out the big takeaways from my work. This chapter has the "cheat sheets," summarizing key points from my journey of school visits, literature research, blog reading, and active learning workshop facilitations.

CHAPTER ELEVEN

The Existential Challenge for Schools
Voices from Our Future

To grasp the enormous importance of corn to America, one must walk, ride, or drive between the western central plains and the Atlantic Coast and envision endless orthogonal extensions, broken only by the low green of soybeans, arrow-straight roads, two stoplight towns, and crow-laden power lines. In the summer of 2003, I drove for ten days with my son, Josh, then a rising junior in high school, on a college visit tour from Baltimore to Indianapolis, and other than the center of a few big cities, I don't believe we were out of sight of cornfields for fifteen minutes the entire trip. In that July the corn was tall, thick, and emerald green. By the time we got to northern Iowa, we understood the nightmare tales of children becoming lost among the towering, endless, tasseled stalks.

In the fall of 2012, I drove for hours and then days and then for two weeks across a heartland in the grip of the worst drought since the Dust Bowl, and never saw a green field of corn, never more than sad stunted ruble of withered, dun-colored, chest-high stalks. Climate change poses an existential risk to human culture that has developed over the past 20,000 years. Existential is sometimes an overused word, but in the case of climate change it is not. Forty years ago scientists predicted exactly what is happening now, except they underestimated the rate of change by a century. Sea levels will rise. Rainfall patterns will shift the productive grain belts to higher latitudes, not in one year of drought, but over a relatively few decades. The shabby, burnt cornfields of the summer of 2012 will become increasingly common.

There is another inevitable effect of climate change that all the models predicted decades ago: an increase in the number and severity of violent weather events. Following physical laws, heat must be transferred from the equator to the poles, and the most efficient pathways for this flow of heat are ocean currents and large weather systems like hurricanes. Big hurricanes. Some of those storms will water cornfields; some will destroy coastal cities and towns. We will either adapt to these changes or suffer major disruptions in food supply, infrastructure, economics, and the very fabric of our culture.

Education is undergoing a period of existential change that threatens the future of traditional schools for many reasons. Many authors have exhaustively discussed two of these: rapid changes in technology and tectonic flattening of global political-economic spheres. The sum of human knowledge will soon be doubling every year; education is in the knowledge business and can't keep up. This is no more in doubt than is global warming; data do not lie.

There are other deep forces at play that have only begun to appear at the edge of most educators' radar screens: rapid changes in the relationship between consumer demand and producers; the nature of informal virtual social interactions; and physical laws that govern the development of interactive systems. As long as schools were largely isolated entities responsible for a relatively defined, predictable, repeatable mission, these drivers were weak or irrelevant. Now, as technology has allowed massive interpersonal connections to evolve quickly and with ever-decreasing costs, consumer demand is reorienting entire markets, and the flow of knowledge capital is aligning with new pathways of creation, distribution, and consumption.

Educators frequently are isolated from changes in the rest of the world; the "ivory tower" metaphor is based in reality. In this chapter I will introduce the reader to four people from outside the mainstream of traditional education whose voices I find profoundly relevant to the future of what we imagine "school" will be in the next decade. These thought leaders are widely followed in their respective fields and give us critical perspectives that frame big, real issues facing education today and in the future. The stories of school innovation I found around the country are taking place in irreversible response to the framework that these voices help to illuminate.

Shoshana Zuboff:
Mutation and Disrupted Capitalism

My friend and "thought-colleague" Thomas Steele-Maley introduced me to Shoshana Zuboff and her husband, Jim Maxmin, on a visit to their home in Maine. Zuboff, now retired, was one of the first tenured women at the Harvard Business School, and they are both highly sought-after international consultants. We talked for five hours. Believe me, you wish you were in that room. Much of the following section is similar to an article I published in *Independent School Magazine* in February 2014, as I "introduced" the ideas of Zuboff to school leaders.

In addition to Zuboff and Maxmin's book *The Support Economy: Why Corporations Are Failing Individuals and the Next Episode of Capitalism* (2002), Zuboff is in the process of writing another book about major shifts in capitalism and consumerism, including a focus on education. Her 2010 article in *McKinsey Quarterly*, "Creating Value in the Age of Distributed Capitalism," is an absolute "must read" for school leaders. I summarize her key points in the following paragraphs with her kind permission.

Zuboff argues that consumer capitalism is fundamentally changing from "a *mass production logic* based on standardization and high volume throughput to a *distributed logic* based on providing people with the tools, platforms, resources, and relationships that enable them to live their lives as they choose." This shift to what Zuboff calls a new "distributed capitalism" is occurring in a wide range of consumer markets, including publishing, music, retail, health care, education, and more.

According to Zuboff, "Major shifts like this have historically developed through a process of *mutation* that drives fundamental economy-wide change. While *innovations* improve existing frameworks, *mutations* combine social, economic, and technological components in an internally consistent and wholly new institutional framework." Zuboff insists that the so-called "disruptive innovations" described by Clayton Christensen and others do not meet this standard, and that is why, as she puts it, "despite so much that is supposedly disruptive, there is relatively little genuine disruption taking place." In a school setting, for example, introducing computers and tablets has *disrupted* the classroom, but has not yet fundamentally *mutated* how learning takes place.

What does this mean when we strip out the business school language? It means that we have moved from a time when large, powerful companies said to their customers, "This is what I have to sell you, so buy it," to a new relationship where customers tell companies, "This is what I want, so sell it to me." Just think of the era of music on CDs giving way to iTunes and customized playlists, and how that has changed the music industry. Zuboff points out that Henry Ford's discovery of mass production was the mutation that shaped twentieth-century capitalism. She argues that "iTunes does for distributed capitalism what Henry Ford and mass production did for managerial capitalism; it introduces a whole new operating system for how to realize value for individuals."

> *We have moved from a time when large, powerful companies said to their customers, "This is what I have to sell you, so buy it," to a new relationship where customers tell companies, "This is what I want, so sell it to me."*

Zuboff cites a number of factors that indicate when a sector is ripe for mutation. Based on my school visits and subsequent work with school leaders all over the country, I find three of these factors are particularly relevant to the landscape of public and private education:

• *Trust between the producer and the consumer has fractured.* Zuboff points out that the General Social Survey of American moods and values shows a ten-point drop (from 38 percent to 28 percent) in trust in educational institutions from 1976 to 2006. Customers constantly evaluate educational options for their children and are ready to shift when they find one that improves their perception of value. Compared to a decade or two ago, consumers have vastly more educational options from which to choose as they continue to lose trust in the traditional system.

- *The sector has high levels of fixed costs that could be shifted to, or subsumed by, more flexible, lower-cost collaborators, competitors, or networks.* Schools have very high fixed costs, mostly wrapped up in people and large, expensive facilities. The key transactional medium of the current system, knowledge, is increasingly available through alternative, lower-cost, more tailored mechanisms that are available both in person and virtually.

- *Your end users have needs and desires that you have yet to imagine.* Schools provide services that are largely unchanged from decades ago. Vanishingly little effort is spent on imagining future alternatives that meet consumer needs and desires outside of the traditional school structure. Most schools today assume that because students came to them in the past, they will continue to do so, even as the needs and desires of those customers change in important ways.

As changes like these occur, Zuboff says, successful institutions, and indeed entire industries, dispassionately evaluate which assets of the existing framework have real value in a mutated landscape. Assets that can generate real value through customization are retained while others are jettisoned, particularly those with high fixed costs. New products and services that are more customizable to individual consumer demands bypass older products and services that have been largely pushed at consumers. In the face of these pressures, schools will have to focus on their core competencies and let go of the pieces that cost a lot to deliver but that do not deliver differentiated value in the eyes of their customers.

> *Nearly everything a school does today can be effectively outsourced* except *the powerful relationships that grow between students and teachers and between peer students, and the culture and traditions that make a school such a powerful part of young people's lives.*

Over the past year I have asked hundreds of educators (and some parents and students) to consider everything that their school does, and to decide which functions can and cannot be taken over by a competitor, often at a lower cost due to advances in technology. It is a difficult discussion, because we all want to believe what we do is critical to the success of our organization. But after some soul-searching, the results are almost identical in every group: Nearly everything a school does today can be effectively outsourced *except* the powerful relationships that grow between students and teachers and between peer students, and the culture and traditions that make a school such a powerful part of young people's lives.

Marina Gorbis: Rise of a Socialstructed World

Marina Gorbis, director of the Institute for the Future in Palo Alto and author of *The Nature of the Future: Dispatches From the Socialstructed World* (2013), says that a new network of relationships is forming across a wide range of sectors where individuals join forces to replace products and services that have traditionally been supplied by large corporations and organizations. This process, which she terms "socialstructing," involves "moving away from a dominance of the depersonalized world of institutional production." The changes "threaten many established institutions and offer a wealth of opportunities for individuals to empower themselves" (Gorbis, 2013). Gorbis and her colleagues at the Institute for the Future see the rise of a new framework of societal connections that allow individuals "empowered with technologies and the collective intelligence of others in the social network to take on many functions that previously only large organizations could perform," more efficiently, and at a lower cost. She sees this evolution taking place in finance, health care, education, and science. Start-up entrepreneurs find financing through Kickstarter; professionals share free expert advice over chat communities; programmers collaborate to develop free open-source software purely because they want to; students can direct a telescope at the Harvard observatory simply by logging on and entering a request.

Many of the key points that Gorbis cites in this evolution from institutional to personalized production are coincident with Zuboff's view of current global trends and, as we will see, with highly predictable physical laws as well:

• Value flows through a much larger number of widely distributed nodes, ultimately residing at the level of the individual person. In the case of education, the value that flows through the system is *knowledge*. Each student, teacher, parent, school, and classroom can act independently of the others.

• Socialstructing allows scale to be achieved *without* large organizations. The cost of everything from communication to distribution of goods and services is driven down.

• Humans increasingly focus on what they do best and leave the performance of repetitive tasks to computers, machines, and robots. Humans can focus on determining "the deeper meaning or significance of what is being expressed; social and emotional intelligence; novel and adaptive thinking; moral and ethical reasoning."

Socialstructing manifests in education as "microlearning"—learning driven by "individual desires and needs" rather than by an externally imposed set of objectives and demands. Where the current system invests time, people, and money only in programs that may succeed at a very large scale, in a microlearning environment scale is achievable, and success is measured, at the level of a single person or school, or a few schools. Learning institutions leverage the strengths of connected individuals who cannot be replaced, at least yet, by computers. Institutions mine value from interpersonal relationships, mentoring, and strong social settings. Individuals gather in real and virtual space based on their interests and passions, not for profit or to pass a test. Gorbis reminds us that this shift is not revolutionary, that "the foundations of this kind of education lie far in the past," with Socrates, Plutarch, Rousseau, and Dewey.

> *Socialstructing manifests in education as "microlearning"—learning driven by "individual desires and needs" rather than by an externally imposed set of objectives and demands.*

Adrian Bejan:
Knowledge Flow and the Constructal Law

There is supporting evidence in the physical world that our system of learning is perched on the edge of fundamental and inevitable reorganization that is largely beyond our control. Adrian Bejan, a world-renowned professor of engineering at Duke University, is the creator of the constructal law, what many have called the fourth law of thermodynamics. The constructal law states, "For a finite flow system to persist in time (to live), its configuration must evolve in such a way that provides easier access to the currents that flow through it." As detailed in his book *Design in Nature* (Bejan & Zane, 2012), and as I discussed with Bejan in a discussion on my blog site in 2013, he and his collaborators have shown that *all* flow systems, be they highways, blood vessels, veins in a leaf, hospitals, or rivers, develop in such a way as to *increase the efficiency of flow* through the system, resulting in system-wide structures with remarkably similar and predictable topographies.

Bejan agrees with me that the constructal law applies to the system of K–12 education. "The current grass-roots contributions to K–12 education are in accord with the constructal law, not against it. [We see] the early design of a new flow system, like the new rain falling on the smooth plain, and like the Internet in its early stages. In time, the better ideas contributing to this global K–12 flow will attract more users, and will become bigger nodes, trunks and big branches. The natural emergence of hierarchy (i.e., tree-shaped flow structures) is already happening in this new way of distributing knowledge on the globe. It has been this way with every new technique of spreading ideas."

Why is this structural organization so critical to education now? Prior to the last decade, knowledge passed through a relatively small number of largely isolated or weakly connected pathways: individual schools, poorly connected teachers, writers, universities, publishers, and libraries. Knowledge flowed, but at an infinitesimal fraction of the speed and magnitude that it does today. That paradigm has now exploded into a vast multidimensional neural network of knowledge creation, consumption, and management that is accessible to anyone with a mobile computing device, which will soon include almost everyone on the planet. I call this global system the "cognitosphere"—just the fifth global system of interconnection to have evolved in 4.5 billion years on the planet, along with the lithosphere, atmosphere, hydrosphere, and biosphere. The cognitosphere includes both the body of knowledge as it exists and evolves, and the process of creating, teaching, transferring, managing, and learning that knowledge.

This system includes and will increasingly optimize an extraordinary, and currently lightly tapped, neural network of educators, students, media, businesses, formal and informal organizations, parents and grandparents. A thousand years ago, information was created in small, isolated villages or towns and transferred around the fires at night. A hundred years ago, information was created and passed through a highly restricted network of educated professionals and academics. Thirty years ago, global telecommunication was still "iffy," and data transfer often required a primitive image scanner and an analog telephone. Today these connections are global, nearly universal, fluid, permeable, dynamic, collaborative, instantaneous, democratic, and constantly in a state of rapid evolution. K–12 education is one set of connector-transmitters within the cognitosphere, particularly critical in the transfer of knowledge through time, from the past to those who will create new knowledge in the future.

The future success of schools will be determined by how well they are connected to other knowledge-based sources, not their legacy reputation, the size of their endowment, or where their graduates went to college a decade ago.

Just as towns grew up along railroads in the Old West and withered where they were bypassed, the constructal law requires that the now-connected system of learning (education) will develop along predictable patterns that *maximize the flow of knowledge through the system*. Knowledge-based entities (schools, universities, individuals, companies, social media groups, crowd- and open-sourced interest-based collaborations, research labs) that facilitate knowledge creation and flow—that fully develop the dynamic, creative, externally focused, adaptive processes that I found percolating at innovative schools around the country—will form the healthy, vibrant main nodes and trunks of this system. Schools that remain rigid, internally focused, isolated, and focused on knowledge consumption, regardless of their history, fame, or financial strength, will tend to wither. The constructal law, supported by what people like Zuboff and Gorbis see evolving across all sectors today, demands that the future success of schools will be determined by how well they are connected to other knowledge-based sources, not their legacy reputation, the size of their endowment, or where their graduates went to college a decade ago.

Gary Hamel:
Balancing Our Innovation Portfolio

In his book *What Matters Now* (2012), Gary Hamel, an expert on innovation and change management, argues that the principles of management in almost all organizations are primarily a function of *control*. Managers are deemed to be good at their jobs if they control variables in ways that are favorable to a set of assessment and operating results. Frequently this control is most efficiently accomplished by managing those variables right out of the workplace equation. In an increasingly competitive environment, one stressed by increasing ranges of options for our goods and services, we need to introduce *freedom* as a counterbalance to the principles of control. Freedom requires people to have the resources to experiment, dream, test, try, and fail.

Hamel cites two primary reasons that organizations are late in responding to existential threats from the outside. First, the threats have to be *really big* to gain the notice of top leadership. Leaders are busy people, and whether they are responding to the demands of shareholders, boards, employees, or customers, even the best leaders can focus on only a few things at a time. Everyone who crosses the leader's path believes that what *they* see as most important is, in fact, most important. Almost all of them are wrong. Leaders have to be able to identify the truly existential challenges and opportunities and focus on those. Unfortunately, the ability to do so is not what got most school leaders promoted to their leadership positions.

Second, many top leaders are heavily invested in the status quo and fight to preserve it rather than looking for opportunities to become more nimble. Schools are not an exception. As in other industries, the barriers to competition in our traditional niche are dropping. The first response to the specter of externally imposed change is usually to hope it goes away. The second response is to take a cautious approach, to stay away from the bleeding edge of change. As we have discussed, schools are risk-averse organizations and are therefore more likely to take a small, hopeful shot at change and wait to see whether it hits the mark. Hamel says that one-shot solutions do not tend to be sustained over time; changing the organizational DNA takes real commitment.

Schools need to rebalance their portfolios to allow more experimentation and more risk that will generate long-term growth.

Schools are heavily overweighted to preservation of tradition at the expense of innovation. If you think of an investment portfolio, a good portfolio is balanced between conservative instruments that preserve capital and more risky investments that generate a greater return. Schools need to rebalance their portfolios to allow more experimentation and more risk that will generate long-term growth. If well designed, this rebalancing yields an equilibrium between what the school has always done that made it successful in the first place and what they need to attempt to stay competitive in the long run. Hamel's argument is that our conservatism is rooted in the principles of management that we have all grown up with, and if we do not tackle that core issue, our organization will be left behind as others that engage in a more rapid pace of experimentation lead the way in terms of customer satisfaction. This is exactly what so many experts with vast vision and experience from outside education—along with people like Zuboff, Gorbis, and Bejan—see in our immediate future.

REFLECTION

These threads form a tapestry that challenges the very core of what we call "schools" today. Education is not an island, protected from the megatrends that have radically altered how individuals interact with a wide range of products and services. Agile, nimble networks of individuals and fluidly evolving organizations that meet personalized demands will increasingly replace large organizations that have successfully dictated products and services to consumers in the past. Falling costs for communication and rising abilities to create and share knowledge will increase overall system efficiency, driving expensive humans to focus our efforts where they create the most value. Even though it is inevitable, the evolution of this new system is not smooth and predictable; traditional organizations (schools) will not have long lead times to adapt to new competitors. Alternative learning mechanisms will continue to develop in the background and then emerge seemingly overnight. Consumers increasingly have the technology and comfort with social connections to select knowledge and learning suppliers that meet their short- and long-term needs.

The evidence of these changes in education is everywhere: the explosion of MOOCs at the college level; access to academic content via free open sources like CK–12, iTunesU, and many others; the dramatic growth in online learning at every level from K–12 to postgraduate; radical fall-off in the use of traditional textbooks; personal learning programs like Khan Academy; the rapid rise of charter and hybrid learning schools; crowd-sourced and socialstructed networks of individuals who freely share expertise, answer questions, and collaborate on research; competency-based learning standards and adaptive learning platforms that focus learning on each individual, not the population as a whole. None of these were driving forces in education a decade ago; all of them are powerful forces today, routinely accessed by millions of learners around the world—and increasing at incredible rates.

In the time it takes to move this book from final edit to publication and distribution, new players, approaches, and learning services will have exploded on the scene; some that appear strong today will start to show signs of weakness and fade away. Some schools and school leaders won't see the changes or hope they will go away. Like corn farmers in the American heartland, some will go out of business, giving way to systems that are better adapted to the prevailing environment, while others will innovate in response to global change. Effective school leaders are already recognizing the nature of these existential changes, just like rising global temperatures and shifting rainfall patterns, and are responding in how they imagine and how they "do" school. Where that reaction takes place at a truly foundational level, we are changing the very fabric and underlying conditions of education. How that change is taking place, and the laws driving a new system of learning, are the subject of the next two chapters.

CHAPTER TWELVE

Leaving the Past Behind
The Assembly-Line Model of Education

The road is not a black asphalt line across the country; it is a complex machine, built to connect distant points of terra firma, a self-contained system with food, water, air, fuel, shelter, way-finding, security, communications, and repair. I could live on this road forever, never straying more than one quantum on ramp and off ramp right or left, for as long as my credit card holds a charge. The pieces are all here, interchangeable, from the massive twenty-lane belts that rip in and out of Los Angeles, Chicago, Boston, and New York City, to the two-lane byways that roll through green Missouri backwoods and the humid lowlands of the Mississippi Delta.

It is utterly impossible for me to conceive of an America where roads do not lead everywhere, where a lonely wanderer can't pick a spot on the map and just go—yet that was the America of my parents' generation. The vision, design, the indomitable forces of will and market demand that went into creating this road system are beyond my comprehension—until I think of the Internet and personal computing devices, software, call centers in Bangalore, factories in China, and the phone on my dashboard mount that has more computing power in it than the space shuttle did when it was retired a few years ago.

My goodness, we humans are good at building things of wonder! Some we are glad we built, and some we wish we had not; I leave the discussion of the Glen Canyon dam for another time. But we did not just build a road and then leave that road to be a road. We created a world within a world, with sunrises and sunsets; rain, snow and fog; day and night; food and outlet centers, little grass parks and picnic benches—just like the real world, but built for the sole reason of getting "me" from here to there.

The Assembly Line

What does it *actually mean* when we say our traditional schools follow an industrial age assembly-line model? How does an assembly line work? How is that different from what we want learning to look like? What did the designers have in mind when they built, and changed, and tweaked our learning model? Which processes do we want to change, and which do we want to keep the same? What is our learning system good at? How do we know?

Social engineers designed the schools of today, and in order to answer these questions we need to look at schools through the lens of what is common to all engineered systems, be they dams, roads, computer chips, robots, or human-made molecules.

The education system in the United States and most of the industrial world worked extremely well for about 150 years. The education system was designed in the nineteenth and early twentieth centuries to solve the problem of a workforce inadequately prepared to meet the demands of industrial economies and to help a diverse population contribute to evolving democratic societies.

Measured against the original design specifications, assembly-line education over the past 150 years has been a remarkable success.

In his award-winning TED talk, Sugata Mitra argued that the education system also provided a large corps of minimally trained, interchangeable civil servants to govern expanding colonial empires. Many people say that our system of education is broken, but they are wrong. Measured against the original design specifications, assembly-line education over the past 150 years has been a remarkable success. More students entered and progressed through a system of knowledge transfer than at any other time in human history. Increasing numbers of students graduated, ready for further training in colleges, universities, or trade schools or instead to immediately enter and contribute to exploding industrial econ-omies. Despite resistance and lagging inequities, education has become available to an increasing segment of the population. Teaching evolved from a profession for ill-prepared high school graduates to a respected, if still underpaid, career that is the focus of preparation and ongoing profes-sional development at many colleges and universities, as well as through a multibillion-dollar industry.

Over the past several decades and more intensely in the past ten to fifteen years, the assembly-line model ceased to meet its design specifi-cations for two reasons. First, the Internet exploded the boundaries of once-controllable sources of information. The basic three-way educational relationship among students, teachers, and knowledge within a bounded school environment has been shattered, along with the mechanical con-trol of the original system design. These boundaries simply do not exist any longer. Second, the environmental demands that drive postsecondary education have fundamentally and irreversibly changed. The collapse of communism in the former Soviet Union, the development of a more pragmatic single-party-directed system of Chinese capitalism, flattened eco-nomic relationships between an ever-growing supply of inexpensive labor and wealthy consumers, and growing entrepreneurial focus in young, populous democracies like India and Brazil have reorganized global eco-nomic, political, and cultural environments. The world faces rising existential challenges in the areas of energy, environmental sustainability, climate, and health. The challenges of the past are not the challenges of the future, and the environment in which we need to address those chal-lenges has similarly changed.

What is the real nature of an industrial age, engineered assembly line? What is the baseline of the educational system we are trying to change? To make the rest of this chapter relatively simple and somewhat playful, I will use two sample subjects: a farmer and a maker of "widgets."

Understanding the Problem

The first step in engineering design is always to understand the problem. The rest of the design process, and ultimately how well the process works, rest on this accurate definition of the problem. Our farmer faces a very basic problem: He is trying to keep himself and his family from starving by consuming, selling, or trading his crops. Farming is a pretty easy problem to define: How do I get the most, best, or most marketable harvest while expending the fewest resources on land that I have access to? Beyond that, there are a million smaller questions that farmers ask that will influence the actual design of their work. Asking the right questions at the right time is critical to creating an effective process. In other words, it does no good to add more fertilizer if the problem is a plague of locusts.

Our widget maker also faces a basic problem: making a product that meets or creates a need that she can sell for more than it costs to make (with a bit of profit). Each process in her assembly line on the factory floor or at the job site may involve a complex series of steps, any one of which, improperly designed, can lead to failure of the product. In other words, it does no good to add yeast to a loaf that is already in the oven.

In the mid-nineteenth century the problem in education was that we were not producing nearly enough people with the knowledge and skills needed to fill the jobs created by the growing industrial economy. The response to this problem was a function of the social and economic environments of the time. Our education system was designed according to the prevailing Newtonian view, in which discrete objects of matter can be accurately categorized, measured, and controlled according to a clear set of defined laws. The system solved the problem, providing an explosion of opportunity and access unrivaled in the history of humankind. The assembly-line educational system was never perfect, but it met the needs better than any other system of education that preceded it.

Efficiency

A well-engineered process is efficient. A process that uses fewer resources is a better process than one that uses more resources to produce the same outcome. The farmer's desired outcome is to produce the largest consumable crop possible with the least application of resources. The farmer considers the amount and type of seed to use, the application of fertilizers, the use of labor or labor-saving mechanical equipment, the season of planting, and irrigation practices. The farmer may choose to grow a more resource-intensive crop, but only if the resulting yield is somehow "better" than the crop that needs fewer resources. *Better* might mean more crop volume, a higher price at market, or improved nutritional value.

Our widget maker designs a process to build her widgets to a specification that makes them attractive to potential buyers. While the farmer gets help from nature, the widget maker may need to supply most or all of the basic materials and energy to drive the process. She calculates the amount of different materials; the type and amount of energy required to shape the materials; the application of skilled and unskilled labor; the location of the processing facility relative to the supply of materials, energy, and labor; and her market. The more efficient the process, the lower her unit cost per widget, and the more competitive her product is for her customers.

A critical and often overlooked measure of efficiency is the amount of *waste* or *drag* generated within the process. Almost all man-made systems generate waste. The formation of and need to eliminate waste at some point in the process reduces efficiency. In other words, waste takes away from profit. As we will note later, healthy ecosystems are generally waste-free, as a healthy, balanced ecosystem recycles waste.

Schools are often measured based on their efficiency: the number of students and quality of students, based on quasi-objective exams, who are eligible to move to the next grade and ultimately to graduation. A school that moves more students along this pathway with a given number of resources is considered "better" than a school that does "less" with those resources. We often overlook key variables in this calculation, of course—that is, the capabilities and internal resources of the students and families who compose a school community. Different schools have vastly different levels of built-in inefficiency, or drag. Public schools don't get to choose their students as private schools do. Virtual schools don't have the "drag" cost of a physical campus. Charter schools don't have the "drag" of the same level of regulation as noncharters. Schools in wealthy areas don't have the same "drag" of providing safety and social supports required by schools in poorer areas. In summary, efficiency is a messy, inaccurate, and often misleading way to measure schools, but we still try to do so.

Simplicity

A corollary of efficiency is *simplicity*. If the same product or service is generated with fewer parts, that process is more efficient, because fewer things can go wrong. If our farmer could farm a single crop on a single plot of land, planting and harvesting once a year with no reliance on chemicals and irrigation systems and crop rotations, he probably would. Our widget maker will work to minimize the steps on the assembly line or the number of moving pieces in the final machine, reducing the likelihood that something will go wrong in the manufacturing process. In a modern analogy, computer programmers will use the fewest number of coding commands that achieve the desired outcome. Simple solutions are more elegant than complex ones.

Early versions of the educational process were very simple and highly efficient, as they required relatively few resources. Mid-nineteenth-century education was a simple system of one-room schoolhouses and poorly trained teachers. With little bureaucracy and almost no hierarchy of oversight, the system was simple but not very productive in terms of the number of children who received anything more than the most basic education. Over time, the process has become vastly more productive but much more complicated. Many more students receive extensive education, but large bureaucracies with multiple layers of decision making and many competing stakeholders sap efficiency. Money is diverted to support the system outside of the direct educational experience. Decisions that move the process in one way are later changed to move it in another way, resulting in real wastes of time, money, and intellectual energy. Today, schools are expected to produce an entire life-support mechanism that extends well beyond learning basic academic knowledge. While the list varies by demographic, state mandate, and the public-private divide, schools are expected to provide academics, extracurricular outlets like sports and the arts, basic parenting skills, transportation, basic health care, food, law enforcement, social welfare support, psychological services, language translation, and a clean, safe, physical environment. In other words, what was conceived and designed to be a simple system is now not simple at all.

Manage and Control

A well-engineered process is manageable or controllable. The more control our farmer has over the key aspects of his crop process, the more predictable the outcome. If he is using a greenhouse, he can control essentially every element of the growing process: temperature, light, water, seed, soil, time, nutrients, and atmosphere. If he is growing crops in a field, he can only control or manage some of these. If he does not get enough rain, he can build an irrigation system. He can plant seeds that are attuned to the projected climate. If his soil is poor he can add fertilizer. In each of these he can manage or control the time, amount, and cost in order to meet his goals of a healthy and plentiful harvest. Our farmer also has control over a well-defined boundary. Farmers rarely harvest beyond a boundary line, because of ownership questions, of course, but also because of the need to control the cultivation process. Inside the boundary, he can control more aspects of the environment than if he were just to go spread seed out on the prairie and hope for the best. This is perhaps the fundamental difference between farmers and gatherers, and in almost every case, farmers realize a higher yield per unit of resource than do gatherers.

For our widget maker, a miss of a tiny fraction of a percent in key ingredients, or a speck of dust in the clean room, turns a high-priced computer chip into a useless wafer of junk. The entire process—design, selection of materials, the skill set of the workers, and quality inspection of the final product—is geared around control and effective management. The ability to control the entire process depends on the ability to control a physical boundary, like that containing a factory, including security, cleanliness, continuity of energy supply, and the like.

Public education is controlled by government through a vast array of laws, codes, oversight, assessment, and the power of the purse.

Education has become increasingly controlled over the last century. Public education is controlled by government through a vast array of laws, codes, oversight, assessment, and the power of the purse. Many groups with specific political, social, governmental, ethnic, and economic agendas work to influence resource allocation. They frequently disagree about how to apportion money, power, and autonomy. Ultimately it is up to a combination of federal, state, and local governing bodies to decide how, when, where, and why to apply controls.

The boundary of the process of education is both tight and protected. Students are required to attend school for a prescribed number of years; schools are open for a fixed number of days each year; and governments in faraway places dictate much of the subject material. The obstacles to competition have been high in the past, though competitive alternatives like charter and online schools are now starting to tear significant holes in these boundaries. Private and charter schools are less regulated by government, so the systems of control tend to be internal rather than external. These schools can change or experiment with their programs, and they largely control where and how to allocate their resources. Private and charter schools are limited by their ability to attract and retain customers, without whom they would be out of business. Even the physical boundaries of most schools are increasingly rigid and highly controlled, as we deal with legitimate concerns about student safety and security. Like a well-controlled factory, students at many schools enter in the morning through a wall, gate, fence, or door that clearly delineates the boundary between "school" and "world".

Measurement

An important aspect of control is the ability to measure or assess various stages of the process and the eventual outcome. Our farmer watches his crops grow and makes midseason corrections: more water, an application of fungicide, sending out the kids to weed the rows. He measures how much crop he harvests, and by adjusting variables and keeping track of the results, over time he or his successors will develop a process that optimizes their results based on objective measurement.

Our widget maker may measure environmental controls to make sure the plastic is the exact right temperature and composition before it is molded. She may have inspectors check the quality of the welds before the next panel is added. She will take a sample of the millions of ball bearings that roll out of the mill and do a statistical analysis that tells her whether most of the bearings are within the design specifications. If she wants to stay in business long, she will have a way of receiving both objective and subjective assessment back from her customers, and she will use those data to continuously refine her internal process and controls.

Both public and private education are heavily measured. Measurement systems have changed dramatically over time, and many educators believe this ongoing vacillation is one cause for the seeming inertia in the overall system. Standardized tests measure the amount and type of knowledge, and to some extent skill sets, that students have acquired and can exhibit on a test. These data are matched against standards of where students "should be" at various stages of the process. When students are deemed to have completed the education process at around age eighteen, various other measurements may be applied to see how well the system is working: graduation rates, standardized test results, college entrance statistics, or employment data.

In a rapidly changing world, measurement systems rapidly become obsolete.

The ability to accurately measure or assess the effectiveness of any system rests on what we are measuring *for*. In a rapidly changing world, measurement systems rapidly become obsolete. The data may be less relevant, or even irrelevant, to the fundamental problem that the process is designed to solve. If, for example, our farmer has been growing lettuce using pesticides, and now the market demand is only for organic lettuce, it does not matter how much nonorganic lettuce he grows; his measurement of yield in terms of heads of lettuce per acre is no longer relevant. The relevant measure is "heads of *organic* lettuce per acre," which means he has to design a way to measure the "organic-ness" of lettuce.

Education is now at that point where we are spending more time assessing (via standards and standardized tests) for a product that is increasingly outdated. Most educators agree that we should be teaching skills that our students will need to succeed in this more unknowable future, yet measurements are still largely stuck in testing mastery of content. The Common Core standards seek to change this, but it very much remains to be seen whether this new set of standards is a step in the right direction; if so, whether it is a big enough step; and whether measurement of any fixed set of standards is merely the same stale loaf in a new wrapper.

Scalability

A well-designed process is scalable, and almost always starts small, with the ability to grow into production mode when we are confident with the results of pilots and tests. Our farmer sets aside a few acres to try a new seed strain or a new pesticide. He borrows, rents, or leases a new combine or thresher before making a huge capital investment. He learns to farm on ten acres before he takes on a thousand acres. Our widget maker may design and build a whole series of models, some of which work well, others that completely fail, and still others that fall somewhere in between. She knows that all the parts as individual elements may actually perform as they should, but it is not until you put them all together, and until the process of actually putting them all together works, that you know whether the process succeeds. In order to reduce her risk in time, money, and other resources, the widget maker starts small and then scales up.

Our education system did not arise fully developed; it has been through a continuous process of slow change for more than 150 years and in some ways for thousands of years. Pilot projects, lab schools, spin-offs, tests of new curriculum—these are vibrant and ever-changing aspects of the education landscape. New ideas develop, make their way through a subset of the system, are measured and retooled; then some are widely adopted, while others fall by the wayside for any combination of reasons. A few, usually dictated by large government-led decisions that span many years, are scaled up to become widely adopted steps in the overall educational process.

Many participants are involved in the process of modeling and growing educational ideas to scale. These constituents frequently disagree, so the time required to go from small to large scale can be extremely long. Large schools and school systems are very slow to change, as the process must proceed through the model and scaling stages. If the rate of change in the world is increasing, then the problem statement we are solving for is also changing at an increasing rate. The process and time requirements of scalability become a serious liability of the entire system.

Repeatability

A well-engineered process must be repeatable, or our farmer would eat well one year and starve the next. Our widget maker would quickly go broke if she invested in a process that fell apart after the first successful production run. For their work to be repeatable, both the farmer and the widget maker depend on two things: a process that lends itself to repetition and the ability to record and pass along knowledge about the process. The process cannot be highly dependent on one person or set of circumstances. If a crop grows only when annual rainfall exceeds the average by 50 percent, the number of years of successful harvest is, by definition, quite limited. If construction of an electronic device requires a rare component that is frequently out of supply, the process is impractical.

The institution of education has developed rigid sets of internal controls to ensure that the services it provides are predictable and repeatable. Many teachers teach largely the same material in the same way year after year. Content and expectations are standardized by age group and curriculum level. The process does not depend on an individual instructor or content delivery system. Yet repeatability is highly sensitive to the rate of change. When change occurs over a period of many years or decades, mechanisms for ensuring repeatability are easy to maintain. Teachers can be trained or retrained; new curricula undergo extensive longitudinal trials. But when the rate of change increases, as is now the case, the ability of the process to ensure repeatability becomes highly stressed. We do not have time for all that training and all those longitudinal studies before the target moves again.

Repeatable processes must be easily *explainable*. Our farmer may pass the practice of successful farming to his children through direct experience in the fields. Our widget maker may hire apprentices or interns who become fully embedded in the process only after they have shown a degree of expertise. In some cases, the children or apprentices may need to understand not only *how* the process works, but also more complex, abstract concepts such as *why* the process works the way it does, or what to do when things go wrong. Maps, organization charts, guide books, flowcharts, line diagrams, and a thousand other representations are essential to capturing and transferring the knowledge base that is critical to the system's sustainability. The assembly line does not depend on the designer to function; it is knowable to others who are tasked with its effective operation.

We have multiple blueprints for the modern process of education: state standards, shared textbooks, published curriculum units, degree training programs, cookie-cutter campuses, grades, divisions, subjects, and legal codes. These blueprints are not identical in every city and every school, but educators can move from state to state and even around the world and fit pretty well into a new school, a new organization, a new classroom. The similarities of public, private, faith-based, charter, choice, magnet, and virtual schools are vastly greater than their differences. All standards, including the Common Core, are an attempt to ensure this need for repeatability and explanation. Even if the standards are designed to shift the balance of learning from content to skills, wider use of common standards, by definition, increases the degree to which the system acts like an assembly line.

> *Even if the standards are designed to shift the balance of learning from content to skills, wider use of common standards, by definition, increases the degree to which the system acts like an assembly line.*

Upgradable

Even effective processes must be subject to intentional upgrades and revisions. Both our farmer and our widget maker are the inheritors of thousands of years of previous work, which included millions of tests, failures, revisions, and retrials. All systems are subject to externally imposed impacts: a new strain of pests, climate change, a new high-yield seed, a strong competitor, a better mouse trap, rising levels of education in Asia, new lawmakers in the state capital, mines in the Straits of Hormuz. A good process accommodates revisions either ahead of, or in reaction to, these changes, while retaining the repeatability that allows it to operate effectively with a minimum of disruption.

Schools suffer mightily from this tension between repeatability and the need to upgrade and revise. External forces require that schools change in order to prepare students for a world that is changing at an increasing rate. Yet schools are built around systems that have been massively repeatable and slow to revise in the past, with the forces of inertia almost always more powerful than the ability to change. When change *is* contemplated, it must be repeatable across large, complex, highly diverse systems, which makes change monolithic by definition. Unfortunately, our experience regarding successful innovation over hundreds of years tells us that monolithic, one-size-fits-all change is rarely successful.

> *Schools are built around systems that have been massively repeatable and slow to revise in the past, with the forces of inertia almost always more powerful than the ability to change.*

REFLECTION

Like the time before highways, the Internet, commuter airplanes, telephones, and fast food, it is hard for us to conceive of the time when the US school system was not a massively connected girdle that covered the social map. Yet the system we have today arose in just a few decades in the late nineteenth and early twentieth centuries, almost as quickly as Eisenhower built the transcontinental highway system.

We celebrate these leaps, these constructs that have brought the world to heel and helped us pursue our collective needs, wishes, and dreams. We are vastly better at building than at tearing down. Our predecessors similarly and rightly celebrated when they cleared forests, dammed rivers, mined coal, tilled land, pumped oil, and harvested the seas to build, light, warm, cool, and feed growing cities and towns with roads, schools, and families. But now we know that some of what we built in the past has outlived its useful life, has turned harmful, and we struggle to find the will to change, to tear down what does not work and build something better.

Our process of education is now failing in light of rising external demands that exceed the ability of the process to meet them. The key failure is that it is an engineered process and not another type of system that would be better suited to more effectively meet those rising external demands. Can we imagine a system that is more attuned to the changes in the world beyond school walls? Can we intentionally evolve a system over which we do not have ultimate control? I believe we can find the answer all around us in the natural world, as we will see in the next chapter.

CHAPTER THIRTEEN

A Better Model
The Natural Ecosystem of Learning

It is hard to find the good in West Texas, driving endless miles with nothing but long horizons on all points of the compass rose. Nothing lives on the brown expanse, nothing will grow here where the flats refuse to channel proper rivers and streams—nothing, that is, except mesquite trees with hundred-foot taproots and car-sized tumbleweeds that must steal moisture from wispy clouds that never seem to deliver even the promise of rain.

Small Last Picture Show *towns dot West Texas where rare temporary rivers flow in the late summer or even rarer springs pound crystal clear water to the surface from some ancient aquifer—dots here and there on a barren map where native Americans camped as they rotated through the endless llano, and later ranchers filled old tin troughs for herds of tough, stringy longhorns. A few lucky folks stumbled on thousand-acre tracts of no-good range that happened to sit atop reservoirs of sweet Cretaceous oil. Towns grew and busted with the oil fields, leaving behind burnt-out houses, wind-torn billboard signs, and rusted oil pumps frozen forever in the half-up position.*

And then there is the West Texas wind, a nasty, evil, constant wind that drives grit through every seal and filter, cold in the winter and a furnace in the summer. That wind has been here for millennia and is going nowhere soon, not like the water that comes and goes with drought and monsoon, or the oil that plays out in a generation or two. The wind is here to stay, and so now the West Texas horizon is broken by a growing crop of enormous windmills, a giant's orchard planted by the tough people of this tough land who know how to find promise when it would elude most of the rest of us, just like those thorny mesquite that send roots down, down, down until they find water to tap. Windmills are growing like weeds in West Texas, the perfect crop for this desolate ecosystem, plants that make money for the little towns and faraway investment partners for as long as the infernal wind continues to blow across the plains.

Natural Ecosystems

An ecosystem is a community of organisms and the environment in which they live. An ecosystem is defined by its living (organic) and nonliving (inorganic) elements, and the relationships, functions, and processes that connect the elements in various ways. Unlike engineered processes, which are human-made constructs created and adapted over time to solve a problem, natural ecosystems evolve purely in response to a set of environmental conditions.

Schools that recognize the need to prepare their students for a changing world are knowingly or unknowingly in the process of converting from an engineered process to a model based on the laws that govern natural ecosystems.

The mission of education is to prepare our students for their future. That future now arrives at a rate that exceeds our ability to design responses through the relatively sluggish processes of social engineering. If we want our students to be effective in this rapidly changing environment, they need to become independent of a slowly evolving, externally driven design model. An ecosystem contains the set of life forms that can best exploit the current environmental conditions at a point in time and space, having followed a generally accepted set of guiding principles and physical laws, including Darwinian evolution, to arrive at that condition. Schools that recognize the need to prepare their students for a changing world are knowingly or unknowingly in the process of converting from an engineered process to a model based on the laws that govern natural ecosystems.

Evolution

The strongest and most unique process that takes place within a natural ecosystem is evolution. An engineered process can evolve only through redesign by an outside human element (although man-made, self-evolving systems rooted in some form of artificial intelligence will likely be familiar to us in the next decade or so). In a natural ecosystem, species evolve and adapt to meet the changing conditions of their environment. Sometimes the pace of change is overly swift for some elements of the ecosystem; then, certain species fail while others continue to thrive and still others fill the void. The introduction of nonnative plant species along waterways in the American Southeast resulted in replacement of some species by the kudzu plant, while other plants continue to thrive. The riparian ecosystems of those areas look quite different from their appearance fifty years ago, but they still exist as successfully functioning systems.

Sometimes, though, the pace of change or the degree of stress outstrips the ability of the ecosystem to evolve as a whole. Critical elements are lost, and entire ecosystems cease to exist in a familiar form. Sixty-five million years ago, the impact of a meteor near what is now the Yucatan Peninsula put so much dust into the atmosphere that species extinctions exceeded 85 percent worldwide, causing the catastrophic collapse of many global ecosystems. Similarly, during the ice ages, a drop in annual temperature and the development of massively thick ice sheets physically obliterated a number of ecosystems, while other systems became reestablished at more temperate latitudes.

In our current education system, change requires a complex combination of economic, political, social, and professional compromises that will always take a very long time and may well result in no change at all. As soon as we learn to use one technology, another better technology is available. As soon as one text is approved, some of the content is out of date. As soon as we decide that universal objective testing is the best method to ensure that no child is left behind, we recognize that universal objective testing drives test preparation that is antithetical to good learning. In an ecosystem model, schools will restructure to take advantage of evolutionary tendencies, not fight against them. Rigid, prolonged decision-making is replaced by real-time collaboration among faculty, staff, students, and the community, unencumbered by the mindset of traditional boundaries. People and ideas that enhance learning of critical skills receive more resources, while ideas, people, and structures that resist these changes are either gradually or radically eliminated. Entire schools and school systems that fail to provide learning needed for the future success of their students are subjected to Darwinian deselection as consumers leave these schools to seek alternatives.

Diversity

Diversity is a measure of how many different elements are present in a system, regardless of the population or amount of each element. Coral reefs and rain forests are the two most diverse ecosystems on the planet. One reason for this diversity of species is that these ecosystems also have a high degree of inorganic and topographic diversity. Coral reefs are most robust in areas where ocean currents and the seafloor combine to produce high levels of both nutrients and sunlight that support the bottom of the food chain. Rain forests prosper where water is abundant and in soils where nutrients can be recycled throughout the system. In both reefs and rain forests, the structure of the biosphere itself provides many physical opportunities for species to evolve in specialized niches, resulting in a high level of biodiversity. At the opposite end of the spectrum, ecosystems that exhibit low levels of diversity, like a desert or a deep cave, have fewer of the elements required to support a complex ecosystem. Such ecosystems are not necessarily less healthy, but because they are far less diverse, their health is more fragile.

As educators, we understand that a broad distribution of viewpoints and attitudes provides a more complete education than a narrow range of exposure; breadth is more representative of what our students will face in the real world. Ensuring that school communities are integrated along racial, ethnic, cultural, socioeconomic, and gender lines helps to provide this diversity. Educational ecosystems are also healthier if they include and embrace a diversity of ideas and approaches to the process of education. Monocultures can lead to environmental malaise.

Diversity is as important to our schools as to a pond or a forest. Schools that have a monoculture of learning, where everyone is doing the same thing and there are few test projects in the pipeline, are particularly susceptible to changes in the external environment. Systems that exhibit multilevel diversity are more adaptable to environmental change and are more resilient in the face of stressors like decreased funding, rapid evolution of technology, changing

Just as a healthy ecosystem has a store of diverse DNA to draw upon in times of environmental stress, schools that support a diversity of ideas and approaches have a store of options that can be put into use quickly when challenges arise.

needs of employers, and changing demographics. Just as a healthy ecosystem has a store of diverse DNA to draw upon in times of environmental stress, schools that support a diversity of ideas and approaches have a store of options that can be put into use quickly when challenges arise. Schools with this kind of diversity have pilot projects in development at all times, ready to bring to scale. Such schools are testing options for programmatic mutations, similar to the genetic mutations that occur in nature. Some ideas die out; they are not suited for the environment. Others are ready at the right time, and they succeed quickly and may even take over as a new learning tool, like 1:1 wireless computing, design thinking, online courses, project-based learning, differentiated instruction, expeditionary learning, or flipped classrooms.

Interconnectedness

Ecosystems are characterized by the degree to which the various living and nonliving elements are interconnected. Most ecosystems have a food web that starts with the conversion of sunlight, water, and carbon dioxide into plant growth and the upward transfer of those elements through the system as animals eat plants and then are themselves eaten by other animals. The food web is one example of interconnectedness, but there are many others. Most ecosystems include complex relationships among nutrients, fluids, gases, and many different competing and mutually supporting animals and plants. These relationships are not simple and linear. They are often multilateral and multidirectional. Some relationships are symbiotic, where two species are completely dependent on each other.

The engineered process of education has created largely one-way relationships. External bureaucracies set high-level policy that is handed to administrators; administrators oversee implementation of policy at their respective sites; teachers deliver material to students; students absorb the material and regurgitate it, demonstrating that they have retained knowledge. In contrast, the ecosystem model embraces web-like connectedness of people and ideas. Traditional organizational charts that promote largely vertical hierarchies of authority and responsibility are morphed to promote much more frequent interdepartmental and inter-scholastic collaboration. Distributed authority promotes faster and more nimble experimentation with new ideas, recovery from failure, and direction of resources to places where ideas are percolating most quickly and away from areas of stasis. The student-teacher relationship becomes increasingly bidirectional, as teachers recognize their role as lead learner or co-learner in a fluid learning environment. Students and teachers at con-

Students and teachers at connected schools share common learning opportunities in a rewarding web of idea creation, development, and distribution.

nected schools share common learning opportunities in a rewarding web of idea creation, development, and distribution, in which students have the opportunity also to teach, and teachers have the opportunity also to learn.

Resilience

When stress does occur, some ecosystems are resilient, while others are fragile. Generally, the healthier, more diverse, and more adaptive an ecosystem is, the more resilient it is to an induced change. Longer warm seasons in the mountains of the southwestern United States are stressing pine forests by extending the life cycle and lowering the mortality of pests that damage or kill the trees. The forests are fragile since they are not healthy. In a relatively short period of time, areas that are now forest ecosystems will become grasslands.

Diversity increases resiliency, as the loss of one species may not cause the loss of all species. If, however, the species that is lost is a critical link in the web of relationships that defines the ecosystem, this loss may indeed signal the collapse of the system. This is the effect we see today in tropical reef systems, where relatively slight increases in ocean temperatures threaten some of the coral species that build the reef itself. In that case, an ecosystem that has been spectacularly successful for tens of millions of years by exhibiting a high degree of resiliency is threatened by collapse of one critical element of the system.

An ecosystem that adapts is always stronger relative to the prevailing environment than one that does not. Schools that are structured to adapt rather than structured to solve a particular problem will be more resilient to unforeseen changes in the environment. Schools that encourage distributed authority, development of "skunk works" pilot labs, and coffee shop–style professional collaborative networks provide integrated regenerative capacity to the system. Once these functions are embedded, they become part of the culture of the school and support natural, ongoing adaptations. The school is not reliant on external direction or the ideas and charisma of one senior leader who may leave in a year to meet new challenges; that resilience is self-contained and self-generating.

Permeability

Ecosystem boundaries tend to be very different from those that are typical of a human-designed process. A few ecosystems are defined by a relatively clear boundary, like the edge of a pond. More frequently, both living and nonliving parts of an ecosystem fade out at the edges. The population of a species decreases, the soil gradually changes in response to the underlying geology, or the average water or air temperature changes enough that the species of one system merge with those of an adjacent ecosystem. We can say that the boundaries of ecosystems are sometimes *flexible* (they change in time and space, though the ecosystem itself is unaffected); they are often *permeable* (species penetrate or share ecosystems that may not be their home base); and they are *unintentional* (they are defined purely by underlying conditions).

The boundaries of our educational system are undergoing a radical shift that cannot be accommodated within the current model. Until very recently, the boundaries of K–12 education were highly impermeable, largely described by single teachers in physical classrooms situated within physical schools transmitting knowledge captured in printed books. From time to time we could include within this boundary an outside lecturer or a daylong field trip. Parents and grandparents contributed knowledge when asked to help with homework or volunteer in the classroom.

Trying to restrain education within the traditional boundaries is like forcing black bears to forage in Manhattan.

With the development of the Internet and relatively cheap mobile computing devices, enormous holes have been torn in those impermeable boundaries. Trying to restrain education within the traditional boundaries is like forcing black bears to forage in Manhattan. Schools are becoming open, connected, flexible learning nodes, physical or virtual spaces within which knowledge is accessed, shared, managed, and created. Students and teachers collaborate with each other seamlessly, creating and sharing knowledge that transcends the bounds of traditional student-teacher and student-student relationships. Students and teachers can communicate with a limitless number of colleagues across a vast and increasingly efficient global neural network, what I have dubbed the *cognitosphere*, obliterating the traditional restrictions within four-dimensional space and time.

Schools increasingly insert students into the community outside the physical school walls. As noted in chapter 8, school has become "a place we meet, not where we necessarily learn." Magnet and charter schools draw students outside of their home neighborhoods; home-schooled children may never go to a central school meeting place; expeditionary schools home-base in a traditional school building but spend a large percentage of time off campus, using the nearby community as a real-world classroom; blended and hybrid schools meld a physical school with online learning and day care. Each of these developing, adapting learning nodes is a subset of the learning ecosystem, just as every pond is a subset of the global hydrosphere.

Free Flow of Energy and Resources

Ecosystems use and distribute energy and other resources in ways that maximize efficiency and minimize waste. Energy is consumed at each step, first in the creation of plant material and later by each consumer that lives off the lower level of the food web. In contrast, nutrients are free to flow in all directions throughout the ecosystem. Nutrients are consumed, passed along, and recycled by scavengers and decomposing organisms. Some are retained by the system, while others are transferred out of that system but are available to other ecosystems, like dead marine life that falls from the shallow, sunlit surface to be recycled by bottom-dwelling denizens of the dark, cold ocean depths.

The primary resources that nourish the educational system are money, people, knowledge, and time. As we understand the limitations of the assembly-line system, end users increasingly demand more direct control over the use and distribution of resources, as viewed through the lens of their individual self-interest. Private schools, charter schools, and online education are "species" that attempt to localize and customize decisions about the allocation of these resources. Students and teachers access knowledge resources where and when they want, both on and off campus. Decisions are increasingly made at the level of single classrooms, between individual students and their teachers, or by students themselves with little or no direction from an adult. Courses are offered for different lengths of time and at different points in the year; students might take a trimester off of their traditional school to work at an internship or in a design studio; summers are commingled with the normal autumn-to-spring schedule to capture opportunities for innovative course design; online courses free up student schedules during the day. Significantly, unlike traditional schools with their repetitive, unidirectional flow of resources, these ecosystem-like resource relationships are flexible over time. They move with and support, rather than inhibit, rapid evolution and change. If we think of resources in a traditional school flowing along the largely orthogonal lines of the organizational chart, we can think of resources in a school eco-system moving more like spices in a constantly stirred pot of savory stew.

Building Structures

Organisms build structures that are reflected in the ecosystem's success. Natural systems build these structures for themselves, in contrast to engineered systems, which are designed and built by someone outside the system. Think, for example, of the coral reef or the rain forest. The elegant process of photosynthesis results in plant structures of myriad shape and form. Those structures provide growth niches and habitat as well as food for other plants and animals. Structures as humble as a flat, smelly algal mat in a marsh are critical to the success of multiple species in the ecosystem.

The main structures within the factory model of education are classes, subject-grouped or grade-level departments, divisions (elementary school, middle or junior high school, and high school), schools, and districts. Decision making, resource distribution, and collaboration take place largely within these structures, as they have been designed and maintained for that very purpose. This built-in mechanism perpetuates change-resistant silos of interest. In the ecosystem model, structures evolve to meet changing needs based on shared

In the ecosystem model, structures evolve to meet changing needs. Groups and processes form, dissolve, and re-form in order to imagine, test, develop, implement, and sometimes kill off new ways of learning.

interests and the success of the overall ecosystem. Groups and processes form, dissolve, and re-form in order to imagine, test, develop, implement, and sometimes kill off new ways of learning. These structures have defined authority that is recognized throughout the school system, and that authority ebbs and flows with the changing needs of the entire school community. Group structures are fluid, drawing people in based on particular strengths that are needed to adapt, not based on seniority or positional authority. Groups and committees devolve and disband as needs pass. Distributed connectivity among an amorphous set of knowledge-based networks where ideas are developed and exchanged becomes the critical structure for the health and success of an adaptive organization.

Is Your School an Ecosystem?

Does the foregoing discussion mean that we have no control over the direction of schools? Does it mean that natural systems disallow human design and impact? No! We humans are very much part of the ecosystem, the apex species, and our ability to imagine, think, plan, design, and build are utterly critical to the success of the system. Engineers are not excluded from successful natural ecosystems; they are embraced within them. We merely have to recognize that ecosystems follow a set of laws over which we, the human inhabitants, have limited control. We do not get to select these laws any more than we get to decide whether gravity or thermodynamics should or should not apply in the natural world around us. We must simply understand how systems work, see which models fit best, and then design our systems to take advantage of these natural strengths and weaknesses. Based on our understanding of ecosystems, the following questions can help drive an understanding of a school's organizational ability to make this fundamental shift:

• Who or what brings resources into the school and ensures that they are distributed in ways that maximize the health of the overall school system? Is this the role of just one top-level administrator, or will resources be better applied if a group is responsible for ensuring they are distributed in ways that support the success of the entire system?

• How does your school develop and maintain diversity of individuals and groups (species) within the system? What are the types of diversity that are critical to the health of a school, and how are those decisions made? Is diversity narrowly defined by race, gender, or ethnicity, or does it include point of view, talents, and passions?

• Who ensures or oversees evolution in response to environmental change? How does the school monitor the external environment to promote proactive, not reactive, response to change? Is adaptability deeply embedded in the responsibilities of many people or narrowly reserved for a few?

• How does the school maximize connections with other schools, people, and knowledge systems, to ensure and enhance permeable boundaries? What incentives are in place to increase the flow of knowledge in and out of the school?

• Does the school create the time, place, and resources for all individuals to safely, vigorously grow and interact with others? How are these responsibilities the same and different for students and adults?

• Are there mechanisms in place to monitor the evolution, and sometimes extinction, of jobs, roles, departments, classes, subject areas, programs, events, traditions, or budget items?

• Is waste (both physical and programmatic) recycled into useful products or eliminated from the system when recycling is impossible? Does the school look at sustainability from both the environmental and operational points of view? Are people, programs, and events retired if they expend more resources than the value they return?

An ecosystem that continuously adapts to external stresses with smaller, nimble adjustments will be more stable in the long term. The ecosystem will be more productive as highly impermeable physical boundaries, rigid controls, and "knowledge tariffs" break down and individual students and teachers develop productive ideas into fully functioning processes. The ecosystem will evolve organizational structures that are more attuned to innovation through distributed leadership and decreasing rigidity of the learning model. Knowledge and time will differentially flow where they are needed by each individual learner rather than by the homogenized needs of the student and staff population as a whole. Preparation for the future is utterly woven into the capabilities of the ecosystem itself. It cannot be outpaced by a near or far future that includes completely unknown variables; the system adapts to meet those environmental challenges.

> *Preparation for the future is utterly woven into the system itself. It cannot be outpaced by a near or far future that includes completely unknown variables.*

Exemplars

Throughout this book I have referenced schools I visited that I believe can provide examples of a transformed learning experience. In this section I have synthesized the empirical evidence from many such schools into a holistic model of evolving best practices. Since the end of my trip I have been asked many times, "Which school is the most innovative? Which should be our model? Who is doing it all?"

I hope the reader will look to the many specific examples I have cited in previous chapters (and very possibly to a school across town that I did not visit!). I also hope that the many schools I did and did not visit that are piloting marvelous programs will not take offense if I try to answer that question.

Three public and two private schools that I visited stand out as examples of schools that have adopted many attributes of the evolving learning ecosystem discussed in this chapter. There are many other outstanding examples that I did not visit.

- Science Leadership Academy (SLA) in Philadelphia may be the iconic high school in the United States today. The school has an extraordinary ethos of entrepreneurialism and innovation focused on student-centered learning. The students and teachers maximize resources despite a lousy physical environment and disastrously low levels of public funding. They thrive on "quirky" thinking, and are willing to test and fail rapidly. If we could replicate SLA in every community across the country (and there is no fundamental reason we cannot), the future of our system of education, and indeed the future for our students, would look bright indeed.
- From the board of trustees to the youngest student, Mount Vernon Presbyterian School in Atlanta is breaking entirely new ground when it comes to understanding and systemically mapping everything they do to a forward-looking, unbounded, open-to-the-unknown future. Their ability as an organization to imagine, shift, test, analyze, adjust, and try again—all while keeping a strong eye on traditional, strong academics outcomes across grade levels—is remarkable. They combine the data gathering, analysis, and design of great engineering with the fluid dynamism and adaptability of a thriving natural ecosystem.

• Design 39 Campus in Poway has yet to open its doors, but when it does, I believe the full support of a large public district will ensure the success of the school's vision of an evolving, differentiated learning pathway for each student. The model represents a fundamental shift in resource flow and relationships, away from an industrial one-size-fits-all model to a customized web of student-centered support. The school's self-evolving governance system scales the strengths of private and charter schools into a large, diverse public school environment.

• Presbyterian Day School in Memphis has developed a complete cultural comfort with educational entrepreneurialism. Supported by leadership that does not just allow but expects teachers to try, fail, succeed, learn, and then do it all over again, educators at the school have built a differentiated learning system that is ready to go to scale. The adults and students at the school are completely comfortable in a frequently changing environment that seeks to adapt to external changes, not buffer against them.

• The unique governance structure upon which the public Denver Green School (DGS) is built would make it an exemplar, even if the academic program were not also a model of ecosystem learning. DGS has created a system of distributed leadership among the adults and students that amplifies nimble decision making and promotes all members of the community as educational leaders. Teachers focus on their own professional growth and that of their colleagues; students contribute to the main learning themes in an interdisciplinary environment that celebrates a true diversity of perspective and thinking; the boundaries between "school" and "community" are increasingly blurred. By empowering many leaders, the school serves as an incubator for those leaders to grow, develop, and then go out and leverage their knowledge across other learning environments.

I don't mean to say that these schools are "better" than many others that I visited or did not visit. I do believe these schools are great exemplars, as are all the other schools I have cited in this book. Will they continue on their paths when charismatic leaders depart? If market conditions change? If strong public stakeholders weigh in for or against the paths the schools are creating? Time will tell.

A Fundamental Change

I don't believe we can tweak the industrial age model at the margin and meet our current and future goals in education for three reasons. First, current social and economic conditions require students to learn a set of skills (we sometimes refer to these as twenty-first-century skills or "21C skills") that exceed mere command of a specific knowledge base. If formal education pathways are not reformatted to include a heavy focus on these skills, students will go elsewhere to acquire them, leading to systemic irrelevancy.

Second, while formulaic approaches to teaching these "21C skills" are valuable in starting to break the industrial model of learning, those same formulaic approaches are, by definition, a continuation of the industrial model. We have recognized for decades that skills like collaboration, creativity, and effective communication are key for success in the information age, and yet it has taken decades to even *begin* to prioritize these key drivers in our learning experience. These are the skills that are needed for the present and the "near past," but there is no guarantee that they are the skills needed for the unknowable future.

Third, the rate of change in the world has increased to the point that we will never again have the luxury of centuries or decades, or perhaps even years, to recognize, design, develop, test, and deploy new lessons for our students. Interconnectivity is increasing knowledge development and transfer at a rate that is vastly faster and more efficient than our ability to keep up with it.

There are only two logical outcomes. One is that the system fails to meet its own core mission of preparing students for the future at a time when the "unknown" is much closer to us than it was in the past. Failure is possible, in which case the system will become extinct and will be replaced by something completely new and different.

> *Self-evolution is the mechanism that best prepares for future ambiguity and unknowns, not for the present or the "near past."*

The second is that the system regenerates around the paradigm of self-evolution, both for students and for the system itself. Self-evolution is the mechanism that best prepares for future ambiguity and unknowns, not for the present or the "near past." Self-evolving learners and school ecosystems will respond to environmental stresses, rapidly test alternative success strategies, and embrace healthy and favorable adaptations.

Education has begun to adopt tactical, perhaps even strategic, responses to the changed environment. Many are Newtonian responses: reaction to an applied force. These have been great first steps (better than ignoring reality and not reacting at all), but tactics and strategies from within the existing framework will not succeed if the framework is truly mutating.

REFLECTION

The first time I saw the word *ecosystem* used to describe a process of learning more attuned to the future needs of our students was in Thomas and Seeley Brown's book *A New Culture of Learning* (2011). The word resonated with me; I have utterly adopted the authors' metaphor of the teacher as a farmer who sets out the boundary fences of inquiry for her students and allows them to evolve as learners within those fences. Teacher as farmer is a more accurate description of the future than "guide on the side"; a farmer is not on the "side" of anything. The farmer-teacher is a part of the ecosystem, the resource that sets the boundary fence, breaks through some of the hard topsoil, ensures plenty of water and sunlight, helps keep the weeds down, and does some judicious pruning and training of her germinating seedlings.

I see the word *ecosystem* used freely now, perhaps too freely, to describe makerspaces, incubators, design labs, digital collaborations, professional learning networks, and more. But mere use of the term does not make a system "eco." True ecosystems share one critically important attribute: Ecosystems are not designed by humans. Instead, humans exist within ecosystems. In my view, great learning and education do not "act like an ecosystem." Great education *is* an ecosystem. There is a big difference.

Why split this hair? Because the most important element of a natural ecosystem, the function that no engineered system yet developed has been able to copy, is also the outcome we most want for our students. *Ecosystems are self-evolving.* They don't need external designers to make them better; they get better, more well adapted to changing external conditions, all on their own. We, the people in the ecosystem, can help or hinder that process, but we are *in* the process, not the external determiners of the process.

Of all the things we say we want for our students in order for them to be successful and happy living in a rapidly changing world, the one that is most important is that they become *self-evolving learners*. They will only learn how to do that if they spend time in a self-evolving learning ecosystem, one in which they and their teachers and parents and the community coexist, subject to the governing laws of ecosystems. This will be a big leap for schools, and bigger for large complex districts than for small, nimble organizations. How the heck do we make that leap? How do schools, like some of those I visited, large and small, public and private, let go of their past reliance on an external designer? How do adults, who have spent their professional lives following a template handed to them, create their own templates? How can students and adults immerse themselves in a system that can both change quickly and preserve its essential and defining qualities? We find the answers in a different way of thinking and planning the future of our schools, which is the subject of the next chapter.

CHAPTER FOURTEEN

Taking Action
A New Paradigm of School Strategy

Left Denver in heavy rain, making time on I-70 East just shy of the Kansas border. Every warning light explodes in neon green on the dashboard of my Prius. Slow down and hug the side of the highway. Bad luck; this section of the highway is under construction so there is no shoulder. Big rigs blowing by with a foot or two to spare kick up a gritty mist. Next town: Goodland, Kansas. One mechanic, pull in, lots of big diesels, tractors, nice folks, but no one in the good town of Goodland knows much about Left Coast hippie hybrids. Scan the engine computer. Call the Toyota dealer in Denver. Something about an inverter and cooling. Recommends I "get it to a dealer." Gee, thanks; nearest dealer is two hundred miles in exactly the wrong direction. Reset the warning lights. Back out on I-70. Twenty miles later, car starts shuddering. Blown back right tire. Picked up a nail at that garage in Goodland. Cold, windy, spitting rain. Nothing for miles but drought-stunted corn and mowed-under wheat. And this is only Day Five. I've visited four schools. Three months and sixty schools to go.

Stop and think; consider options. Still no shoulder on the highway. Put on the flashers and wait for help? No, going to be dark soon. Time to suck it up, get a little wet and dirty. Unpack the car onto the side of the road and put on the baby spare. Thankfully I'm travelling light and luckily it is the right tire and not the left as big-rigs whip by. Thank God for smartphones; garage sells tires ten miles back in a one stop-sign town that could have served as the set for a bad zombie movie after everyone has died. Tire can't be fixed. Buy a used one. Back out on the road. Only three hundred miles to Kansas City.

Fifty miles down the road, and all the warning lights flash back on. Slow down. Dark now, dark as only the plains can get dark on a cloudy night. Call the Toyota dealer in Hays, 120 miles east. Service department is closed. Sales guy says, "Keep going if you can," so I do. Thirty miles later, the car quietly glides to a stop like it just wants to lie down and sleep. Dashboard says the hybrid battery is drained. Can't see a single light either east or west. Call AAA, and between the two of us we figure out where I am, which is a long way from the nearest highway off-ramp, let alone the nearest town. Give thanks again for GPS and Google Maps, which I bet would have saved a few pioneers with broken wagons back in the day (and wondering whether wagons drawn by both mules and oxen were called "hybrids"). Tow truck is on the way. Shut off engine. Wait. Fifteen minutes later, on a whim, punch the start button and the battery starts flowing again. Call AAA back and put the tow truck on hold and continue east, hugging the shoulder, thirty-five miles per hour for two hours, flashers on. Lights of Hays in the distance are like the blessed rays of dawn. Comfort Inn. Will be at the Toyota dealer first thing. Rearranging meetings in Kansas City and hope this is fixed tomorrow. Bad day. Warm, dry place to sleep; could have been a lot worse.

New Paths to Strategy

Education is not broken, but it does need some major repair. The road ahead used to be fairly predictable. Education, both public and private, operated like a utility. Usage and operation each year was based on usage and operation the previous year, with maybe some new technology or a new metering system or a revised rate sheet thrown in. This is not a metaphor; it is an accurate description. The key driver of public schools is the stipend per pupil the school receives from the public coffers. Private schools are driven by admissions demand. Strategic planning has largely been an exercise of projecting attendance and funding levels, and tweaking what we have done in the classroom in the past to accommodate the customer supply, just as an electrical or water utility would do.

But the world is changing, and so is our vision of students prepared for that world. At nearly every one of the schools I visited on my journey, and at thousands more, educators, parents, and students recognize the significance of rapidly evolving external stresses. Some schools are still playing defense, tweaking the existing industrial age assembly-line model of education and relying on an outmoded model of strategic planning that bases future options largely on a framework of what has been done in the past. I propose that we need a different kind of forward-focused strategic thinking that builds foundations based on evolving future value, not on past successes and failures. Like any good thinking, this process will start with making sure we are asking the right questions and solving the right problems. We will cast off the outmoded notion that strategy is something undertaken by a committee once every few years, and begin to build comfort and capacity with a growth-based culture of imagining that continuously bubbles and percolates in, through, and around the whole school.

We need a different kind of forward-focused strategic thinking that builds foundations based on evolving future value, not on past successes and failures.

School strategy consultant Kevin Ruth (2011) believes, as I do, that most school strategic plans look and sound the same because

> the overwhelming majority followed some sort of template: "let's restate our mission, principles, a brief history, and our philosophy, and follow up that section with a verbose section of 'strategies,' 'goals,' or 'objectives.'" Template planning does one thing *really well*, however: it produces comprehensive and highly predictable "to-do lists." True innovation is rarely found there. (Ruth, 2011)

Ruth cites Richard Rumelt, who said in his book *Good Strategy Bad Strategy* (2011) that we should not reduce strategic thinking to an exercise in deductive reasoning:

> The problem with treating strategy as a [deductive] exercise is that systems of deduction and computation do not produce new interesting

> ideas, no matter how hard one winds the crank. [. . .] Treating strategy like a problem in deduction *assumes that anything worth knowing is already known*—that only computation is required. The presumption that all important knowledge is already known, or available through consultation with authorities, deadens innovation. (p. 244)

Strategy involves identifying and solving a set of problems, and as I wrote in my book *The Falconer*, the root of all problems is dissonance—

> the difference between the way something is and the way we want or expect it to be. Dissonance immediately leads to questioning: we ask "why," "why not," and "what if" . . . In all cases dissonance, the recognition that "I" have a problem, leads first to questioning and then to growth of knowledge or experience. The individual is directly, in some cases, passionately involved, self-interested in the outcome, in finding answers and more questions and more answers until the dissonance is reduced to an acceptable level. This is the true process of learning. It can be tumultuous, exciting, uplifting, rocky, enlightening, or all of them at once. (2008, p. 105)

It seems that the process of learning, developing, and amplifying organizational strategic capacity has a lot in common with great learning in our classrooms!

Operationalizing Innovation

Successful leaders develop an organizational ecosystem of fertile ground that can nurture ideas and opportunities as they arise. The organization must know, through clear communication from leadership, that value-generating innovation is critical to the mission of the school.

In an interview with Braden Kelley (2010), Rowan Gibson, author of *Innovation to the Core*, says that the biggest challenge facing organizations faced with rapid change is to make innovation a "deeply embedded capability." Schools believe they have always been stewpots of innovation, but it has been in highly siloed, unsustainable ways that fail to percolate throughout the organization. There is little true innovation infrastructure built into most school systems; when good ideas are born they often wither from a lack of supporting mechanisms and resources.

Gibson suggests that companies can operationalize innovation by developing the "demand side" of innovation, creating distinctive innovation managers, innovation space and time, assessment metrics, and the like. When schools put a demand for innovation into their organizational and operational structures, employees will embrace the opportunities, and the DNA will procreate. Gibson specifically calls out the list of essential capabilities he believes are missing from our educational system if we actually intend to "do" school differently in the future:

- Systematically discover new strategic insights
- Come up with radical new growth opportunities
- Recognize a really big idea
- Reallocate resources
- Foster cultural conditions inside an organization to motivate innovation

People like Bo Adams are designing ways to pull skills like this together to create new processes of community-wide strategic involvement. Writing in his blog *It's About Learning* (2013), Bo asked, for example:

> Wouldn't it be interesting to engage in a faculty exercise of recording ten expectations, one each on a Post-it note, and affinity mapping the commonality and differences among a school's tribe of practitioners? Shouldn't we have some level of agreement about the ten most fundamental expectations for schooling in our modern era? Do we? (Adams, 2013)

Over the past several years Bo and I (and many others around the country) have collaborated to think about how to move a school from theoretical deliberations about the essential qualities of a graduate to sustainable implementation of operational innovation. We have asked a thousand questions: How are we going to entrain these common understandings in our day-to-day interactions with students? How do we organize these learning goals into operational statements, and craft them into a series of institutional agreements and processes? How can all members of a school intentionally participate in a highly democratic, interactive, participatory crafting of the main drivers of a reimagined learning experience? We have collectively asked more questions that start with "What if" and "How might we?" than I can count.

Everything we know about the history of successful innovation screams that we must move from theory to action: imagining, designing, testing, piloting, failing, tweaking. And we have to do this in shorter time frames and on a more continuous basis than schools are used to or comfortable with. The process of planning every few years is flawed. Innovation is an ongoing process; it needs to become deeply embedded in our everyday DNA, and at multiple levels of institutional organization. We have to flatten organizational structures, distribute authority and responsibility for innovative thinking, and celebrate implementation on a scale that is radically different from our traditional planning and adoption processes.

Creating Value

Over the past twenty to thirty years schools and school districts recognized that they were complex organizations that needed to plan for the future, not just believe in it. Schools learned to do five-year "look-aheads" according to best practices. Kevin Hendry from the University of Queensland writes in his blog entry "Leading Strategic Conversations" (2012) that strategic planning is evolving in substantive ways that I think are highly relevant to school leadership. Both Hendry and Jim Collins, whom Hendry cites, argue that leadership is now less about the vision of a charismatic or revered individual raised up for others to emulate, and more about creating an ongoing dynamism in the organization for continuous self-evaluation and adaptation.

Strategy has to be linked not only with long-range planning for financial and organizational stability, but with creating value.

In the current fast-paced, fluid change environment, when families have multiple options for their children's education, strategy has to be linked not only with long-range planning for financial and organizational stability, but with *creating value*. This is not a new business concept, but it is one that many school leaders have yet to embrace. There are many definitions of an organization's value proposition. The one I like best for schools is this: *the difference between what you say you are going to do and what you actually do, as viewed through the eyes of your customer.* I have found that many schools, as organizations, are unsure of all three clauses of that definition, which makes value hard to enhance. Many of us think of innovation as the creation of new ideas, or the creation of good new ideas. Schools are full of both, which is a good thing, but that does not mean the school is capable of innovation. Innovation, simply, is implementation of ideas that generate enhanced value for the organization. Successfully innovating organizations sustainably create enhanced value in response to changing consumer demands. In highly collegial and democratic settings like schools, it can be uncomfortable to identify, filter, and support only those ideas that generate enhanced value, but that is what innovation demands. This synergy of value and innovation defines the new pathway of school strategic thinking.

Strategy has largely been the purview of senior leadership; leaders set the agenda and lower levels get it done. Value creation requires a vastly more integrated process of determination and implementation. By definition, all members of the organization (and in particular the front-line teachers) can deliver value.

All members of the organization (and in particular the front-line teachers) can deliver value.

All members of the organization will have much greater buy-in, and will exude that new value to a greater degree, if they are part of the process of actually defining what and how value is delivered in our schools.

We cannot imagine and enact institutional change using the same lenses, maps, and tools that we have in the past. We need to respond to the ideas and insights of thought leaders like Zuboff, Gorbis, and Bejan, described in chapter 11, along with many others. As just one example, Shoshana Zuboff's new genome for the era of distributed capitalism is based on a set of functions that successful institutions incorporate to dispassionately evaluate which assets of the existing framework have real value in a mutated landscape (Zuboff, 2010). The functions are:

- *Inversion:* Smart companies ask, "Who is our customer, what does each need, and how can we help?"—rather than "How can we sell you what we have in the past?" Families have increasing options for educating their children. Schools will leverage technology and focus on pedagogies that actually differentiate learning for individual students to meet the rising consumer demand for tailored services.
- *Rescue:* Value-rich core assets are rescued from a costly industry structure, while non-value-generating assets are discarded. Schools will increasingly focus on strengths that cannot be replicated by online or hybrid alternatives, focusing in particular on the personal relationships and social interactions that physical schools provide.
- *Bypass:* New content delivery systems bypass legacy overheads of the traditional systems. Pure knowledge content is increasingly accessible via digital technologies, which frees teachers and instructional resources to provide more authentic sequences of self-owned discovery, questioning, creativity, and synthesis.
- *Distribute:* Student learning is not concentrated in a physical or organizational space, but in individual space. Learning does not require a classroom as much as assets, activities, platforms, tools, and relationships that may be much more widely distributed, both physically and virtually.

Setting Innovation Horizons

Real innovation frequently gets stuck on the back burner as the adults at school are overwhelmed by the stress of day-to-day obligations. We need sustainable frameworks that will help weave innovation best practices into our cultural DNA. One such conceptual framework I have found, presented in a blog series by Paul Hobcraft (2010), is the Three Horizon model. I think it is a good one for school leaders to reflect and build on, a type of thought umbrella, under which the more comprehensive process of strategic thinking that I propose will flourish. Hobcraft's definitions of the three horizons are set in italics; the commentary is mine:

Horizon One represents the company's core businesses today. This first horizon involves implementing innovations that improve your current operations. Your aim is to keep extending and defending your core business and this is done more through an incremental approach to improve on your existing business. (Hobcraft, 2010)

Horizon One is the most familiar to schools; it is where we look for efficiency and improvement in our current core programs. These improvements are not disruptive and should translate directly to increased value as perceived by our families. The core value that brick-and-mortar schools provide is an ecosystem of powerful relationships between teachers and students that cannot be re-created in a virtual world. Educators who overlook this core value, who believe the quickest route to enhanced value lies in a new set of textbooks, a laptop program, or a new gymnasium, are mistaken and may be misspending valuable resources.

Ensuring that your school continues to provide core values requires that you live your vision statement in every classroom, every day. Schools that claim they want to teach each child as an individual must find ways to differentiate the learning program. Schools that tout leading-edge technology should ensure that investment in programs like 1:1 laptop initiatives actually change how students and teacher-learners access and process knowledge in the classroom. Schools that claim to emphasize creativity might get rid of hard-copy texts and pay their own teachers to create curricula. Schools that value collaborative learning need to align their daily schedules so both students and teachers have time to engage in true intraschool and interschool collaborative learning opportunities.

Horizon Two includes the rising stars of the company that will, over time, become new core businesses. These businesses may be step-outs from the core or related extensions that simply require new capabilities and time to build. This is where you often face that point of disruption, that famous innovator's dilemma described by Clayton Christensen. It is a view of the things that are beginning to change, to threaten what you have as a core. It is the place where those disruptions can offer emerging new business that others will see, if you don't. (Hobcraft, 2010)

Knowledge-based organizations are deeply impacted by disruptions, and leaders have to create organizational structures that leverage Horizon

Two opportunities. In schools, many of these opportunities are related to technologies that change the foundational relationship among student, teacher, and knowledge on which our system of education has rested for hundreds, if not thousands, of years: virtual learning, hybrid courses, overseas campuses, open-source collaborations, partnerships with companies and nonprofit organizations in the community.

These opportunities offer the potential to create added value, but that value creation comes with some real risk. Implementation requires that schools get outside of their traditional methods of program development and decision making. These opportunities require rapid prototyping, acceptance of risk and rewards for risk takers, decentralized decision making, networked and cooperative program development, and often uncomfortable revisions to the traditional boundaries of time, space, subject, and age.

> **Horizon Three** consists of nascent business ideas and opportunities that could be future growth engines. Horizon Three innovations are the ones that will change the nature of your industry. It is where there are real possibilities of completely new ways of doing things . . . where the mindset has to be more fluid and adaptable. Often there may be no right or wrong to these different views and often they simply cannot be grounded in "hard" evidence but clear scenarios that embrace these different perspectives need broad discussion and eventually emerging consensus of where to explore and not. (Hobcraft, 2010)

This is the realm of the future of education—the mutations that Zuboff describes, the emerging growth of Gorbis's socialstructed relationships. The third horizon is where we contemplate a future that may look vastly different from anything we now call a school. This is the realm of "what if" scenarios, where we reimagine and redesign the alignment of vision and resources in ways that are significantly different from today. Even discussing this horizon is very uncomfortable for many educators and school organizations. They see it as a threat much more than an opportunity to grow and evolve. Yet history is clear: Institutions, no matter how strong, are not immune from these mutations. As I wrote in *Independent School Magazine* in 2014:

> For some, these challenges to fundamental traditions and structures will seem unnecessary or perhaps even dangerous. The resistance

sounds like this: "Why can't we just tweak what we have successfully done for years, decades, or centuries? We have always had schools; they are not going to disappear. Our value is too great to lose." But that is what the leaders of General Motors and many other strong, iconic organizations said . . . almost up until the moment they filed for bankruptcy. (p. 46)

How do we grasp this task? Whose job is it to reimagine the nature of things like time, space, and basic pedagogy in schools? Where do we start to look? Our normal reaction is to look away from this horizon or hope that it stays way off in the distance. Like the very real threat of global warming, these issues and opportunities are just too big and scary relative to the burdens of daily life. Unfortunately, that reaction flies in the face of reality. Horizon Three exists whether we like it or not. The great news is that organizations that grab these opportunities will be the educational leaders, the great schools of tomorrow.

> *Organizations that grab these opportunities will be the educational leaders, the great schools of tomorrow.*

Zero-Based Strategic Thinking

Is the task too great? Will it overwhelm us as we also conduct the daily business of school? I don't think so. While we see increasing evidence of market change, disruption, and even mutation in education, there is still time for effective educational leaders to leverage core values and sustain the broad outlines of the entity "school," albeit with significant programmatic evolution. To do so, schools need to do two things. First, they must adopt many of the successful *operating tactics* that successfully innovating schools and other organizations have embraced, as I have described in this book, and that are available all around us. Second, educators need to embrace a new value-centered and

> *Zero-based approaches start with justifying every aspect of the system from the ground up; there are no legacy assumptions just because something worked well in the past.*

vision-driven *zero-based strategic thinking model* (the name first popped up at a New York State Association of Independent Schools workshop in 2013) that can lead to fundamental changes in our learning model.

Zero-based approaches start with justifying every aspect of the system from the ground up; there are no legacy assumptions just because something worked well in the past. Rather than stopping our work to reflect and define our goals once every three to five years, this kind of thinking is ongoing as the school community develops the tools for and comfort with questioning, prodding, discussing, and evolving strategy. Rather than one huge bite every half decade, strategic thinking becomes a constant process of frequent little bites and lots of chewing. Rather than allocating the responsibility for strategic *planning* to a relatively small committee, we build and nurture increased capacity for organization-wide strategic *thinking, learning, and growing*.

Does this approach mean schools should discard a formal planning process? No. It means that schools must challenge what they do and how they do it at a very fundamental level, with a clear recognition of the external challenges they face and with no guarantee that "school" of the past is a clear indicator of what "school" will be in the future. This process starts with a set of three questions that I believe most succinctly link a school's vision to a sustainable value proposition:

- Does your school have a forward-leaning vision of students as self-evolving learners prepared to access, filter, consume, create, and manage knowledge in an ambiguous future?
- Has your school aligned available resources at the systems level to ensure learning-centered education in support of the vision?
- Are you effectively communicating the differentiated value your school offers to both the internal and external communities?

In my visits I found that schools that are committed to creating these three building blocks have a solid foundation upon which to construct a sustainable strategy that promotes innovation. Schools that lacked continuity or clarity about these three steps have not yet built a foundation able to sustain innovation.

In the current environment, traditional strategic planning processes embrace fatal flaws. Traditional processes often fail to ask open-ended questions that can expand the frame of future possibilities. Brainstorming sessions are based largely within a framework of what the school has done in the past and how that performance can be improved upon. A committee of stakeholder representatives then goes through a process of idea prioritization and consensus approval before mapping the results into a set of focus areas and goals. Rarely does a traditional strategic plan state that something from the past will be discarded.

Few members of the school community have any real connection to the school's strategic consciousness. They are asked to yield that responsibility to a representative of their silo group and then asked to validate the planning committee's results. Most members of the school community who are asked to implement strategy have little, if any, personal connection to an all-school vision or the plan they are supposed to support. Strategic thinking is viewed as the job of a senior leadership team, when in fact it should be the job of everyone in the community.

The distributed model of organizational innovation demands that we shift this approach at all levels of the school. What does this shift look like? As Bo Adams and I presented at a conference in 2014, if we use the outmoded model of strategic decision making at schools as a baseline, the shift to more distributed, growth-focused, creative, and systemic thinking looks like this:

- *From brainstorming* within *the frame to questioning that* expands *the frame.* Traditional strategy sessions start with open brainstorming, with everyone free to contribute ideas. Since we are all captives of our experience, the pool of ideas reflects those experiences. To overcome this bias, effective thinking and problem solving starts with asking questions that expand potential options—questions like "What if . . . ? and "How might we . . . ?" In the zero-based model, we reduce the fallacy of deductive reasoning by testing all of our assumptions, including those that define the organization itself (Rumelt, 2011).

- *From coalescing ideas around what we* have *done, to building vision around what we* might *do.* In a traditional process, we take the product of our brainstorming and group the ideas together; we have already started to construct a perpetually self-reinforcing system based on what has been successful or comfortable in the past. In order to break out, to innovate, we need to mine the deep wishes, desires, and aspirations of the school community, what Bo Adams calls the unique *ethnography* of the school, to work toward a reimagined future.

• *From covering all the bases, to imagining what school looks like without "bases."* It is remarkable but not unexpected that many school strategic plans look the same; they cover the same bases because they arise from people looking at the future through a predictable set of lenses based on silos of stakeholder affiliation. When we change those lenses, we can ideate, imagine, find problems, and seek solutions by looking through a very different set of shared, organization-wide, vision-driven lenses such as purpose, pedagogy, leadership, curriculum, assessment, and professional growth.

• *From creating a comfortable action plan that angers no one, to designing systemic capability that amplifies innovation.* As I have said, schools are generally highly collegial organizations, and decisions tend to accommodate all viewpoints whenever possible. Strategic plans are notoriously inclusive, not unlike party political platforms, ensuring that all stakeholder interests receive equal weight. The zero-based model requires that we justify strategic decisions, not as stand-alone activities, but as part of a well-mapped system that aligns the resources of the school directly in support of a focused vision.

Schools using a zero-based approach will push themselves into thought-generating exercises that schools have not generally used in the past. Each school and district is unique in its specific challenges and opportunities; each will develop a customized set of probing questions that challenge the status quo, prompt an authentic reimagining of the future, and lead to concrete actions in response to that unique set of conditions. Rather than generating a guiding document once every five years, strategic

> *Schools using a zero-based approach will push themselves into thought-generating exercises that schools have not generally used in the past.*

discussions become the norm at faculty meetings, parent coffees, and administration roundtables and retreats. The community embraces an ongoing process of questioning, design, and implementation, which in turn builds *Since the process is driven by the community, each school's plans will be more unique, less of a cookie-cutter version of the previous plan or the plan of the district or school down the road.* ownership and community-wide support for outcomes.

What sorts of questions can we ask and what kind of self-assessment might a school undertake with this zero-based approach? How can your school begin to construct a new culture of building strategy in a learning-centered way rather than in terms of interest-based silos? Here are some ideas to get started:

- Ask questions that challenge, break, or discard the foundational concepts and traditions of "school," and test those against our best imagining of what the future might hold.
- Examine the geometry of the organizational chart to ensure that it promotes rather than inhibits innovative practices.
- Objectively review which school functions could be shifted to, or subsumed by, a lower-cost competitor.
- Develop a consensus profile of risks and rewards that allow change to occur more quickly and with community support.
- Test what educators at the school *really* know about the dreams and aspirations of their current and future clients, rather than assuming that families want to consume what the school has provided in the past.
- Map resources like time, space, curriculum, and personnel against key elements of the school's vision statement.
- Imagine alternative futures that include learning mechanisms and relationships dramatically different from those of today; look for signals that those futures may be in progress; and test ideas that amplify the school's ability to operate effectively in a range of those possible outcomes.

Since the process is driven by the community and participants are given the authority to think without preconditions, each school's plans will be more unique, less of a cookie-cutter version of the previous plan or the plan of the district or school down the road. A good zero-based strategic thinking process in schools will have at least five common elements:

• *The process is frequent and participatory.* Traditional five-year strategic planning cycles are completely out of phase with the rate of change in the world around us. Schools are knowledge-based organizations suffused with rapidly changing technologies and information. Strategic discourse must become frequent, perhaps even continuous (few successful knowledge-based companies in Silicon Valley rely on five-year planning cycles). In this way, strategic thinking becomes embedded in the cultural DNA of the school. Professional development days and parent events include real work among all members of the school community and inform strategy on an ongoing basis. Students, particularly in the older grade levels, are included in strategy-level discussion.

• *The process is forward looking.* Traditional school strategic plans tend to look backward, preserving legacy structures and practices. Such plans rely heavily on what the school or district has done in the past and propose changes relative to that baseline. The assumption is that both internal and external conditions and major drivers in the future will be largely the same as they have been in the past. This assumption is no longer valid. Effective planning recognizes the valuable lessons of the past without allowing those lessons to constrain or overwhelm futures that are dramatically different.

• *The process is outward looking.* Traditional strategic plans and planners have been inwardly focused; most people involved in the strategic planning process are part of the legacy school or district system. They know the existing system very well but know much less about rapidly changing conditions outside of education. Schools are being driven to change by regional, national, and global economic, social, technological,

Zero-based thinking breaks through the interests of specific groups in favor of long-term institutional sustainability founded on success of the institution as an integrated ecosystem, not success of the individual parts.

and demographic evolution that is outside the experience or expertise of many of those in the school system itself. Effective planning will access and leverage external perspectives. Effective plans will merge the powerful knowledge of *how students learn* from the educational experts with knowledge of *how organizations innovate* from experienced change agents.

• *The process is global, not narrow.* Individuals and groups involved in traditional strategic planning processes represent and defend narrow foci of interest. Hoping to not disappoint any interest group, traditional plans end up as a list of goals that attempt to enhance or defend those interests. Zero-based thinking breaks through the interests of specific groups in favor of long-term institutional sustainability founded on success of the institution as an integrated ecosystem, not success of the individual parts.

• *The process is value-based.* By going through a frequent zero-based thought process, the organization generates ideas and programs that have the potential to enhance future value, cutting loose legacy programs and pilot projects that do not. Value for the customer (student and family) becomes the driver of what the school will do in the future, rather than the entrenched interests of teachers, administrators, a school board, or a remote government oversight agency.

This approach identifies assets and opportunities that are critical to customer value and builds sustainable school-wide systems that support enhancement of that value proposition. A zero-based starting point leverages—rather than discards or overlooks—practical, insightful, and sometimes quirky ideas worthy of strategic discussion. These are exactly the questions and ideas required to create expanded opportunities for value growth. These are the questions that all successful start-ups, incubators, innovators, and entrepreneurs ask when they are searching for ways to realize value for end users and grow market share at the expense of traditional service providers. This process does *not* dictate that schools of today are obsolete. It *does* dictate that we focus on constant enhancements in learning that recognize both the needs of individual children and the rapid changes in the world around us.

REFLECTION

The new roadmap of school strategy that embraces and builds on innovation is evolving right now and will continue to do so; that is the nature of a self-evolving organization. During 2012–13, I worked with hundreds of educators, parents, and even students from schools around the country. Although each workshop or learning day was different, at every one we took about eight minutes to generate sticky notes with questions that started with the words "What if" and that challenged some fundamental structure, process, program, or tradition at participants' respective schools. I archived all of those questions, and as of January 2014 I had more than two thousand of these questions in my database.

I have always loved "What if" as the most important question to ask, because, unlike typical questions—why, what, where, when, who— "What if" leads to multiple answer options (Lichtman, 2008). It is the question that gets us outside the current frame most quickly—but it is also the question that schools ask least frequently. After covering the walls with colorful Post-it note mosaics of "What if" questions, the workshop participants pondered their collective creative wisdom and discussed ways to actually move their schools forward in a new and better way. Some of the best questions that really excited the participants were asked by students, some as young as fifth graders. And in each session, after reviewing the powerful outcomes of this short, simple exercise, I asked the participants, "How many of those questions that you all just generated in the last eight minutes did you contemplate or discuss in your most recent strategic planning process?" Of the hundreds of participants over numerous sessions, no one ever raised a hand. If that fact does not scare you onto a different path of strategic thinking for your school, I don't have anything that will.

Based on the opportunity to work with so many educators, I have built an extensive toolkit to help school teams find their unique on-ramps to the innovation highway from wherever they currently are. Prompting adults and students to ask "What if . . .?" is one of the more simple tools in that kit. I dislike the idea of coming to a school or a conference and talking "at" a large room of people about my work and findings. I find that antithetical to what we know about learning. But I *love* working "with" educators, prompting them with this constantly evolving toolkit to find, unpack, map, design, scale, and leverage the ideas that are percolating just below or at the surface of their communities. That toolkit is already very much in use, and the great news is that I don't have to drive ten thousand miles in my Prius all by myself to help schools move forward!

CHAPTER FIFTEEN

Signposts
The Big Ideas That Mark the Road

In the late fall, with the end of my journey in sight, a few schools called and asked if I could stop in for a visit in Houston, Fort Worth, Santa Fe, Albuquerque, and Phoenix on my way home, and I politely declined. Eighty-nine days was long enough. I was worn out, my memory banks were full, and I wanted to get home, see my wife, enjoy a family Christmas, and start to put all my thoughts together.

Deadheading from Dallas to San Diego is a long, lonely, full-on, two-day, butt-sore drive. I stopped in nameless gas stations to get the same gas, the same big caffeine-laced diet soda, and the same sandwich or burrito that I could somewhat safely eat with one hand on the wheel and the cruise control stuck on 70. When you leave Dallas you also leave behind the changing green and autumn colors of the eastern third of the United States and reenter the perpetual browns, tans, coppers, and duns of the Great West, unbroken except for the predatory spread of Phoenix and the irrigated patchwork of the California Imperial Valley, where we have managed to wring all but the last drops out of the Colorado River before it flows south to Mexico and the muddy upper reaches of the Sea of Cortez.

Thank goodness I do my best thinking on walks and long drives. With sixty-four schools in my rearview mirror, I started to sift and filter what I had seen and heard. While I started this three-month trip with simple goals, I had brought with me thirty years of thinking about education, fifteen years working at a school, and two years studying the arts of innovation and change. At gas stops and stretch stops and the one-night layover somewhere west of the Texas–New Mexico line, I jotted down notes on my Big Ideas pad. And then I was home, turning off the last highway at sunset, onto the familiar back roads of San Diego County, and darn near kissed the ground when I dropped down my own steep driveway. Checked the vital statistics of my trip (9,957 miles and 48.3 miles per gallon). Patted my Prius on the hood. Unplugged my phone/MP3 player/GPS. Stretched my back. And went to bed.

The road to transforming schools is not one-way, two-dimensional, or straight. Some of the key signposts that mark this road, like learning itself, fit into more than one of the chapters in this book or don't fit into any of the chapters, but are important on their own. Some just bear repeating so the reader who has hopefully earmarked, underlined, or highlighted some of the previous pages can leave with a summary of those ideas that swirled onto my Big Ideas pad over the past three years. Here they are.

Wisdom

For millennia, the primary mission of the institution of education has been the transfer of knowledge. That is no longer the case. Knowledge transfer can take place without institutions. To the extent that actual schools have irreplaceable value, it is in the relationships and sense of community they provide. One of my high school students, in 1998, told our seminar, "We would all trade a lot of knowledge for a little bit of wisdom." That pretty much sums up the value of schools today and in the future. Students recognize that it is this wisdom, understanding of the life experience, that they gain from their teachers and their peers with whom they spend such a large chunk of their early years. It is these relationships that generate the essential qualities that most educators seek for their students: that they become happy, productive, caring, sustaining citizens of a civil society. School communities must ask: What is a school's purpose in a time when the acquisition of content knowledge is in the student's pocket? How can a school help students to be wise?

Pedagogy

What are the common elements that I saw in those classrooms and hallways, studios and community gardens, labs and makerspaces, where student and teacher passions for learning, the joy of discovery, boil up, and everyone is eager to share just one story, one picture, one lesson, when the love of learning has the power to transcend and transform lives? I stewed over that question as the miles rolled by, whittling it down to a thought, then a single sentence, then a phrase, and then just three words. And then I got rid of two of them.

"Dewey."

On this trip, educators and students showed me what *they* thought of as their most innovative programs, what *they* felt was going to change education to prepare our students for the future, and in every single case I believe John Dewey and the other giants of the Progressive Era, more than a hundred years ago, would have pretty much nodded their heads and said, "Yep, told you so." Project-based learning, flipped

Learning is founded in passion, which is founded in engagement, relevance, and the experience of the learner.

classrooms, design thinking, expeditions, collaborative work groups, makerspaces, differentiated learning programs, transdisciplinary courses, mutated schedules, teacher Twitter chats, performance-based assessment—the roots of all of these are found in the core lessons of Dewey: Learning is born of passion, which is founded in engagement, relevance, and the experience of the learner.

The myth persists that learning content and developing wisdom and contextual skills must somehow compete for time in the classroom and in our lives. Dewey taught us that this is a false dichotomy: All of us, students and adults, learn content *better* when we learn it through the experiential acquisition of context and skills. Dewey also told us, "If we teach today as we taught yesterday we rob our children of tomorrow" (1916). If schools can set their teaching compass to the simple lodestar of Dewey's progression from experience to engagement to passion to learning, we will go a long way toward moving off of the assembly line and into the learning ecosystem.

Leadership

We have to stop, right now, talking about "teachers" and "school leaders" as if they were two different groups. Very simply, all educators must see themselves as leaders, and educational systems must support them as such. Organizations that remain mired in highly vertical decision structures, which rely on the site leader as the primary change agent, will never break out of the industrial organizational model. Boards and chief executives must set the tone; demand a system of distributed authority; create an appropriate risk profile; build comfort with continuous growth and change; and nurture fluid, collaborative, multilateral relationships based on situational, not positional, authority. On my trip, this culture was the easiest measure of effective innovation to observe and quantify. Where schools were developing this culture and expectation of distributed leadership, where both adults and students were *expected* to take ownership of their own learning and growth, the school was on a path to significant change. Where this model of "leadership ownership" was lacking or cursory, or was left to develop on its own, the schools were largely stuck in a traditional mode with, at best, a scattering of loosely connected innovation brushfires.

> *Where both adults and students were* **expected** *to take ownership of their own learning and growth, the school was on a path to significant change.*

Aligning Systems

The real work of change is to remake a sustainable organization at the systems level. At many schools I visited, I asked teachers, students, and administrators how much of what they do each day has fundamentally changed in the past five years. In many schools, change and innovation are still largely perceived in terms of new computer technology and little else. At nearly every school I visited on my trip, and dozens I have worked with since, leaders can point to *something* that is very different from ten or even five years ago. Many schools have checked the box of "twenty-first-century innovation"; brushfires of innovation are burning and, over time, those fires may spread at these schools. But at a number of these schools, there is no systematic, intentional alignment between what is considered innovative in a classroom on one hall and what is considered innovative in a classroom on another hall. The adults and the students do not share a common understanding of what *innovation* means, or why the school is trying new things. Where school leaders take this more "organic" approach, substantive change takes a minimum of seven to ten years. At that rate, changes we make today in response to the needs we see today are out of date well before they even begin to take effect.

Other schools have placed innovation squarely on the front burner of their strategic stove. Students and teachers at these schools feel that up to *90 percent* of what they do in the classroom is fundamentally different from what they were doing just five years ago. Budgets are transparently aligned with a new, widely validated, and clearly understood set of student outcomes and adult expectations. Communication of a forward-leaning vision is not the sole responsibility of the site leader or the communications department, but is also expected of and supported by classroom teachers, bus drivers, and, yes, students. Teachers in one classroom or grade level know what pilots are being trialed across campus, and why, and when they succeed or fail. Teachers dig down into the pedagogy of the learning system and map it throughout the school. Successful innovation is designed to touch *all* students, not just those who happen to be assigned to the most creative and risk-taking teachers. Schools that take this much more intentional approach can fundamentally change in three to five years the way that most or all students learn.

Finding and Developing People

Most teachers are naturally optimistic and energetic; they love kids and recognize great learning when they see it. Adults are absolutely key to the success of learning. Most grew up in a very traditional school setting; that is what they know. In order to change our schools, we have to "paint the picture" of what a learning ecosystem looks like. This means exposing our educators in person and virtually to the many, many brushfires of classroom and organizational innovation that are burning in this country and around the world so educators can actually *see* a learning ecosystem in action and how innovative organizations work. Then we need to provide the resources—most critically, time—for them to retool their professional skill set and gain comfort with the learning ecosystem as opposed to the learning assembly line. Finally, we must adopt adult performance assessment tools that reward adults as lead learners, co-learners, risk-takers, and owners of their own professional evolution.

Change in schools will accelerate dramatically if new teachers are hired who demonstrate a cultural comfort with change. In private and charter schools, and in public schools where site leaders are allowed to hire teachers based on selected skills and attributes rather than seniority, we see a vastly accelerated pace of change at the classroom level. This does *not* mean that site leaders fire everyone who is unwilling or unable to transform their classrooms overnight. It means that by increasing the balance of the faculty who are naturally comfortable with a more fluid, less rigid, more evolutionary set of working conditions, many of those who are less naturally comfortable will be exposed to methods and outcomes they can adopt for their own professional evolution and growth.

> *Change in schools will accelerate dramatically if new teachers are hired who demonstrate a cultural comfort with change.*

Anchors, Dams, and Silos

A majority of educators I met on the trip and in my subsequent work believe that we have to change our system of learning—that we do, in fact, have to get off of the assembly line. Therefore I had to ask the question: "What is holding us back?" I found three answers.

First, we need to cut through the *anchors* that hold our teachers back from being co-learners, lead learners, farmers, coaches, and mentors with our students (I borrowed the term *anchor* from Steve Davis, director of diversity and communications at the Pomfret School). Those anchors represent the attachment our teachers feel to the assembly-line framework of subject, time, and space that define the quantum packet of traditional education. The traditional school has reinforced in teachers the idea of "my subject, my time, and my classroom." Once teachers and administrators let go of those anchors, many feel an enormous weight has been lifted from their shoulders. They are free to explore learning *with* their students rather than having to serve as the conduit of content.

The major external *dams* of school innovation are standardized college entrance exams and the criteria used by college admissions offices to select students. College admissions is a top goal for US students and their families, and in the selection process many colleges still heavily weigh performance on standardized tests, including the SAT, ACT, and Advanced Placement exams. Schools allow creative, engaging pedagogy and programs at lower grade levels, but, fearing a drop in college admissions, struggle to maintain that approach to learning in high schools. Several schools I visited, and many others around the country, have successfully broken these dams to innovation—dropping AP courses, building highly rigorous alternative courses with greater depth and relevance to the students, and creating their own authentic student performance assessments, without any negative impact on college matriculation statistics.

Over time, schools have constructed *silos* that separate people and processes within the organization. Silos limit networking, sharing, and collaborating, and protect traditions of autonomy and authority amongst teachers and administrators. The silos are firewalls that prevent change from spreading throughout a school organization, as if change were a dangerous virus instead of the cure to fear and inertia. Schools that intentionally and sustainably create time, space, and systematic incentives for adults to collaborate—to disrupt the rigid constraints of departments, grade levels, divisions, schools, and transcend the school-world border— begin to see the rapid spread of innovative brushfires.

Not So Hard

People who have been through significant organizational change know that it is often messy, complicated, and uncomfortable. School communities almost always, fearfully, *overstate* the adverse impacts that change will have. They believe there will be "blood on the floor"; that parents will withdraw their students; colleges will look at their graduates less favorably;

teachers will riot or leave in droves; the administration will fire teachers who do not toe the new line. Yet those who have been through a thoughtful, intentional, transparent change process tell us that, almost always, change is not as difficult as we had predicted. These experienced people also tell us that after the first big change, which the organization weathers with less turmoil than expected, the school will have developed the cultural *chutzpah* to tackle the next change, and it is always much easier.

Frequency and Amplitude

Almost all major events in the institutional life of a school or district (strategic planning, accreditation cycles, annual evaluations, professional development days, conferences, retreats, hiring) occur on a "low frequency–high amplitude" basis. These major events don't happen often; we imbue them with great weight; and the results and opportunities they provide are quickly lost under the pressures of day-to-day work. Schools need to flip this. We know as educators that all of us learn and implement skills better if we learn frequently and in small bites. Important activities that guide what we do and how we do it at school, like strategic thinking, professional development, school visits, and self-assessments, should take place on a "high frequency–low amplitude" basis: lots of frequent, small bites, with plenty of time to chew. There is no better example than the opportunity for educators to meet, collaborate, and share ideas about their teaching craft. Some schools are stuck in the outdated mode of allowing teachers to attend a conference once a year or less, where teachers sit in a room with hundreds of others and listen to lectures. These schools think this experience constitutes valuable professional growth. It does not. Other educators, increasingly with the support of their leaders, spend twenty minutes or an hour a week on live Twitter chats or checking their blog feed, or a half-day at weekend unconferences, where they find or develop actionable plans they can implement the next day at school; then teachers dive back in the next day or week or month for more. We know this approach supports good student learning, and that is just as true for adults.

Magnitude

Given the chance to boldly envision the future of learning a decade from now, most educators still see learning taking place in a school that looks pretty much like it does today. Futurists, given the same chance, say the future of learning, like so many of our other evolving industrial and social sectors, will look very different and that the familiar place and structure that we call "school" will not survive global changes that are already in motion. Both cannot be right. This dissonance brought to my mind the geologic Richter scale (Lichtman, 2013c). Most educators see change on a linear scale: big, dynamic, disruptive innovations of the future may be two or three times more impactful than what we have seen in our own life experience. The futurists believe, and I tend to agree, that the scale is logarithmic like the Richter scale and that we are already undergoing global changes that will cause impacts to education greater than the impacts that have already occurred by a factor of ten, or a hundred, or more. Educators should at least consider this possibility: What does a "magnitude 8" innovation look like on a logarithmic scale? What would *learning* and *school* mean if the changes in the next ten or twenty years are a hundred times greater than those we have witnessed in our lifetimes?

Rhythm

Our current system of education is out of rhythm with the rest of the world. A couple of centuries ago, it took weeks or months for news to travel around the globe and decades or centuries for the rise and fall of empires. That time frame has been utterly compressed. In the past twenty years we have seen a complete upheaval of global relationships driven by an expired Cold War; the greatest transfer of wealth in the history of the world from one set of nations to another; a ballistic increase in technological and scientific discovery; a massive, once-in-a-generation economic upheaval that has rewritten the legacy of the American Dream and possibly the promise of a relatively prosperous global middle class; the longest-running war in US history; and unprecedented global environmental changes that threaten species, cultures, and societies that have slowly evolved since the last ice age. Within and to a great extent driving all of this is instant and near-universal access to data, news, and knowledge. In those same twenty years, virtually nothing has changed in the core academic programs at most schools in the United States.

Whether or not you agree with a change like the Common Core standards, it has taken more than a decade to invent, write, and adopt those new standards. And to many, even a massive adoption of new learning standards seems marginal, if not trivial, relative to the changes in the rest of the world. Schools should be *attuned* to the rhythms of the world around us, not isolated from them.

> *Schools should be* **attuned** *to the rhythms of the world around us, not isolated from them.*

Student Ownership

Students are vastly more capable of understanding and using the tools of learning than the traditional system allows them to be. Handing over the expectations and responsibility to students for their learning is both the toughest and most rewarding change I saw in schools, particularly among veteran teachers who are often considered the "best" in the current system. Many of these teachers stay up to date on new technology; have flipped their classrooms; create projects for students to undertake; and provoke their students with questions in the Socratic style instead of lecturing at students. It is tough when we point out that all of this is still teacher-centered; they have not turned over responsibility for asking questions, finding problems, designing projects, trying and failing, to their students. When teachers do so, both students and teachers blossom in a relationship of experiential co-learning that lies at the absolute heart of what we call transformed learning.

Bell Curve

In 2012, researchers Ernest O'Boyle Jr. of the College of Business and Economics at Longwood University and Herman Aguinis at the Kelly School of Business at Indiana University reported on a study of the performance of more than 630,000 people across four broad areas of human performance: academics, athletics, politics, and entertainment. The core finding, which I happened to hear reported by Shankar Vedantam on National Public Radio, is that "a small minority of superstar performers contribute a disproportionate amount of the output."

This research shows that the bell curve is not, in fact, a good representation of much of human performance. These findings should have stirred a massive discussion among educators. Much of our student assessment is still based on bell curve assumptions, when in fact we are probably holding back our student superstars when we set the highest bar as an "A+", a "5" on an AP test, or a 2400 SAT score. Like students, a few superstar employees account for much more of the higher-end performance in our businesses, which means that all of the nonsuperstars are performing at or below our previous conception of average. Doesn't this hold for innovators in our schools as well? It is statistically probable that a few superstar innovators will be responsible for the majority of the good ideas and effective implementation strategies that move your school from where it is today to where you want it to be, or where it will be regardless of "your" intentions. If we do not hire, develop, and support superstars of innovation, it is likely that change in our schools will be slow at best.

In the Coming Year . . .

In just the coming year, with no formal directive, and purely in response to changes in the world around us . . .

- Hundreds of school leaders will try new approaches to management and organizational structure, without a guarantee that they made the right choice.
- Thousands, perhaps even tens of thousands, of teachers will link together for valuable professional learning via social media, many with no prior approval from their supervisors, no support from their school, and no bump in their take-home pay.
- Hundreds of thousands, perhaps millions, of parents will seriously think about new options for educating their children.

- Millions of students will access, manage, or create knowledge in some new way, mostly on their cell phone and other Internet devices, whether or not any adult teaches them how or asks them to do it.
- Millions of students will take university courses online, for free.

LAST SIGNS

In the spring of 2012, I read a beautiful essay in *The Nation*, by Richard Wolin of the City University of New York, on the history and democratic ideals of American college education, as he summarized *College* by Andrew Delbanco. Wolin writes as we all wish we could write, with fluidity, clarity, and the perfect selection of words and sentence structure, like the great nineteenth-century orators who have disappeared in the sound-bite age.

Wolin argues that one of the signature constructs of our American heritage—equal access to a strong liberal arts college education, that fruitful gap between high school and life that should allow young people to reflect, explore, and develop their unique passion in life—may be wounded beyond repair due to lack of societal commitment. College, he argues, is beyond the reach of the poor; admissions are skewed to the privileged classes; and we forfeit depth for haste. I fear he is absolutely right. Many of the same arguments can be made for K–12 education.

I share Wolin's fear that few will find their Walden Pond in the same way our generation or past generations did. I watch bright, talented students multitask in front of LCD screens and find myself wishing that they would go spend as much time in isolated wilderness as I did at their age. But then I see how connected they are, how they can share lives and knowledge with people in ways that I never could when it took three weeks for mail to travel from one hemisphere to the other, and a transoceanic phone call was still rare, difficult, and expensive. I see the audacity with which this generation tackles obstacles of time and space that seemed insurmountable just a decade or two ago. I see not only their belief that the future is right here, but also their desire and ability to grab it, create it, and make things happen in ways that we just don't understand quite yet. Some students in this generation exhibit a pioneering fearlessness, a willingness to do, that may have skipped a couple of American generations, including my own.

I have to wonder whether the yearning for what was perfect in education in the past is not exactly that: a yearning for something in the past. I see the brilliance with which motivated students and teachers tackle their passions, and I think the only real difference between the days of Dewey and today is the rate of change. Are we overly impatient? Of course. More impatient than a generation past? Probably. Is that a good thing? I think it is.

Here is the key takeaway from my trip and subsequent work, the one I want my readers to remember:

Children are naturally creative, adaptive, dynamic, fluid, metacognitive learners, ready to try whatever tool is at hand if given the opportunity. For some students, the chance to grow with these tools of learning is robbed from them by an environment of economic, social, or emotional poverty. And for others, we, the adults, have created a well-meaning but outmoded educational system that robs them of that opportunity, when we should have a system that creates, nurtures, and celebrates it. Some of us have been talking about the need to replace the industrial age model of education for years; some of us for decades; John Dewey and others were talking about it a century ago. It is convenient to think that students need a new set of skills for the twenty-first century, but the truth is that these are the skills that successful people have exhibited across many centuries. If we keep talking about transforming education at the rate we have to date, we will lose another generation or more to an education that is just not preparing our children for their futures.

I passionately urge us all to stop talking and start doing.

REFERENCES

Adams, B. (2013). "Process Post: Mission, Vision, Strategies, Tactics, and Logistics," *It's About Learning* (blog), September 3, http://itsaboutlearning.wordpress.com/2013/09/03/process-post-mission-vision-strategies-tactics-and-logistics/.

Bejan, A., and Zane, J. (2012). *Design in Nature: How the Constructal Law Governs Evolution in Biology, Physics, Technology, and Social Organization*. New York: Doubleday.

Berkun, S. (2010). *The Myths of Innovation*. Sebastopol, CA: O'Reilly.

Blank, S. (2012). "Why Innovation Dies," *Steve Blank.com* (blog), May 1, http://steveblank.com/2012/05/01/why-innovation-dies/.

Collins, J. (2001). *Good to Great: Why Some Companies Make the Leap . . . and Others Don't*. New York: HarperCollins.

Cowan, M. (2013). "Bonus Interview with Megan Cowan," vimeo.com video, http://vimeo.com/47294652.

Crandall, D. (2007). "Learning From Failure." In D. Crandall (ed.), *Leadership Lessons From West Point*. San Francisco: John Wiley & Sons.

Deutschman, A. (2007). *Change or Die*. New York: Harper.

Dewey, J. (1916). *Democracy and Education*. New York: Macmillan.

Dweck, C. (2007). *Mindset: The New Psychology of Success*. New York: Random House.

Folk-Williams, S., Stikeleather, J., and Zanini, M. (2012). "Leader Meter 2.0: Spotting the Natural Leaders in Your Company," *Management Innovation eXchange* (blog), May 8, http://www.managementexchange.com/hack/leader-meter-20-spotting-natural-leaders-your-company.

Fullan, M. (2010). *Motion Leadership: The Skinny on Becoming Change Savvy*. Thousand Oaks, CA: Corwin Publishing.

Gino, F., and Pisano, G. (2011). "Why Leaders Don't Learn from Success." *Harvard Business Review*, April.

Gorbis, M. (2013). *The Nature of the Future: Dispatches From the Socialstructed World*. New York: Simon & Schuster.

Hamel, G. (2012). *What Matters Now: How to Win in a World of Relentless Change, Ferocious Competition, and Unstoppable Innovation*. San Francisco: John Wiley & Sons.

Heathcock, K. (2013). "Transforming Practice," *Teachers.k12albemarle.org* (blog), September 13, http://teachers.k12albemarle.org/kheathcock/2013/09/13/transforming-practice/.

Hendry, K. (2012). "Leading Strategic Conversations," *The Discipline of Innovation* (blog), May 21, http://timkastelle.org/blog/2012/05/leading-strategic-conversations/.

Hobbs, L. (2011). "Mindfulness for Teens at UC San Diego Center for Mindfulness," YouTube video, http://www.youtube.com/watch?v=GYV9pk57cMA.

Hobcraft, P. (2010). "The Three Horizon Approach to Innovating," *Paul4Innovating* (blog), September 10, http://paul4innovating.com/2010/09/10/the-three-horizon-approach-to-innovation/.

Hord, S., and Tobia, E. (2012). *Reclaiming Our Teaching Profession*. New York: Teachers College Press.

Hunter, J. (2013). *World Peace and Other Fourth Grade Achievements*. New York: Houghton Mifflin Harcourt.

Johnson, S. (2010). *Where Good Ideas Come From: The Natural History of Innovation*. New York: Riverhead Books.

Kaiser-Greenland, S. (2010). *The Mindful Child*. New York: Simon & Schuster.

Kelley, B. (2010). "Part 1 of 3: Building a Systematic Innovation Capability," *Blogging Innovation* (blog), March 15, http://www.business-strategy-innovation.com/2010/03/part-1-of-3-building-systemic.html.

Kelley, D., and Kelley, T. (2013). *Creative Confidence. Unleashing the Creative Potential Within Us All*. New York: Random House.

LaPlante, L. (2013). "Hackschooling makes me happy: TEDx at University of Nevada". YouTube video, February 12, https://www.youtube.com/watch?v=h11u3vtcpaY.

Lichtman, G. (2008). *The Falconer: What We Wish We Had Learned in School*. Bloomington, IN: iUniverse.

Lichtman, G. (2013a). "Design of Schools and the Nature of Design via Dr. Adrian Bejan," *The Learning Pond* (blog), January 24, http://wp.me/p2gT3m-ry.

Lichtman, G. (2013b). "Response From Dr. Adrian Bejan on Design of Nature," *The Learning Pond* (blog), January 25, http://wp.me/p2gT3m-rH.

Lichtman, G. (2013c). "Innovation: Are We Overlooking 'Magnitude' with Focus on 'Frequency'?" *The Learning Pond* (blog), August 16, http://wp.me/p2gT3m-BV.

Lichtman, G. (2014). "Zero-Based Strategic Thinking." *Independent School Magazine*, 73(3), 40–46.

McGrath, R. G. (2012). "The Empty Innovation Mantra—Way to Go WSJ!" *Ritamcgrath.com* (blog), May 23, http://ritamcgrath.com/2012/05/the-empty-innovation-mantra-way-to-go-wsj/.

McHenry, I., and Brady, R. (eds.). (2009). *Tuning In: Mindfulness in Teaching and Learning*. Philadelphia: Friends Council on Education.

Moran, P. (2013). "Design 2015: Transforming Learning and Teaching in 3rd Grade," *Superintendent's Blog: News and Information from Pam Moran* (blog), September 30, http://superintendent.k12albemarle.org/?p=1015.

O'Boyle, Jr., E., and Aguinis, H. (2012). "The Best and the Rest: Revisiting the Norm and Normality of Individual Performance," *Personal Psychology*, Onlinelibrary.wiley.com, February 27, http://onlinelibrary.wiley.com/doi/10.1111/j.1744-6570.2011.01239.x/abstract.

Peters, T., and Waterman, R. (1982). *In Search of Excellence: Lessons From America's Best Run Companies.* New York: HarperCollins.

Ramharter, S., and Grams, C. (2012). "Unclog Your Pipes with the Autonomy Reality Check," *Management Innovation eXchange* (blog), May 1, http://www.managementexchange .com/hack/unclog-your-pipes.

Rodriguez, D., and Jacoby, R. (2007). "Embracing Risk to Learn, Grow, and Innovate." *Rotman Magazine*, Spring.

Rumelt, R. (2011). *Good Strategy Bad Strategy: The Difference and Why It Matters.* New York: Random House.

Ruth, K. (2011). "Strategy as Deduction Is Insufficient," *Introit* (blog), August 28, http://introit.typepad.com/introit/2011/08/strategy-as-deduction-is-insufficient .html.

Siegel, D. (2013). UCLA Mindful Awareness Research Center, vimeo.com video, http://vimeo.com/46257447.

Skarzynski, P., and Gibson, R. (2008). *Innovation to the Core: A Blueprint for Transforming the Way Your Company Innovates.* Boston: Harvard Business School Publishing.

Slotnick, D., and Schulten, K. (2012). "Sowing Failure, Reaping Success: What Failure Can Teach," *The Learning Network* (blog), NYTimes.com, May 7, http://learning.blogs .nytimes.com/2012/05/07/sowing-failure-reaping-success-what-failure-can-teach /?_php=true&_type=blogs&_r=0.

Stikeleather, J. (2012). "Innovation Is a Process," *Management Innovation eXchange* (blog), February 9, http://www.managementexchange.com/blog/innovation-process.

Thomas, D., and Seeley Brown, J. (2011). *A New Culture of Learning: Cultivating the Imagination for a World of Constant Change.* [self-published at CreateSpace Publishing]

Vedantam, S. (2012). "Put Away the Bell Curve; Most of Us Aren't 'Average,'" National Public Radio program, May 3, http://www.npr.org/2012/05/03/151860154/put-away -the-bell-curve-most-of-us-arent-average.

Wheatley, M. (1999). *Leadership and the New Science: Discovering Order in a Chaotic World.* San Francisco: Berrett-Koehler.

Wolin, R. (2012). "Democracy and Education: On Edward Delbanco," *The Nation*, thenation .com, May 21, http://www.thenation.com/article/167679/democracy-and-education -andrew-delbanco.

Zaninni, M., Folk-Williams, S., and Komori, M. (2011). "Silo-Busting with Formal Networks," *Management Innovation eXchange* (blog), August 24, http://www .managementexchange.com/hack/silo-busting-formal-networks.

Zuboff, S. (2010). "Creating Value in the Age of Distributed Capitalism." *McKinsey Quarterly*, September.

Zuboff, S., and Maxmin, J. (2002). *The Support Economy: Why Corporations Are Failing Individuals and the Next Episode of Capitalism.* New York: Penguin Books.

INDEX

A

Ability grouping, 114

Abrams, J., 127, 128–129, 139

Accountability: in effective organizational structures, 79; of teachers, 53

ACT, 88

Active learning: change from traditional to, 122; motivation and, 120; student-led, 150–152

Adams, B., 52, 64, 150–152, 231, 239, 240

Adaptability: description of, xviii; diversity and, 213; in ecosystems, 211, 215, 220

Adaptive learning, 114–115

Administrators: distributed authority model and, 68–69; in effective organizational structures, 79; evaluation of, 25; in network/ team structure, 71; tasks of, 79; in traditional organizational structure, 64–65, 68

Advanced Placement programs, 58, 123

Agility, 67–70

Agrarian-driven calendar, 11

Aguinis, H., 256–257

Albemarle County Schools, 19, 106–108, 167

Alexandria Country Day School, 173

Alvar, C., 55–56

Amygdala, 171

Analysis paralysis, 140

Anchors, 252–253

Anderson, J., 141–143

AP scores, 88

Armageddon (Uris), xi–xii

Art classes, 144–145

Asheville School, 124–125, 176

Assembly-line model of education, xviii–xix, 106; control of, 201–202; decision making in, 94–95; description of, 196–197; versus ecosystem model of education, 181; efficiency and, 198–199; main structures of, 218; manageability of, 201–202; measure of, 202–204; problem with, 197–198; repeatability of, 205–206; scalability of, 204–205; simplicity and, 200; teachers' attachment to, 252–253; upgrading of, 206–207

Assets, 187, 234

Attention spans, 84, 137, 171–172